Ireland during the Second World War

MANCHESTER
1824

Manchester University Press

Ireland during the Second World War

Farewell to Plato's Cave

Bryce Evans

Manchester University Press

Published by Manchester University Press
Altrincham Street, Manchester M1 7JA, UK
www.manchesteruniversitypress.co.uk

British Library Cataloguing-in-Publication Data is available

Library of Congress Cataloging-in-Publication Data is available

ISBN 978 1 7849 9249 1 *paperback*

First published by Manchester University Press in hardback 2014

This edition first published 2015

Printed by Lightning Source

Contents

Acknowledgements   *page* vi

1   Introduction: farewell to 'Plato's Cave'   1

2   Anglo-Irish trade and business relations   18

3   Moral policemen of the domestic economy   44

4   Conditions in town and country   69

5   Smuggling   91

6   Church and state   114

7   Coercion in the countryside   134

8   The state and the small man   153

9   Conclusions   177

Select bibliography   187

Index   198

Acknowledgements

My greatest debt of gratitude is to Dr Susannah Riordan of University College Dublin, who provided judicious editorial suggestions, advice and encouragement.

Thanks also to Professor Michael Laffan, Professor Mary Daly, Professor Michael Kennedy, Professor Liam Kennedy, Professor Diarmaid Ferriter, Professor Seán Connolly, Dr Lindsey Earner-Byrne, Dr Stephen Kelly, Dr Maura Cronin, Dr Niall Carson, Dr Neal Garnham, Dr Seamus Helferty, Comdt. Victor Laing, Tom Clonan, Dr Marc Caball and all at the Humanities Institute of Ireland, as well as to Dr Liz Dawson and all the interviewees and staff in the archives listed in the bibliography, particularly the National Archives in Dublin.

My thanks to University College Dublin for the award of an 'Ad Astra' research scholarship, which enabled the initial research, and to Liverpool Hope University for allowing me time to complete it.

Lastly, thank you to three strong women for their support – Marian Carey, Úna MacNamara, and Greta Evans – and also to my father, Peter Evans, for the incessant recital of those jigs, reels and ballads, which probably stirred something in me as a child.

1

Introduction: farewell to 'Plato's Cave'

And here Neutrality, harps, art exhibitions, reviews, libels, back-chat, high-tea, cold, no petrol, no light, no coal, no trains; Irish language, partition, propaganda, propaganda, propaganda, rumour, counter-rumour, flat Georgian facades, Guinness, double Irish, single Scotch, sherry, Censors, morals, rain home to all.

John Betjeman, 10 January 1941

The military and economic expansion of the state

At 11 am, on 3 September 1939, British Prime Minister Neville Chamberlain declared war on Germany. When the Irish government responded later that day, declaring the Emergency Powers Act, Ireland's independence was just seventeen years old, its constitution two years old and its control of the strategic ports barely a year old. The Ireland that appeared in the letters of the poet John Betjeman, press attaché to the British delegation in Dublin during the war, was a place of charm but hardship, anxiously asserting its neutrality as Britain and Europe burned. The political and economic crisis of the Second World War not only provided the acid test of this fledgling independence. Just as significantly, the war marked the high point of centralised state intervention in Ireland.[1] The Emergency Powers Act – from which the Irish vernacular for the war originated – enabled the Fianna Fáil cabinet to pass orders without the need for specific legislation or detailed scrutiny in Dáil Éireann. In these extraordinary conditions, the government hastily formed a cabinet emergency committee, composed of Taoiseach Éamon de Valera and a handful of key ministers, streamlining decision-making and marking the transfer of power from local government to the executive.[2]

In taking these measures, the government's immediate priority was security. In January 1939, the Irish Republican Army (IRA) declared itself at war with Britain and affirmed its non-recognition of the Irish state. On 19 January 1939, Neville Chamberlain's son escaped a bomb attack in Tralee, County Kerry.[3] Between then and March 1940, the IRA carried out a bombing campaign in Britain and just three months into the Emergency pulled off the audacious Magazine Fort arms raid.[4] Moving quickly to neutralise the security threat, the government reintroduced internment and increased its surveillance of the IRA and suspected communist groups.[5] The state also expanded its military capability. Under Frank Aiken, the new Minister for the Coordination of Defensive Measures, there was a massive growth in the armed forces. After the initial recruitment drive of September 1939, the number of men under arms in independent Ireland increased from 7,000 to 19,000.[6] After the fall of France in June 1940, de Valera wrote in his diary: 'Good to organise quickly. We try to avoid sacrifice.'[7] There followed a steep rise in recruitment with 41,000 men in the army by March 1941 and a total of 180,000 in the twin auxiliary bodies the Local Security Force (LSF) and Local Defence Force (LDF) by October 1941.[8] Domestic surveillance was assumed by the army's intelligence wing 'G2', which cooperated closely with the Gardaí. An omnipresent slogan – 'Step Together!' – encouraged both recruitment to the Defence Forces and a wider unifying national élan.[9]

While the security of the Irish state during the Emergency has produced racy narratives complete with Nazi espionage,[10] the economic and social history of the period sits rather timidly beside it. Yet the priority of economic survival was just as pressing for the nascent state as its security. The rushed exercise of state centralisation impacted hardest in the economic realm. The trade disruption that war threatened prompted the government to form a unique new arm of state: the Department of Supplies (1939–1945). Minister for Industry and Commerce Seán Lemass was appointed Minister for Supplies in September 1939, empowered to control the prices and import and export of all commodities, dictating the methods of 'treatment, keeping, storage, movement, distribution, sale, purchase, use and consumption' of all goods.[11] The state's meticulous censorship network kept Supplies informed of profiteering and the evasion of ministerial orders[12] as this new department gradually assumed dominance over economic life.

Other government departments also undertook wide-ranging interventionist projects. The Department of Agriculture introduced an unprecedented degree of state control to Ireland's agricultural sector, evicting unproductive farmers from their land. A huge effort to produce domestic fuel through turf took place under the Department of Local Government and Public Health and later the Department of Supplies. The Customs Service dealt with the increase in volume of items smuggled across Ireland's frontiers. Meanwhile, the Department of Justice and the Gardaí, assisted by the LSF and LDF and a cohort of Department of Supplies Inspectors, addressed the upsurge in crime and black marketing that accompanied the introduction of rationing in Ireland.

The narrative of absence

Despite this, the social and economic history of the Emergency is the subject of a largely deficient historiography which provides little indication of the manner in which Irish people survived the shortages wrought by war. Much responsibility for this rests with one of Ireland's great historians: F.S.L. Lyons. In his majestic *Ireland*

Since the Famine (1973), Lyons used Plato's allegory of the cave to claim that Emergency Ireland was 'almost totally isolated from the rest of mankind'.[13] Ireland as 'Plato's Cave' was born: Lyons's lapidarian, sweeping analogy supplanting the short edited collection on the Emergency published by Kevin B. Nowlan and T. Desmond Williams in 1969.[14] Lyons's synopsis of the Irish Emergency echoed accounts of neutrality elsewhere. British diplomat Clifford Norton, stationed in Berne during the conflict, compared the Swiss people to 'passengers on an air-conditioned ocean liner': they 'could see through the portholes the storm and stress of the weather or the heat of the tropics' but failed to appreciate 'the conditions which the captain and crew were facing and by which they were hardened and influenced'.[15] Lyons's invocation of the archetypal cave was a slicker articulation of the neutral condition. The analogy heavily influenced the historiography which followed it.

A noticeable historiographical tendency subsequently took shape in works about the Emergency written in the 1970s and 1980s. These works focused on the diplomatic construction of neutrality, exploring the *realpolitik* that underlay de Valera's diplomacy. Considerations of everyday life and the state's increased domestic presence were placed to one side as the release of state papers illuminated the neutrality debate. Even the best general survey of the Emergency (published a decade after Lyons) extended 'Plato's Cave' backwards to the 1920s and 1930s, describing independent Ireland as suffering a 'postcolonial blackout'.[16] In this study, Robert Fisk's excellent *In Time of War* (1983), the focus remained almost unfalteringly on political elites. In other publications from this period, any thoroughgoing analysis of Irish economy and society was conspicuous by its absence.[17]

Outside the minutiae of the neutrality debate, Irish society was described in rather puritanical, isolationist terms. Invariably, the widespread popular support for neutrality was presented as indicative of a mute 'bottom-up' consensus in Irish society. The first perceptible charge out of 'Plato's Cave' was signalled by Bernard Share who, in his *The Emergency: Neutral Ireland, 1939–45* (1978), argued that Lyons had exaggerated the stagnation of Irish society.[18] Yet in this study, as in other early histories of the period, the mass of the Irish people appeared in a narrative that was, as Clair Wills puts it, 'all about absence – of conflict, of supplies, of social dynamism, of contact with the outside world'.[19] If Share displayed recognition of the poverty of 'the narrative of absence', he offered little by way of alternative analysis.

By the late 1980s, the historiography of the Emergency was starting to edge away from the marble halls of high political accounts towards 'bottom-up' considerations of life in Ireland. But these early revisions of 'Plato's Cave' tended to dilute the economic impulses driving government action and its impacts by trivialising the narrative of absence. During the Emergency, the widely quoted Myles na gCopaleen contributed some of his most biting satire in the column 'Cruiskeen Lawn' in the *Irish Times*, but his references to the 'plain people of Ireland' sat too long as a waggish substitute for an analysis of social and economic conditions at the time. Leaning heavily on the golden age of Dublin journalism, much of Tony Gray's *The Lost Years*

(1988) substituted diplomatic history with semi-whimsical reminiscence.[20] By the late 1980s, the narrative of absence had gained acceptance at the popular level, offering a survey of social life akin in its depiction of boredom to Patrick Kavanagh's Maguire, subject of his 1942 poem *The Great Hunger*, whose only antidote to the tedium of rural life was to occasionally 'sin' over the warm ashes of the cottage fire. The Irish people of the Emergency, when mentioned at all, resembled the inhabitants of Plato's Cave: metaphorically, they were placed closer to Maguire's cottage fire than 'the fire of life'.

Deprivation and periodisation: the exceptionality of the Emergency

Terence Brown's *Ireland: A Social and Cultural History* (1985) briefly considers whether Irish people were conscious of the cultural stagnation portrayed in much literature of the period. Instead of advancing the more abstract judgments of cultural history, Brown finds 'the economic depredations of the war years all too evident'.[21] Even for those like John Betjeman, who moved in elite literary circles, Dublin may have been gossipy fun, but it was also painfully 'cold, no petrol, no light, no coal, no trains'.[22] But by the turn of the twenty-first century and with the growth of the Celtic Tiger, recounting the extremities of deprivation in twee auld Ireland had become almost hackneyed.[23] This book does not dwell on hardship, therefore, but concentrates instead on the social impact of the *war economy*. In doing so, it reflects a shift in the broader historiography of war, where a focus on military histories in which 'armies and navies come or go, commanded by greater or lesser figures deciding momentous historical issues' has given way to a focus on productive forces.[24]

The material challenges of wartime represent a common thread in human experience. The clear similarities between Ireland and the other neutral European states defy the sometimes stultifying narrative of Irish exceptionalism. On the other hand, there were important differences in the wartime experience of the European neutrals. Therefore, in the following pages, life in neutral Ireland is compared to that in Sweden, Switzerland, Spain and Portugal. These countries, like Ireland, were all 'long haul' neutrals, remaining outside the conflict for its duration.[25] Far from the bliss of life on a neutral 'air-conditioned ocean liner' or the obliviousness of Plato's Cave, each country was subjected to economic bullying by their larger combatant neighbours. This group of five can thus be divided into two, based on the dominant sphere of economic influence they found themselves a part of. For Sweden and Switzerland, it was the continental sphere of Axis dominance. For Portugal, Spain and Ireland, it was the Atlantic sphere of Allied power.

In rejecting the idea that wartime neutrality represented a snug unconsciousness about outside pressures, this study rests on the social and economic singularity of the period. The war brought great disruption to daily routines, life experiences and long-term aspirations. This is hidden from overviews of twentieth-century Irish history, where a politico-centric historiography has tended to place the Emergency in the middle of the period of Fianna Fáil ascendancy between 1932 and 1948. After all, the party won two elections within a year of each other, in June 1943 and May 1944. In keeping with this tendency, the Emergency has been reduced to either an adjunct to the economic 'revolution' of the 1930s or a prelude to the victory of the Inter-party government in 1948.[26]

This trend, witnessed in most general surveys of twentieth-century Ireland, rests on the continuity between Fianna Fáil's protectionist economic programme of the 1930s and that of the 1940s. The political and economic 'break' signified by Fianna Fáil's coming to power in 1932 has been overstated.[27] Even so, by 1939, the party had established itself as more interventionist in power than Cumann na nGaedheal. With the same man (Seán Lemass) at the helm, the centralised, bureaucratic and regulationist ethos of the Department of Industry and Commerce in the 1930s found its natural continuation in the Department of Supplies in the Emergency. Lemass assumed much broader powers during the early 1940s, however. This is obscured by a sixteen-year periodisation which focuses on the political transitions of 1932 and 1948 while underplaying the fact that the scope and influence of the state in everyday life was patently greatest during the Emergency. It is argued here that through the constant issuing of Emergency Powers Orders, state interventionism was accelerated to an exceptional extent. What John Horgan describes as 'the high-water mark of Irish interventionism' was unique to the war years.[28]

In strictly quantitative terms, the exceptionality of the Emergency is less obvious. According to the Department of Industry and Commerce's annually produced *Statistical Abstract*, the average yearly number of people on the live register of unemployment was 73,900 during the Emergency years (from 1939 to 1945).[29] According to data compiled by the Department of Supplies, this figure (for the years 1939 to 1944) was 96,500, reaching an average of 105,000 during the years of the worst shortages (1940 to 1942).[30] The exceptionality of the Emergency era is not obvious from *these* statistics because the yearly average on the live register between 1935 and 1938 was similarly high: 97,311 according to the *Statistical Abstract*.[31] Similarly, the net passenger movement in and out of independent Ireland during the Emergency was minus 10,903.[32] This figure was actually higher in the pre-war years between 1933 and 1938, when the yearly average was minus 15,498.[33] But these figures cloak the atypical mixture of sociopolitical events attached to economic privation in this six-year period.

The Economic War of the 1930s brought increasing prosperity to Ireland's urban centres, where cheaper food and better job prospects won Fianna Fáil much working class support.[34] The dietary standards of Ireland's urban population also improved during that decade.[35] By 1939, Ireland still lacked a significant industrial base. Since 1932, however, Fianna Fáil had expanded infrastructure and established a number of consumption goods industries behind protective tariffs. In contrast to

the social conservatism of William T. Cosgrave's Cumann na nGaedheal administrations, Fianna Fáil's welfare expenditure in the 1930s was considerable as well. The
party increased unemployment benefits (1933) and pension schemes (1935).

The Emergency marked a clear break with this trend as prices and unemployment rose and food supplies waned. Despite the strong political consensus at the
time that national unity was needed,[36] the role of the government reflected anxie-
ties arising from material conditions. J.J. Lee notes that the post-independence
expansion of the state's house-building programme resulted in the proportion of
families living in one- or two-room dwellings falling from 50% to 25% in Dublin
alone between 1926 and 1946.[37] Lee's twenty-year periodisation obscures the
fact that the pace that house building and slum clearance had gathered in the
1930s slowed to a virtual standstill by 1941.[38] The Irish economy limped rather
than strode out of the Anglo-Irish Economic War in April 1938, entering the
Emergency already scarred by the outflow of young people, meagre growth and
industrial stagnation.[39]

The impairments worsened after the fall of France to Nazi Germany in June 1940.
Thereafter, Britain's attitude to Irish neutrality hardened. Ireland suffered a crippling
supply squeeze from late 1940. The priority of Irish self-sufficiency was underlined
by the extensive sinking of merchant ships in the Battle of the Atlantic. As the supply
of fertiliser, feed and fuel withered, the country reverted to burning turf and to travel
by horse and cart or bicycle. The crisis year of 1941 was heralded when petrol pumps
across the state ran dry at Christmas 1940 after Britain cut fuel supplies. It was compounded later that year when German bombs fell on the country, a devastating foot-
and-mouth outbreak occurred and Dublin Castle was ravaged by fire. Due to the
absence of raw materials, industrial production fell steeply. Meanwhile, the response
of organised labour to government restrictions was resoundingly negative. James
Larkin's burning of the Trade Union Bill in June 1941 signified the worst crisis in
government–trade union relations since independence.[40] For the Irish government,
1941 truly was an *annus horribilis*.

Irish agricultural exports, which had thrived during the First World War, were
crippled in the Second by British price controls and farming communities struggled
to cope with the loss of this market. In 1940, Ireland imported 74,000 tons of
fertiliser, a figure below the peace time level but still sufficient to meet demand. By
1941 – the year in which the British attitude hardened – this figure had dropped to
7,000, and for the rest of the Emergency, it sat at zero. Similarly, the 1940 figure for
feeding stuffs was six million tons, falling to one million in 1941 and zero thereafter.[41] The reduction in feeding stuffs and the foot-and-mouth outbreak ensured that
livestock numbers in Ireland fell dramatically during the war. There were three
million sheep in the country in 1940; by 1943, there were half a million less.[42]

Crime also rose. 1945's *Statistical Abstract* noted that 'criminal proceedings have
shown a very serious increase generally since the outbreak of war'.[43] Convictions
for theft in neutral Ireland trebled from 1,160 in 1939 to 3,395 by 1943.[44] In 1941,

the total number of people summoned for indictable offences stood at 8,196; by 1943, it was 10,735. It was not until the end of 1944 that the first decline in the daily average number of people in custody since 1939 occurred.[45] This rise can be linked to the increase in the number of offences listed as criminal under emergency legislation. The contemporary political and religious establishment, however, inclined to blame such trends on moral failings. Surveying the situation at home, an influential vein of opinion in middle-class Ireland held that material shortages caused by the Emergency had led to the sort of moral degeneracy many associated with the British metropolis.[46]

These social concerns were not without their quantitative complement. Urban unemployment figures began to rise in 1938, and by the first six months of 1939, the number of people registered as unemployed in cities and urban districts was 8% higher than in the preceding year. This figure rose steadily during the years of the worst shortages – 1941 and 1942. Rural unemployment displayed similar trends. The number of men out of work in rural Ireland stood at just over 530,000 in 1939. This figure rose to 555,601 in 1941 and in 1942 was well over the 540,000 mark.[47] Alongside the socio-economic 'push factors' underlying migration, the higher waged jobs of the British war economy provided a compelling 'pull factor'. The number of travel permits to Britain and Northern Ireland issued in 1940 was just under 26,000, but rose to 35,000 in 1941 and reached 52,000 in 1942.[48] In 1941, both governments agreed that Britain would effectively control emigration by the issuing of permit cards in Ireland and work visas in Britain. This trend continued throughout the Emergency, with Irish employment exchanges effectively transformed into offshore branches of the British Ministry of Labour, which paid the travel costs of migrant workers.[49]

The British war economy absorbed many young Irishmen and women at this time, but wartime employment opportunities in Britain were not so pronounced that (as Frank McCourt claimed) the working class 'thanked God for Hitler because if he hadn't marched all over Europe the men of Ireland would still be at home scratching their arses on the queue at the Labour Exchange'.[50] In Ireland, the real measure of wartime adversity was the fall in wages in real terms and the rise in the cost of living. In marked contrast to the 1930s, conditions for workers during the Emergency were exacerbated by the Wages Standstill Order, in effect from May 1941, which outlawed strikes for greater pay. Wartime inflation compounded these hard times. According to a conservative estimate of price inflation at the time, wages increased by one third during the Emergency, while the cost of living rose by two thirds.[51] According to a less conservative estimate, these proportions were a staggering 13% and 70%, respectively.[52] Indeed, the Irish cost of living index for all items displayed a rise from 173 in February 1938 to 298 in November 1945.[53] This rise was so steep that an interdepartmental committee was established in November 1943 to discuss ways to alleviate the poverty that was its result.[54] The dramatic rise in the cost of living during the Emergency is illustrated in Figure 1.1.

Base: 1913 = 100

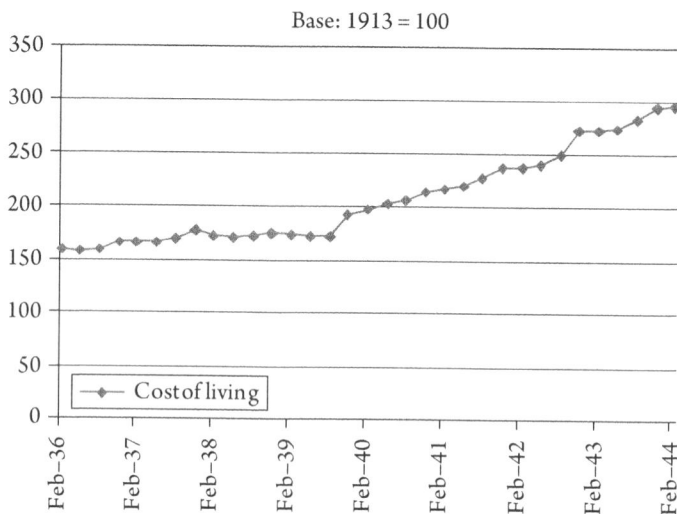

Figure 1.1 Cost of living in independent Ireland by quarter, 1936–1944
(Source: *Irish Statistical Abstracts*, 1936–1946)

Dismantling the narrative of absence

It was not until the turn of this century that histories of the Emergency underwent a fundamental shift, reflecting the social and economic exceptionality of the period outlined above. This transition was telling of the changes taking place in Irish historiography in general. There was a recognition that the 'age of de Valera' interpretation, an approach which often looked little further than the leader for the roots of stagnation, inhibited a fuller understanding of Ireland in the last century.[55] Similarly, histories with diverse narrative teloi were challenging the emphasis of competing nationalist and revisionist narratives on state seizure and state building.[56] In line with these developments, Emergency historiography underwent change as well. The older, familiar neutrality narrative was supplanted by what Geoff Roberts terms 'a new narrative which better encompasses the complexities, contradictions and ambivalences of Ireland's war'.[57]

Gerard Fee's 1996 doctoral thesis provided a harbinger of developments to come. Fee paints a detailed picture of the roles of the church, the state and common people in the management of shortages of food, fuel and clothing in Dublin's low-income areas.[58] Contrary to the passivity found in versions of 'Plato's Cave', Fee demonstrated that Irish people's experience of absence led to greater public engagement with the government. In 2010, Peter Rigney applied a similar focus on the economic role of Ireland's railways amidst Emergency fuel shortages.[59]

The best recent survey of the Emergency was Clair Wills's 2007 *That Neutral Island*. Although professedly a cultural history, Wills struck an admirable balance between economic hardship and cultural experience. Like earlier writers, Wills concluded that

Fianna Fáil enjoyed support for neutrality so resounding that it did much to override still-lingering civil war animosities. The situation of Wills's history within the 'new wave' of Emergency historiography was marked, though. She concluded that economic and social regulation played an important part in consolidating the power of government during the period.[60] Her focus, however, was predominately literary and did not extend to an appraisal of the broader significance of state action and popular reaction in the spheres of production and consumption.

Donal Ó Drisceoil's *Censorship in Ireland* exhibited a similarly nuanced exit from 'Plato's Cave', examining the political effects of Emergency censorship outside a narrative of parties, parliaments and diplomacy.[61] Ireland underwent the strict construction of 'negative propaganda' whereby, unlike other neutral countries, the state attempted to relay the war 'impartially'. Ó Drisceoil depicted such censorship as pursued with 'the sort of puritanical ardour normally applied to matters sexual'. He termed the phenomenon 'moral neutrality'. Censorship, he claimed, was constructed around the notion that Ireland, as a spiritual nation, was aloof from the destructive material conflict taking place in the outside world. A key objective for censorship officials was to define neutrality in relation to moral questions arising from the war. The overriding message was that Ireland had to keep out of the conflict, not just physically, but morally also.[62] This propaganda characterised the Irish people as exceptional, not by virtue of Ireland's neutrality alone, but because this neutrality was indicative of a spirituality absent in other nations.[63] This work extends Ó Drisceoil's conceptualisation of Irish neutrality as 'moral' into the economic realm.

Moral neutrality/moral economy

In 2006, Brian Girvin's *The Emergency: Neutral Ireland, 1939–45* subjected Irish neutrality to reappraisal. In 2012, Fine Gael Justice Minister Alan Shatter went further, describing Ireland's wartime neutrality as 'a principle of moral bankruptcy'. Diarmaid Ferriter responded by accusing Shatter of 'reading history backwards'.[64] The spat illustrated the continuity of the 'moral' status of the Emergency in public discourse. Ferriter's rejoinder attacked the intellectual laziness of much condemnation of the 'De Val-era' as a longue durée of misery and stagnation. De Valera's 1943 St Patrick's Day speech is a case in point. The address has heavily coloured popular historical memory of both the Emergency era and the Irish political elite of the time. In the Taoiseach's dream of Ireland, her countryside would be 'bright with cosy homesteads, whose fields and villages would be joyous with the sound of industry, with the romping of sturdy children, the contests of athletic youths, and the laughter of happy maidens'.[65] The tone of the speech has since been roundly derided. In the words of one commentator, the speech exemplified a reversion to 'primordial' or 'retro-nationalism'.[66] For Tom Garvin, such rhetoric typified the yearning of de Valerite conservatives towards an Ireland 'pious, disciplined and folksy', 'a real-life version of *The Quiet Man*'.[67]

Green dreams aside, the temper of the speech addressed the unique conditions of the Emergency. The speech may belong to de Valera, but the frugal idiom attached to economic hardship was not exclusively his. The view that Ireland belonged out of a war that was 'the fruit of statesmen's follies and human greed'[68] was common. More significantly, a rustic tone characterised much justification of hardship during the war, particularly in combatant nations. In early 1941, with Britain's position in the war appearing increasingly precarious, George Bernard Shaw wrote in the London *Catholic Times* 'Irish ports must be occupied and defended by the British empire, the United States or both'. Prominent Catholic intellectual Alfred O'Rahilly replied by affirming Ireland's right to stay out of 'a competition in atrocity in which victory goes to the competitor who kills and destroys most'.[69] Similarly, rustic sentiments appeared frequently in Irish newspapers at the time. A report from the same year in the *Irish Press* described mourners at the funeral of three women killed by German bombs in County Carlow: 'Men, smoking, not talking - mountainy men, whose feet are on the earth, to whom planes and bombs and calibres of guns are strange language.'[70]

While challenging the staid portrayal of Emergency Ireland has been the distinguishing feature of the recent strides in Emergency historiography, the period is still marked by the absence of accounts offering a critical analysis of changed social and economic conditions in the context of the expansion of state power. The same historiographical advances have exposed Ireland's splendid isolation during the Emergency as myth. The most striking example of shared experience between people in Ireland and those in Europe and beyond at this time was, firstly, scarcity of supplies (particularly food) and, secondly, the effect of state efforts to overcome scarcity and improve productivity. As in every other European nation, the expansion of Ireland's Defence Forces was rapid and pronounced. But, unlike combatant nations, in Ireland government planning and regulation ensured that manpower for the armed services never assumed priority over manpower for economic production.[71]

Tom Garvin has amplified the suitability of the Fianna Fáil hierarchy to the hiatus from the post-agrarian and urban march of modernity that the Emergency provided, arguing that the 'Victorian horse-and-cart economy'[72] caused by shortages sat comfortably with the feudalism of the Catholic Church and the protectionism and clientelism of Fianna Fáil.[73] Yet during the Emergency, the Irish government resorted to fundamentally illiberal state-driven measures in order to increase productivity. In a 1948 election address, de Valera famously conceded that on the problem of emigration, 'we cannot corral the people and say "You must not go out". That is an interference with human liberty and would not be justified except in times of grave emergency'.[74] This statement is as significant in terms of the questions it raises about state interference with human liberty in the period of 'grave emergency' between 1939 and 1945 as it is for the seriousness of the emigration issue in 1948.

As the role of the state expanded during the Emergency, it was the new Department of Supplies which assumed the preeminent role in the domestic management of the Emergency. In 1945, the functions of the department were transferred back to the Department of Industry and Commerce. Subsequently, the latter produced several documents assessing its role during the war. It is clear that the department's civil servants viewed the Emergency as an exceptional period in which social interests took priority over conventional economic objectives. One retrospective explained that a system of price control in ordinary conditions 'sought, where practicable, to provide incentives to manufacturers to increase output' and thus profits.[75] This, the normal situation, contrasted markedly with conditions during the Emergency, which necessitated 'the limitation of profits to levels considered reasonable'.[76] Herein lay a crucial distinction not only between alternative ways in which the economy was regulated but in terms of in what direction, and for whom, the economy was geared. As senior civil servants put it, 'During the war the social advantages of relieving unemployment and developing natural resources took priority over productivity'.[77]

From an official perspective, the Emergency was, therefore, economically as well as historically exceptional. Not only did the independent Irish state face its worst ever supply crisis, but this situation ensured that the mass of the Irish people relied on the government to prevent unfair market practices to a greater degree than ever before. Unsurprisingly, amidst such straitened circumstances, rumours of profiteering and excessive greed were widespread. Among these were allegations that fish were being dumped at sea so that fish would come into the Dublin market at a time which would justify an excessive price to the consumer[78] and that a secret, and sinister-sounding, 'fruit ring' was controlling the distribution of fruit in Dublin.[79] A populist sentiment that demonised the profiteering middleman and the hoarding middle class typified the political discourse surrounding supply shortages: 'The criminals who deal in the black market are not of the Bill Sykes type', declared Seán Lemass in late 1941; 'they are pompous and respectable looking citizens robbing others of their fair share'.[80]

Customary traditions of the marketplace as fair, rather than exploitative, became powerful legitimising notions. The ethic of Irish rationing was based on the notion of just moral reward; the black market, by contrast, was seen by the state as fundamentally socially unjust. During the Emergency, the state not only deployed moral propaganda to discourage black market activity and promote equitable distribution but also took chief responsibility for the *material* assault on 'unfair' market practices. Efforts to establish equitable distribution and increase productivity were also foisted upon the populace by the church. From the pulpit, parish priests regularly decried the black market and emphasised the *spiritual* duty of Catholics to refuse and report offers of black market goods. Catholic discourse promoted social harmony and condemned the black market as aggravating poverty. The Irish bishops repeatedly expressed opinions similar to those of the Bishop of Cork who in 1942 spoke of the 'duty of all' to 'co-operate' in turning their back on the black market so that there would be 'peace and contentment'.[81]

Due to these social and economic pressures, Ireland during the Emergency took on the overtones of moral economy. Moral economy, a term popularised by the English social historian E.P. Thompson, refers to the advocacy of market practices of mutuality and 'fair shares' and an antipathy to profiteering. For Thompson, collective behaviour stimulated by difficult economic conditions was often based around 'a consistent traditional view of social norms and obligations' in which the economy was conceived of as local, fair and paternal; usury and the free market were seen, by contrast, as greedy and immoral.[82] The concept has been most widely used by historians of the eighteenth century but has been applied to many contexts including modern market economies.[83] Many studies of social policy in independent Ireland have concentrated on the political anxiety over the clash of modernity and tradition. In these studies, the 'moral' label has been applied to the social control exercised by the church and the state, with particular reference to *sexual* rather than *economic* morality. As Ferriter contends, it is arguably the privileging of the 'moral' in the Ireland of this time that marks this country as exceptional in a European context.[84] The predominance of the 'moral' in Irish society in the 1940s was particularly evident in the economic sphere but has been generally overlooked by historians.

Commenting on the economic practices in an Irish country town in the interwar period, the socialist politician Noël Browne recalled the dishonesty of haggling for butter, turf and animals. A haggard old horse would be made to look vibrant before a mart by his owner's insertion of mustard and ginger into his rear end. Quite frequently haggling provided 'a sad picture, two desperately poor heads of families each trying to outwit the other for a matter of pence. Such were the imperatives of our competitive society; the farmers could not afford to agree among themselves on a fair price'.[85]

To what extent, then, did Emergency social pressures, market regulation, rationing and price control mark a break with these sort of practices? This book examines the extent to which market restrictions and shortages during the Emergency – which catapulted Ireland back to a 'horse-and-cart economy' – resulted in the emergence (or re-emergence) of forms of *moral economy* in Irish society. It details the multifaceted relationships between the government, pressure groups, the church, the middle class and the rural and urban working class and underclass. It examines whether such interaction provides evidence of a balance and understanding between governor and governed in the negotiation of market conditions, one based on fair price and equitable distribution and a determination to 'Step Together!', or whether a popular alternative conception of 'moral economy' existed in defiance of the state's vision.

A new departure

Fundamentally, measures to ensure economic survival in Emergency Ireland were carried out with the best intention: the prevention of starvation. Nonetheless, the means used to achieve this end demand closer historical scrutiny. While discussing the attitudes of the leaders of the church and state to Emergency conditions, this study also reveals the reactions of ordinary people when faced with the changed economic and social (and indeed moral) priorities created by wartime exigencies. It documents their unwillingness to simply fall in line and do as they were told. As the

Emergency wore on, the membership and support of the Irish Labour Party grew along with working class dissidence.[86] This study, though, provides a bottom-up, rather than an organised labour, history of the Emergency. It explores the response of working people to the government's version of moral economy but concentrates on individuals and communities rather than trade unions.

The main focus of this work is the period from 1939 to 1945. Although analysis extends, in places, to the 'Long Emergency' (shortages and rationing continued until 1948), the unique cocktail which Emergency measures represented had been diluted by that point. Emergency censorship was lifted on 11 May 1945, by which time, the global geopolitical situation – and hence the rationale of moral neutrality – had shifted considerably. Wage controls were lifted in 1946 and the post-war period witnessed a rise in wages, industrial production and population: trends distinctly alien to the Emergency proper.[87]

During the Emergency, consumer capitalism and the use of technology remained at an embryonic stage, unemployment increased, and a grim rise in tubercular and infant mortality rates and malnutrition occurred.[88] Perhaps the most potent symbol of deprivation in Emergency Ireland was the hated black loaf of bread, a one hundred per cent wholegrain staple resulting from Ireland's chronic wheat shortage which first appeared in early 1942.[89] These were hard times indeed, but to point to Emergency Ireland and remark, like the wine shop customer in Dickens's *A Tale of Two Cities*, 'it is not often that many of these miserable beasts know the taste of anything but black bread and death' would itself produce a narrative of stoic resignation. Despite the black loaf, there was the black market – an underground trade in commodities that operated in defiance of the state and the legal system.

With the surge in state regulation came a consequent increase in the engagement of Irish people in illegal acts. According to the church and state, black market activity represented a moral lapse. However, as this study reveals, many people reverted to such actions out of necessity or a refusal to acknowledge the legitimacy of the state's version of moral economy. There seems to be much of 'the fire of life' in border pursuits between customs men and smugglers or in the tensions between the role of the state and the will of the individual. Life was hard during the Emergency but, as this work details, human agency prevailed. If 'Plato's Cave' is to be applied to the inhabitants of Emergency Ireland, the fact that it was also possible for the inhabitants of the cave to escape should not be overlooked. This book reveals the practical expressions and the limitations of that possibility in Ireland between 1939 and 1945.

Notes

1 'Ireland' is used to demonstrate that both the sources used and the historiography discussed reflect a strong 32-county dimension to events. Where differentiation from Northern Ireland is necessary, the terms 'independent Ireland' or 'neutral Ireland' are used interchangeably.

2 Mary E. Daly, *The Buffer State: The Historical Roots of the Department of the Environment* (Dublin, 1997), 249.

3 *The Times*, 19 January 1939.

4 For a good account of public sympathy towards the IRA, see J. Anthony Gaughan, *Alfred O'Rahilly*, 2nd vol. (Naas, 1989), 323.

5 Files referring to IRA and communist activity (1939–1945), Dublin Garda Index to Special Files, 1929–1945.

6 Eunan O'Halpin, *Defending Ireland: The Irish State and Its Enemies since 1922* (Oxford, 2000),161–164.

7 Diary entry for 20 June 1940. University College Dublin Archives (UCDA), Eamon de Valera papers, P150/308.

8 O'Halpin, *Defending Ireland*, 162.

9 For a history of the Irish Defence Forces Emergency Establishment, see John P. Duggan, *A History of the Irish Army* (Dublin, 1991).

10 See Enno Stephan, *Spies in Ireland* (London, 1965); John P. Duggan, *Neutral Ireland and the Third Reich* (Dublin, 1989).

11 Department of Supplies, 'Record of Activities'. National Archives of Ireland (NAI), Department of Industry and Commerce (IND)/EHR/3/15, appendix I.

12 Donal Ó Drisceoil, *Censorship in Ireland, 1939–1945: Neutrality, Politics, and Society* (Cork, 1996), 61.

13 F.S.L. Lyons, *Ireland since the Famine* (Bungay, 1973), 557.

14 Kevin B. Nowlan and T. Desmond Williams eds, *Ireland in the War Years and After* (Dublin, 1969).

15 Clifford Norton to Foreign office, 13 February 1945. Cited in Neville Wylie, 'Switzerland: A Neutral of Distinction?, in Neville Wylie ed., *European Neutrals and Non-Belligerents during the Second World War* (Cambridge, 2002), 334.

16 Robert Fisk, *In Time of War: Ireland, Ulster and the Price of Neutrality1939–45* (London, 1983), 358.

17 For top-down accounts of Emergency diplomacy focusing on de Valera's relations with British representative Sir John Maffey and American representative David Gray, see Lord Longford and Thomas P. O'Neill, *Éamon de Valera* (Dublin, 1970), 374–414; Joseph T. Carroll, *Ireland in the War Years* (New York, 1975); Tim Pat Coogan, *De Valera: Long Fellow, Long Shadow* (London, 1993) 521–629; Robert Brennan, *Ireland Standing Firm and de Valera: A Memoir* (Dublin, 2002), 178–182.

18 Bernard Share, *The Emergency: Neutral Ireland, 1939–45* (Dublin, 1978).

19 Clair Wills, *That Neutral Island: A Cultural History of Ireland during the Second World War* (Dublin, 2007), 10.

20 Tony Gray, *The Lost Years: The Emergency in Ireland 1939–45* (London, 1988).

21 Terence Brown, *Ireland: A Social and Cultural History, 1922–1985* (London, 1985), 175.

22 Betjeman to John Piper, 10 January 1941, in Candida Lycett Green, *John Betjeman Letters*, volume one (London, 1994), 278.

23 See some of the criticism levelled at Frank McCourt's *Angela's Ashes: Memoir of a Childhood* (London, 1996) as summarised in Diarmaid Ferriter, *The Transformation of Ireland, 1900–2000* (Dublin, 2005), 361.

24 Alan S. Milward, *War, Economy and Society, 1939–45* (London, 1977), xii.

25 In his survey of European neutrals, Neville Wylie distinguishes between non-belligerents which later joined the war effort and 'long haul' neutrals. See Wylie ed., *European Neutrals,* 1–10.

26 R.F. Foster's *Modern Ireland, 1600–1972* (London, 1988) devotes just four pages (559–563) to the Emergency; in Lyons's *Ireland since the Famine,* the Emergency forms a small part at the end of the 'ascendancy of de Valera' section (555–558); Ferriter's *Transformation of Ireland,* likewise, situates the Emergency as part of the 1932–1945 section (358–450).

27 J. Peter Neary and Cormac Ó Gráda, 'Protection, Economic War and Structural Change: The 1930s in Ireland', *Irish Historical Studies,* 27, 107 (1991), 252–255.

28 John Horgan, *Seán Lemass: The Enigmatic Patriot* (Dublin, 1997), 110.

29 Department of Industry and Commerce, *Statistical Abstracts,* 1940–1946.

30 Supplies, 'Record of Activities'. NAI, IND/EHR/3/15, p. 42.

31 *Statistical Abstract,* 1940.

32 *Statistical Abstracts,* 1940–1946.

33 *Statistical Abstract,* 1940.

34 Neary and Ó Gráda, 'Protection', 255.

35 David Johnson, *The Interwar Economy in Ireland* (Dublin, 1989), 41.

36 John A. Murphy, 'The Irish Party System', in Nowlan and Williams eds, *Ireland in the War Years,* 148–149.

37 J.J. Lee, *Ireland 1912–1985: Politics and Society* (Cambridge, 1989), 193.

38 Mary Muldowney, *The Second World War and Irish Women: An Oral History* (Dublin, 2007), 119.

39 Cormac Ó Gráda, *A Rocky Road: The Irish Economy since the 1920s* (Manchester, 1997), 1–8.

40 Finbarr O'Shea, 'A Tale of Two Acts: Government and Trade Unions', in Dermot Keogh and Mervyn O'Driscoll eds, *Ireland in World War Two: Neutrality and Survival* (Cork, 2004), 222.

41 James Meenan, 'The Irish Economy during the War', in K.B. Nowlan and D.T. Williams eds, *Ireland in the War Years and After* (Dublin, 1969), 34.

42 Department of Supplies, 'Historical Survey'. NAI, IND/EHR/3/C1, part IV, p. 161.

43 *Statistical Abstract,* 1945, 162.

44 *Irish Times,* 6 February 1943.

45 *Statistical Abstract,* 1945, 162.

46 Wills, *Neutral Island,* 128.

47 *Statistical Abstracts,* 1938–1945.

48 Supplies, 'Record of Activities'. NAI, IND/EHR/3/15, p. 42.

49 Mary E. Daly, *The Slow Failure: Population Decline and Independent Ireland, 1920–1973* (London, 2006), 146.

50 McCourt, *Angela's Ashes,* 247.

51 Emmet O'Connor, *A Labour History of Ireland, 1824–1960* (Dublin, 1992), 137.

52 Mary E. Daly, *Social and Economic History of Ireland since 1800* (Dublin, 1981), 157. Liam Kennedy puts these figures at 27% and 70%, respectively. See Liam Kennedy, *The Modern Industrialisation of Ireland 1940–1988* (Dublin, 1989), 6.

53 *Statistical Abstracts,* 1940–1946.

54 Supplies, 'Record of Activities'. NAI, IND/EHR/3/15, p. 46.
55 See Ferriter's introduction to *Transformation of Ireland* for a challenge to the negativity of the 'Age of de Valera' school. See also Ferriter's *Judging Dev: A Reassessment of the Life and Legacy of Eamon De Valera* (Dublin, 2007).
56 David Lloyd, *Ireland after History* (Cork, 1999), 77.
57 Geoffrey Roberts, 'Three Narratives of Neutrality: historians and Ireland's War', in Brian Girvin and Geoffrey Roberts eds, *Ireland and the Second World War: Politics, Society and Remembrance* (Dublin, 2000), 179. A notable recent exception to this trend is Brian Girvin's *The Emergency: Neutral Ireland 1939–45* (London, 2006).
58 Gerard Fee, 'The Effects of World War II on Dublin's Low-Income Families, 1939–1945' (unpublished PhD thesis, UCD, 1996). See also Lindsey Earner-Byrne's *Mother and Child: Maternity and Child Welfare in Ireland, 1920s–1960s* (Manchester, 2007).
59 Peter Rigney, *Trains, Coal and Turf: Transport in Emergency Ireland* (Dublin, 2010).
60 Wills, *Neutral Island*, 424.
61 The treatment of the period in Ó Drisceoil and Wills contrasts markedly with Benjamin Grob-Fitzgibbon's unenlightening *The Irish Experience during the Second World War: An Oral History* (Dublin, 2004). Grob-Fitzgibbon's exaggeration of the burlesque ribaldry of wartime Dublin smacks of the bacchanalian narratives of Irish greed and plenty conveyed jealously in the British wartime press.
62 Ó Drisceoil, *Censorship in Ireland*, 285–287.
63 An extreme political example of this belief is to be found in the fascist Ailtirí na hAiseirghe movement. See R.M. Douglas, *Ailtirí na hAiséirghe and the Fascist 'New Order' in Ireland* (Manchester, 2009).
64 *Irish Times*, 4 February 2012.
65 *Irish Press*, 18 March 1943.
66 Richard Kearney, *Postnationalist Ireland: Politics, Culture, Philosophy* (London, 1997), 157.
67 Tom Garvin, *Preventing the Future: Why Was Ireland So Poor for So Long?* (Dublin, 2004), 63.
68 See John O'Doherty, 'The Catholic Church in 1939', *Irish Ecclesiastical Record*, 55 (January–June 1940), 1–14.
69 Cited in Gaughan, *Alfred O'Rahilly*, vol. II, 325–326.
70 *Irish Press*, 6 January 1941.
71 Milward, *War, Economy and Society*, 217–218.
72 Garvin, *Preventing*, 81.
73 Garvin, *Preventing*, 62–111.
74 *Irish Press*, 3 February 1948.
75 Department of Industry and Commerce, 'Observations regarding Price Control', *Report of the Committee of Inquiry into Taxation on Industry* (Dublin, 1955), 115.
76 Industry and Commerce, 'Observations', 115.
77 *Report of the Committee of Inquiry into Taxation on Industry*, 10–11.
78 Peadar Doyle, *Dáil Debates*, vol. 80, col. 1205, 29 May 1940.
79 Untitled memorandum on fruit supply in Dublin city. NAI, Hilda Tweedy Papers, 98/17/5/5/43.
80 *Irish Times*, 13 December 1941.
81 Daniel Cohalan, cited in *Irish Independent*, 28 May 1942.

82 E.P. Thompson, 'The Moral Economy of the English Crowd in the Eighteenth Century', *Past & Present*, 50 (1971), 76–136.

83 For a good application of moral economy to modern societies, see James C. Scott, *Weapons of the Weak: Everyday Forms of Peasant Resistance* (Yale, 1985). For the application of the term to actors in a modern market economy, see Thomas Clay Arnold, 'Rethinking Moral Economy', *The American Political Science Review*, 95, 1 (2001), 85–95. Tom Bartlett has argued that the militia riots at the end of the eighteenth century marked the end of moral economy – 'that balance, that tacit understanding, between governor and governed' – in Ireland. See Bartlett, 'An End to Moral Economy: The Irish Militia Disturbances of 1793', *Past & Present*, 99 (1983), 42. It has also been argued that moral economy in Ireland was more enduring. See, for instance, James Kelly, *The Liberty and Ormond Boys: Factional Riots in Eighteenth-Century Dublin* (Dublin, 2005).

84 Diarmaid Ferriter, *Occasions of Sin: Sex and Society in Modern Ireland* (Dublin, 2009).

85 Noël Browne, *Against the Tide* (Dublin, 1986), 22.

86 See Niamh Puirséil, *The Irish Labour Party, 1922–1973* (Dublin, 2007). See also Kieran Allen, *Fianna Fáil and Irish Labour, 1926 to Present* (London, 1997). For Seán MacEntee's relationship with organised labour as Minister for Industry and Commerce, see Tom Feeney, *Seán MacEntee: A Political Life* (Dublin, 2009), 112–128. For the activities of the radical left, see Mike Milotte, *Communism in Modern Ireland: The Pursuit of the Workers' Republic since 1916* (Dublin, 1984). For liberal opposition to the growing conservatism of the party, see Andrée Sheehy-Skeffington, *Skeff: The Life of Owen Sheehy-Skeffington 1909–1970* (Dublin, 1991).

87 Daly, *Social and Economic History*, 158.

88 See Browne, *Against the Tide*; Liam Price, *Dr. Dorothy Price: An Account of Twenty Years' Fight Against Tuberculosis in Ireland* (Oxford, 1957); James Deeney, *To Cure and to Care: Memoirs of a Chief Medical Officer* (Dun Laoghaire, 1989). For a good oral history of the disease's impact in the rural west, see Brenda Ní Shúilleabháin ed., *Bibeanna. Memories from a Corner of Ireland* (Cork, 1997).

89 See Ciarán Bryan, 'Rationing in Emergency Ireland, 1939–1948' (unpublished PhD thesis, NUIM, 2014) for the negative nutritional effects.

2

Anglo-Irish trade and business relations

I have discovered that the real cause of the differences between these two countries is spiritual and will not be cured until God wills it.

John Betjeman, 20 April 1943

The 'corporation sole'

To John Betjeman, Anglo-Irish tensions boiled down to differences in national temperament. During the war, however, the principal differences between the two countries were very much material. Ireland's political elite began planning for wartime supply shortages some time before the Emergency began. As early as 1935, Minister for Defence Frank Aiken established an interdepartmental committee to report on essential materials required in the event of a major European war.[1] By 1935, Aiken – a farmer and former IRA strongman from County Armagh – had held the Defence brief for three years. The following year, against the backdrop of general European militarisation and major civil conflict in Spain, plans were drawn up by Aiken and others for the economic survival of the country as a neutral state.[2] In November 1937, Minister for Industry and Commerce Seán Lemass, other ministers and high-ranking civil servants were informed by the British Food Department that 'complete economic control' would be exercised by the British government in the event of war. This, they warned, would lead to the 'absence of a free market in the U.K.'[3]

These early indications of disruption to normal trading conditions between Ireland and Britain prompted the establishment of the Emergency Supplies Branch of the Department of Industry and Commerce in 1938. The new branch came under the control of Lemass. An immaculately attired, pencil-moustached young Dubliner, Lemass had worked with Aiken in de Valera's anti-treaty political camp for well over a decade.[4] His new branch was devoted to the anticipation, assessment and organisation of Ireland's supply needs if a significant European conflict developed.[5] The latest extension to Lemass's ministerial powers, his new branch would expand rapidly over the next seven years or so, exacerbating key interdepartmental and interpersonal rivalries within de Valera's cabinet. Aiken and Lemass did not see eye to eye on many issues and, as Lemass accrued more power, his major cabinet rival Seán MacEntee – a right-leaning Belfast nationalist – would lose much of his.

After Britain and France declared war on Germany, the hurriedly enacted Emergency Powers Act gave the government the power to 'make provision for the control of supplies and services essential to the life of the community'.[6] The state now took on extraordinary powers to regulate economic activity. To facilitate this, Taoiseach Éamon de Valera announced a 'rearrangement of the functions which are carried out by the members of the Government'. There would now be 'a Minister in charge of supplies so that he will be able to give his whole time to that very important service'.[7] Shortly thereafter, the Emergency Supplies Branch was upgraded to a department of state and Lemass appointed Minister for Supplies.

When the Emergency Supplies Branch of Industry and Commerce was established in September 1938, it was described as 'the nucleus of an organisation for central purchasing and selling'.[8] During the Emergency, this objective was put into practice as economic control was centralised in Lemass's hands. As Minister for Supplies, Lemass controlled the 'treatment, keeping, storage, movement, distribution, sale, purchase, use and consumption' of all goods.[9] In this role, to quote Ronan Fanning, he 'assumed the role and status of an economic overlord'.[10] This term reflects the extraordinary hiatus from normality that the Emergency represented and the extraordinary powers that Lemass assumed as a consequence. His was certainly a leviathan portfolio. The Ministers and Secretaries Act (1924), which defined ministers and departments of state, was even amended in 1939 to allow the Minister for Supplies to act as a 'corporation sole'.[11] The new minister had the power to control all prices and profits in Ireland, control a wide range of industries and police the domestic market.[12]

In carrying out his new brief, Lemass relied on Departmental Secretary John Leydon and Assistant Secretary John Williams. The hagiography surrounding Lemass and T.K. Whitaker – the two men credited for Ireland's 'Economic Turn' away from protectionism in the 1960s – has nudged Leydon out of popular historical memory. Born to affluence in County Roscommon in 1895, Leydon was a devout Catholic and a talented senior civil servant. Having transferred to the Irish Free State civil service in 1923, Leydon joined the Department of Finance and rose quickly. In 1932, he was offered the post of secretary of the Department of Industry and Commerce by the outgoing Fine Gael administration. Lemass, the incoming Minister for Industry and Commerce, renewed the offer, and Leydon joined him as secretary of Industry and Commerce and, during the Emergency, secretary of the Department of Supplies.

In existence exclusively for the six-year duration of the Emergency, Supplies formed a critical part of the state's strengthened executive. Unfortunately, the paucity of the department's records presents a problem for historians analysing its work. There are three reasons why the volume of extant papers does not reflect the department's elevated role and status. Firstly, Lemass and Leydon encouraged working practices that were novel, revolutionary even, in the civil service at the time, favouring action over lengthy memoranda and encouraging the use of the telephone.[13] Secondly, there was a shortage of paper during the Emergency and therefore correspondence was economised. Finally, some of the records of the department were lost or destroyed. Fortunately, the Department of Industry and Commerce compiled a thorough post-war overview of Supplies' ephemeral but highly significant history: the 'Historical Survey'.[14] This vast civil service document (the authorship of which is uncertain) numbers just under 700 pages. Frequently overly praiseworthy of the department's efforts, it nonetheless provides the most illuminating account of the management of Ireland's economy during the Emergency. It is discussed, in detail for the first time, in the following two chapters.

British sea power

Due to the size of its fleets, the United Kingdom represented Ireland's economic lifeline during the Emergency. Around two thirds of Ireland's imports came from the United Kingdom and nearly all her exports went the opposite way.[15] Relations with Britain had been reasonably healthy since the Anglo-Irish Trade Agreement of April 1938. Later that year, Leydon shuttled back and forth to London. He received assurances from the British Board of Trade of a 'square deal' on shipments of tea, sugar, coal and agricultural machinery.[16] The altered priorities of a war economy were to change this happy situation. Just after the outbreak of war in September 1939, Leydon was summoned to London at the urgent request of the British Board of Trade. Although discussion was confined to 'the next two or three weeks', Leydon returned to Dublin to inform Lemass that a number of 'unsatisfactory' export controls had been hinted at by senior British civil servants.[17]

Leydon's worries could be traced back to his minister's failure to establish a merchant navy during the 1930s. This meant that Ireland entered the war totally dependent on British shipping. British companies imported essential bulk cargoes like wheat, maize, timber and fertilisers as well as coal supplies. Ireland had been well placed to take advantage of the low prices for vessels during the shipping depression of the 1930s but, on a number of occasions, Lemass declined the opportunity to establish a merchant marine.[18] This strategic failure would become clearer as war drew closer. In 1926, there were 152 steam ships registered in Ireland; by 1937, this had fallen to 141; and at the outbreak of war, neutral Ireland had just 56 ships (none of which were of ocean-going standard) at her disposal.[19]

In June 1939, with world war looming, the Irish crew of the ship *Normandy Coast* walked ashore at Dublin Port in an act of protest against the transfer of the ship's port of registration from Dublin to Liverpool.[20] Three months later, in September 1939, there occurred a similar act in the Port of Holyhead when the British crews of three vessels refused to sail under the Irish tricolour.[21] The Irish crew who walked off the *Normandy Coast* worried that if they stayed aboard their vessel under the red ensign, they would find themselves under attack from German U-boats. At the outbreak of war, the Irish government instructed all Irish-registered vessels to fly the Irish flag, and the protesting sailors wanted it hoisted. But this, as the British sailors at Holyhead argued, was illegal since a ship's flag was determined by its country of *ownership*.

Lemass's top officials already knew that this was the case. Back in February 1939, Leydon had fretfully instructed civil servants in Industry and Commerce to draw up a memorandum illustrating just how dependent Ireland was on other countries for essential supplies.[22] When the report reached Leydon's desk in April 1939, it made for alarming reading. The bulk of Ireland's imports came from Britain and its commonwealth. The value of shipping shares held by Free State residents was pitiful. In the British and Irish Steam Packet Company – the largest and most important shipping company to Ireland – only £158,000 of the £1,342,000 share capital was Irish. Of all the ships in Irish ports, a mere 5% were Irish-owned. The memo made it clear that 'if war should break out we are at the mercy of the United Kingdom' and that 'economic activities of this country could be completely paralysed'.[23]

With war only months away, Ireland's supply of key commodities such as coal, wheat, maize, petrol and timber was completely at the mercy of the British. Leydon described the memo as of 'vital importance' and instructed it to be circulated to ministers immediately.[24] By this stage, though, it was too late. The newly formed Emergency Supplies Branch of Industry and Commerce frantically consulted Whitehall on whether British-owned ships would be requisitioned en masse from Ireland as part of the war effort. But the British had already made this cynical calculation. As early as the Munich Crisis of September 1938, the British Board of Trade decided that in the event of a conflict, the well-worn tactic of economic blockade would cut off maritime trade, forcing neutral shipping into British hands because of the lack of other markets.[25]

Ireland's dependence on Britain was most vividly illustrated by Ireland's perilous reliance on shipped imports at a time of fierce marine warfare. Nine Irish ships were sunk by U-boats in 1940, with the loss of fifty-eight men.[26] In April and May 1940, Lemass and James Ryan – Wexford farmer, medical doctor and the Minister for Agriculture – travelled to London where Anthony Eden, Neville Chamberlain's Secretary of State for Dominion Affairs, informed them in the most gentlemanly manner that the 'elimination of competition' on shipping was coming, a regrettable consequence of Britain's highly centralised war economy.[27]

The message, for all its mannerly delivery, was clear: Ireland would no longer be able to charter her own ships. It now seemed likely that Lemass would have little choice but to make concessions to the British in return for access to shipped imports but after France fell in early June 1940, Taoiseach Éamon de Valera turned down the British offer to end partition in return for the use of Irish ports. The following month, August 1940, the British began to turn the screw. The British Ministries of Food and Shipping requested that British merchant vessels be allowed to use Irish ports.

Lord Fred Leathers, British Minister for Shipping, wrote to new British Prime Minister Winston Churchill, expressing confidence that the Irish government's weak economic position would force them to agree to this deal, which would have brought all Irish shipping under British control.[28]

Irish policymakers now faced a tough choice. The deal would have given Ireland much-needed access to food and fuel cargoes. Leathers assured Churchill that to Ireland, a country reliant on shipped imports but without a merchant marine, the offer was too good to be turned down. Senior Irish civil servants agreed that there was a 'strong economic argument' in favour of granting the British these facilities. On the other hand, the agreement was likely to place Irish civilians at the mercy of *Luftwaffe* bombs. As Leathers justified the deal to Churchill, the subtext became clear. It would 'relieve the heavy concentration of large vessels' in British ports.[29] As this would have meant the extension of heavy German bombing to Ireland, and Dublin in particular, the deal was turned down at a subsequent Irish cabinet meeting.

In refusing the British offer, Irish policymakers ensured that for the rest of the war Ireland would suffer an agonising supply squeeze aimed at coercing Ireland into the war on the Allied side. The decision not to facilitate British shipping was based on the rationale that neutrality would have been compromised and German aggression would have followed. Interestingly, though, the Allies viewed similar concessions to German shipping by neutral Sweden as tolerable. American observers, writing in 1942, regretted that the Swedish were assisting the German marine but noted that this was within the definition of neutrality as defined by international law.[30] Back in 1940, with the Nazi war machine at its formidable peak, the Irish government calculated that the German high command would not take such a benign view.

A short time later, Churchill announced a total economic blockade against Germany. Any ship transporting cargo through this blockade had to obtain a 'navicert'.[31] As well as cutting off continental Europe from the world's food supplies, this piece of British red tape was prejudiced against Ireland as a neutral. Ireland was the only country – aside from Syria and Liberia – where navicert control applied to both imports and exports.[32] This, as Irish officials noted, was an 'absolute and indiscriminate application' of the rules applying to neutral states, ignoring both Ireland's geographical position and its practically pro-Allied disposition.[33]

In the following months, Britain's stance hardened further. Germany's occupation of Norway and France had given her bases on the Atlantic which increased the range of U-boats in the war against British merchant shipping. In response but also as a nudge to neutral Ireland to join the war effort, the British imposed strict trade restrictions in January 1941, and the relationship between the two countries became increasingly strained. As Robert Fisk attests, Ireland was the victim of a British squeeze on supplies intended to coerce de Valera into joining the Allied cause.[34] This move was also motivated by British domestic concerns. By autumn 1940, the Board of Trade, along with other departments, was becoming increasingly anxious to transfer all available economic production to a total war footing.[35] Ireland's isolation was aggravated in January 1941 when the British government tore up the previous year's chartering arrangements, citing the 'exigencies of war'.[36]

These conditions necessitated the formation of Irish Shipping Ltd. Set up in March 1941, the company was able to secure fifteen ships in total; most of these foreign vessels laid up in Irish ports.[37] This sorry situation is illustrated by the fate of seven Irish commercial tankers that Britain had bought from Ireland in September 1939. As British cargoes for Ireland started to dwindle by early 1941, Leydon asked for them back. Unfortunately, by this stage, four of the seven had been sunk. When Supplies asked again in January 1943, they were informed that only one had survived German U-boat attacks.[38] The bulk of Ireland's ramshackle shipping was concentrated on importing grain from the United States and the Lisbon trade route.[39] The company's first ship, *Irish Poplar*, was a Greek merchant vessel which had been found drifting and abandoned by Spanish fishermen after being bombed; it had been stripped of everything of value by the Spanish, and on its first voyage, its mainmast collapsed.[40]

Ireland's subservient position to British shipping is demonstrated on two occasions when relations between Supplies and the Irish Censorship Board noticeably deteriorated. Both concerned the publication of sensitive stories about shipping. On the first occasion in May 1941, Michael Knightly, Irish Chief Press Censor, had allowed newspapers to publish a false story about the arrival of a cargo of oranges, lemons and wines. An angry John Leydon informed Thomas J. Coyne, Assistant Controller of Censorship, that he had telephoned his office the previous evening and received an 'explicit assurance' that the stories would not go to press.[41] Coyne replied in a very apologetic tone asking Leydon to forgive 'our incompetence'.[42] When censorship officials repeated the oversight in April 1944, allowing the press to reveal British supremacy through the refusal to issue licences to Irish ships, Leydon was apoplectic. He wrote to Coyne claiming that the story's publication was 'simply calamitous'.[43] Coyne, in turn, reprimanded Knightly for allowing the story, one which 'is likely to have the most embarrassing consequences for the government'.[44]

These examples demonstrate Supplies' supremacy over the domestic departmental scene but also the woeful state of Irish shipping. With Ireland's small merchant fleet unable to guarantee sufficient supplies for the country, considerable Irish resilience was required to secure essential supplies from Britain. Often, the Departments of External Affairs and Supplies had to engage in 'special and repeated representations' to the Irish High Commissioner in London, John Dulanty, because after the restriction of supplies from Europe in June 1940, direct representations to British firms and departments were not effective. Even the success of these representations 'depended, to some extent, on whether the official concerned was or was not well disposed towards this country'.[45]

Supplies did occasionally succeed in securing special exceptions to the squeeze. The trade in hides with Britain stopped in that year after a large consignment was

seized by the British Leather Controller, but Lemass was able to secure the continued supply of Donegal hides to Northern Ireland.[46] Similarly, after the British
imposed bans on the import of Irish cottage industry products in early 1941,
Supplies successfully lobbied for the exception of cotton-string gloves and toys
made in Gaeltacht areas.[47] Leydon could also rely on influential British figures, most
notably British Minister for Food Lord Woolton, to make representations on
Ireland's behalf. On one occasion after unsuccessful lobbying by Leydon, it took the
prediction of 'famine conditions in Ireland' by Irish peer Lord Granard to secure the
release from Britain of chemicals used to prevent potato blight.[48]

Yet throughout the Emergency, the British wielded the economic weapon. British
officials' refusal to export fats and oils essential to Ireland in October 1942 led to the
immediate addition of soap to the Irish ration book.[49] Consequently, three small
Irish merchant ships based in Lisbon were forced to undertake a hazardous voyage
to Angola to get five thousand tons of oils and fats.[50] These Allied blockades were
viewed as mercenary by officials from Supplies. The Historical Survey noted bitterly
that German officials had often proved more flexible than the Allies when it came to
allowing passage for shipped imports heading to Ireland.[51]

Notwithstanding the occasionally benevolent British official and the fact that
Leydon normally enjoyed good relations with several top British officials,[52] representatives of Supplies often effectively went cap in hand to their British counterparts. This pose was rarely struck, however, and Irish officials maintained an attitude
of sturdy independence. This is conveyed in the Historical Survey, which attributes
much verve and dynamism to Supplies in managing the supply crisis. This verdict is
mitigated by the crucial consideration that the concentration of economic functions
under its auspices had as much to do with trends emerging across the Irish Sea as it
did with its own energy. The British war economy was organised on a highly centralised basis.[53] On numerous occasions, the British Ministry of Food and Board of
Trade exerted pressure on its Irish counterparts to exert more control over trade.

Ultimately, Britain's lead proved decisive in the course which the department
took. Supplies regularly came in for heavy criticism from the British Board of Trade
for allowing Irish enterprise too much independence. Where there existed a number
of importers for a certain commodity, rather than a monopoly, British authorities
forced Supplies to establish itself as the central importing agent for that commodity,
effectively controlling the entry of all goods.[54] Even in instances where departmental
papers claim that Supplies set up central importing bodies under its own initiative
– such as the non-profit Tea Importers (Éire) Ltd, established in July 1941[55] – the
timing is suggestive of British pressure. If private Irish firms continued to export
without adhering to British restrictions, the British Board of Trade would flex its
muscles and force Supplies to restrict exports.[56]

When it came to supplies essential to public health, the British outlook was
generally a pragmatic one, regarding it as an issue which (for the good of Britain
as much as Ireland) necessitated a common approach. For instance, the smallpox

vaccine for the island of Ireland was produced in Dublin, with one third of it sent north of the border. When, in 1942, the manufacturer complained to Supplies that capillary glass tubes, an essential component of the vaccine's packaging, had run out, the British authorities were more than happy to grant Supplies' request for glass tubing, particularly since the shortage occurred in the wake of a serious smallpox outbreak in Glasgow.[57] Similarly, when trade agreements conformed to Britain's interests, Supplies was able to wring concessions. Supplies had no difficulty procuring asbestos fibre from the United Kingdom because a significant tonnage was used to manufacture asbestos cement products for export to Northern Ireland.[58] Likewise, the Irish Cement Company was able to readily secure machinery and parts from Britain and, in late 1942, even coal.[59]

This contrasted markedly with Britain's general reluctance to release machinery, which forced the government to postpone planned capital projects such as the Poulaphouca Hydroelectric Scheme in County Wicklow.[60] Despite repeated representations by the department, neither would the British authorities exchange finished metal for any amount of the 10,000 tons worth of scrap metal recovered annually from Atlantic shipwrecks on Irish shores.[61] Resorting to desperate measures, by 1943 Supplies was engaged in an odd legal dispute with British authorities over rubber washed up on Irish shores from Atlantic wrecks. Rubber was usually carried on the decks of ships due to its bulk and consequently was often jettisoned by merchant ships caught in severe storms or under U-boat attack. The Irish assured their British counterparts that 'any rubber salvaged which could be identified as British property would be surrendered'. This concession was, as the Survey contentedly recorded, a 'safe promise' because 'rubber is usually dispatched in *unmarked* bales'.[62]

The unwillingness of British officials to swap supplies for the sea's tragic bounty contrasted with their keenness to take Ireland's beer: through barter if necessary. In 1938 and 1939, Ireland exported around 800,000 barrels of beer annually. In 1940 and 1941, this figure leapt to the 900,000 mark. This increase was due to the rise in demand for beer from the rapidly expanding number of men enlisted in the British military and in British war work. By the end of 1941, however, wheat was becoming seriously scarce in Ireland. Consequently, Lemass imposed export restrictions on the malting of barley and banned the export of beer altogether in March 1942. Faced with a thirsty garrison of American and British troops in Northern Ireland, the British agreed to release stocks of wheat held in the United States and coal in return for beer, and in 1943, the department was able to secure agricultural machinery in exchange for beer.[63]

For Lemass, an avid gambler, beer was a rare but reliable trump card. Nonetheless, the Historical Survey overstates the ease with which barter arrangements were agreed. In fact, Foreign Affairs records indicate that, unsurprisingly, the agreements were reached only after stormy exchanges between the two sides. After the British complained of the 'acute' beer shortage in Belfast following Lemass's restrictions, a hasty agreement was drawn up whereby Britain would exchange badly needed

stocks of wheat in exchange for Irish beer.[64] The export ban was lifted only temporarily, however. A short time later, Guinness complained that they did not have
sufficient coal to produce enough beer for both the home and export markets.
British officials agreed to release more coal to Ireland if Leydon would give them
the assurance that the extra coal would be used exclusively by Guinness to produce
more beer.[65] Leydon, displaying a characteristic honesty, cited the desperate public
need for coal in Ireland and therefore refused to give his assurance. The deal collapsed. Later attempts to secure fertilisers and machinery were met with the British
Ministry of Food's high-handed insistence that 'barter arrangements were not
looked upon with favour' and that they preferred a 'gentleman's agreement'.[66]
Leydon, quite reasonably, replied that experience had proven such agreements
were 'useless'.[67] Barter proved a highly volatile business, and when Ireland did succeed in securing fertilisers and machinery in return for beer, it was in the face of
strong opposition from the United States Combined Raw Materials Board and the
British Ministry of Agriculture. Often, the quantities received after fierce bargaining were described as 'most disappointing'.[68]

From 1944, with the end of the war in sight, the situation improved. From 1944
to 1946, Lemass felt confident enough in the sustainability of British demand to
hand over the beer negotiations to Guinness. Guinness received stocks of barley in
return and, on Lemass's instruction, allocated it proportionately to smaller breweries.[69]
Leaving negotiations to Guinness, an established pre-protectionist company which
Lemass did not trust, indicated a slow return to economic normality and the slow
receding of the state's interventionist role. Yet these green shoots of recovery in trade
relations between Britain and Ireland reflected a geopolitical and economic situation in which the Allies were in the ascendant. They also emerged from the fact that
as the Emergency progressed, Ireland turned increasingly to economic autarchy and
Supplies learned to take a harder stance with Britain. Trade talks were commonly
bad tempered and characterised by threats of suspension from both sides. As the
Emergency wore on, the list of items prohibited for export became more geared
towards the preservation of home stocks than British demands.

When conditions demanded, the Irish export list was also opened to the needs of
other departments. The Department of Agriculture, for example, generally wanted
free exit for agricultural produce;[70] the Department of Defence, for its part, wanted
to preserve all non-ferrous scrap for the manufacture of munitions.[71] Whereas other
departments of state, desperate for imported British goods, urged a conciliatory
approach to the British,[72] Leydon and Lemass often maintained a hard line. 'For
heaven's sake make it clear that you are not trying to force our hand', urged a friendly
official from the British Dominions Office to Leydon in trade talks in 1943.[73] Refusing to heed such advice in this and other instances, Supplies favoured presenting the
British with the fait accompli of halting beer exports and testing the British
response.[74] It was a risky strategy with very high stakes, but barter arrangements had
reached a stable footing by 1944. While uncomfortably at the mercy of British trade

for much of the Emergency period, Lemass and Leydon's poker-faced demeanour worked more effectively as the conflict drew to a close.

Fundamentally, though, British sea power subjected Ireland to a crippling economic squeeze. Ireland was not the only neutral country to fall victim to such economic bullying. Sweden and Switzerland were dependent on Germany, the dominant power in the continental economic sphere, for coal and fertilisers. In the prelude to war, Switzerland moved fast to lessen its economic dependence by buying up steamers and freighters.[75] While Ireland, a country with a large seaboard, failed to establish a merchant marine, landlocked Switzerland secured the designation of Basel as a 'Swiss seaport'.[76] As the war progressed, however, the Swiss were subjected to the iron fist of the German *Kriegsmarine*.[77] Sweden, likewise, was subjected to economic exactions. The country was dependent on the Allies for food and fuel supplies, and the Anglo-Swedish shipping agreements, signed early in the war, gradually gave way to Allied threats to withhold oil supplies and bomb Swedish factories.[78] The Germans, too, ensured that they received their pound of flesh for respecting Swedish neutrality.

Although ostensibly friendly towards Germany, Spain fell within the Allied Atlantic sphere of economic influence. Consequently, the Allies forced the country's ruler, Francisco Franco, into neutrality by threatening to cut off oil supplies.[79] By the end of the conflict, they were still forcing the dictator's hand, cutting off supplies in 1944 in order to stop Spanish exports to Germany. Likewise, for Portugal's Prime Minister António de Oliveira Salazar, the price for retaining long-standing Luso-British trade agreements was an economic squeeze. As well as suffering naval blockades, Portugal was subjected to the British policy of pre-emption: the over-buying of commodities in order to cut off trade with the Axis.[80] Ireland, as a neutral in the same sphere without a merchant navy, was forced to endure economic subservience for the duration of the Emergency: this was to decisively impact the domestic management of the war.

The 'economic overlord': Lemass and Irish enterprise, 1939–1945

Domestically, the amount of elbow room that Supplies took on was bound to rankle with some of those seated at the head table of the Irish economy during the war years. The Historical Survey reveals that from its inception in late 1938, Supplies clashed with Irish manufacturers and banks. In large part, though, the department's decisive interventionism in the home market was influenced by British pressure to centralise economic control, ensuring Ireland conformed to the economic needs of British war socialism.

Anticipating that war on the continent would result in a severe restriction in supplies – a situation grimly realised with the fall of France in June 1940 – officials from Supplies instructed Irish manufacturers and importers to lay in at least six months' reserve stock of supplies.[81] Manufacturers consented but were angered by the government's refusal to grant them guarantees against loss. Lemass had, in fact, tried to secure such assistance previously by asking Irish banks to reduce interest rates for the purpose of the scheme but was met with their refusal to grant such concessions. The Historical Survey notes bitterly that 'the Irish banks who, in 1938/39, would not advance money for the purchase of raw materials, were at a later date prepared to gamble it on the survival of the British Empire by investing in British government loans'.[82]

These early exchanges set the tone for the remainder of the Emergency. In 1940, Lemass accused the Irish Federation of Manufacturers of 'dictating' to his department.[83] The department was consistently irritated by the willingness of Irish industrialists to enter into private negotiations in Britain, where they made commitments with long-term consequences for the nation's trade without consulting the government.[84] Large businesses were frequently uncooperative with the department's efforts to compile statistics and conserve reserve stocks. This was particularly the case with non-Irish businesses: in 1939 and 1940 Irish Shell, Irish American Oil and Texas (Ireland) repeatedly refused Lemass's requests that they lay in stocks of petrol.[85] Irish Dunlop similarly refused to lay in stocks of tyres without advance capital from the government.[86]

The department deemed that this situation was due to the dichotomous relationship between private enterprise and the state in general, rather than the fickle attitude of *foreign* enterprise towards the welfare of the state. All traders, whether domestic or foreign, the Survey noted, held a 'natural opposition' to the interference of the department in their affairs. This situation existed because 'the primary object of all traders is to earn as high a profit as possible', an outlook which was unacceptable in the unique circumstances created by the war.[87] Supplies, on the other hand, possessed the 'primary purpose of protecting the interests of the consumer'.[88]

This conflict with the interests of Irish capital clashed with Fianna Fáil's protectionist policies of the 1930s, when native businesses were protected by tariff walls. Mary Daly has argued that Fianna Fáil's involvement in the Irish economy during the 1930s was conducted on an ad hoc basis with Lemass both conceding monopoly powers to foreign businesses and retaining close informal links with native businessmen.[89] The state took on a strident role, but key economic initiatives and profits still remained in the hands of Irish private enterprise. During the Emergency, by contrast, a significant departure in Fianna Fáil's 'economic revolution' occurred.

Tension between the Irish state and owners of private capital was intensified, of course, by British pressure. But the department was also spurred by what was perceived to be its economic cause. In a social climate infused with moral neutrality propaganda, Supplies, donning the armour of moral economy, attempted to assert control over production. In the case of salt supplies, for example, Lemass imposed a monopoly on imports in 1941 in order to force reluctant manufacturers to build up reserve stocks.[90] In late 1942, as supplies of this essential foodstuff dried up, Supplies stepped into the market to limit its sale and distribution.[91] The preservation of sugar stocks, moreover, was one of the 'success stories' of the department.[92] Although such measures fell short of the implementation of full state management of the

economy, they were certainly strong-arm tactics aimed at ensuring equitable distribution. A 1944 departmental memorandum makes it clear that one of Supplies' key
aims in relation to capital was to restrict profits within reasonable limits, thereby
keeping the level of prices down in general.[93] This represented an involvement of
government not only in technical decision-making but also in anti-inflationary price
control designed to preserve social harmony: what was not only necessary, but
socially and morally desirable.

In implementing this policy, Supplies came to an agreement with businesses over
the maximum percentage rate of gross profit they could accrue. Legally, this was
achieved through three main Emergency Powers Orders.[94] In practice, adherence to
percentage profit rates was secured through the 'considerable volume of control
exercised by informal methods'.[95] These 'informal methods' involved dictation by
Lemass and Leydon more often than genial agreement. According to Tom Garvin,
Lemass possessed an inborn preference for the dynamism of capitalism[96] Nonetheless, the application of free trade telos to this period is anachronistic. During the
Emergency, Lemass's preference was for heavily regulated state capitalism. This
reality does not contradict the narrative of Lemass's celebrated 'pragmatism'. Lemass
was confronted with the fact that Ireland did not contain an established entrepre-
neurial class of the pedigree of neutral Switzerland, for example. Whereas Swiss
bankers and businessmen were afforded privileged influence on federal policymaking during the war, in Ireland the leash was much tighter.[97] Therefore, under Lemass,
the state would lead the way.

This ethic was captured in the retrospective analysis of the department compiled
after the war, where its mission was defined as to 'counter the activities of speculators
or unscrupulous firms'[98] in order to protect 'the general interest in a period of great
difficulty'.[99] The internal departmental retrospectives in which these quotes appear
are likely to have been scrutinised and amended by Leydon himself, raising the possibility that they are marked by a subjective hindsight. However, there is little reason
to doubt the sincerity of the benevolent aim of protecting the 'general interest'
against profiteering. The evident virtue the department placed on its undertaking
rested on the sheer severity of the supply situation. Hence, the conviction in central
command of the economy within the Irish government reached its 'high-water
mark'[100] during the Emergency. To the President of the Irish Federation of Manufacturers, these trends represented a regrettable socialisation of the economy. Writing
to Lemass in 1946, he lamented the increasingly 'oligarchic' character of Irish business, attacking the 'delays and indecision inherent in bureaucratic control'.[101]

Todd Andrews, Managing Director of the Turf Development Board during the
Emergency, credits John Leydon with securing the equitable distribution of clothes
and fuel through the war years, claiming he was 'ruthless in dealing with the numerous spivs and black marketers which a rationing system inevitably spawns'.[102] This
squares with a letter the latter wrote to de Valera in 1945. De Valera had appealed for
clemency on behalf of an erstwhile associate convicted of a rationing offence in

1943. Leydon exhibited clear disdain for such patronage, insisting to the Taoiseach 'we must support the Gardaí in confronting these people of standing'.[103] Leydon's attitude reflected the department's ostensibly unswerving opposition to patronage exemplified in Lemass's well-publicised 1941 invective against the 'pompous and respectable looking citizens robbing others of their fair share'.[104] These assessments elevate the agency of Lemass and Leydon because they suggest a personalised and principled leadership. Although at this stage of his political career support from his own party was rarely better than lukewarm for Lemass,[105] de Valera had rewarded him with a position that befitted his patent work ethic, innovative mind and proficiency. Leydon, in his role as departmental secretary, proved a more than capable lieutenant, and they 'complemented each other admirably'.[106]

When it came to the role of the state, though, Lemass was not the statist radical some of his contemporaries reckoned.[107] In 1944, he reassured manufacturers and retailers: 'this state is based firmly on the principle of private commercial enterprise and the sooner we can allow private enterprise to have free play again, the more rapid will be our return to better conditions'.[108] Lemass's tone in this speech does not go so far as to suggest that these assembled businessmen were collectively the grey eminence directing Emergency economic policy from behind the scenes, but it does highlight the fact that for all the aggrandisement of their functions, both real and prospective, Supplies could not ultimately rule out collaboration with private enterprise. The department's Historical Survey gloomily acknowledged that 'traders will have learned that even when they do nothing to secure supplies they still share in the benefits of supplies obtained through official action' and that 'in a period of shortage money can be made almost without effort'.[109] For its part, the department conceded that cooperation with trade groups was an 'essential feature' of import arrangements; indeed, in some cases, the equitable distribution of essential supplies was left entirely to private businesses.[110]

In what is otherwise a somewhat glowing portrayal of the power, reach and autonomy of the department, this admission of reliance on private business softens the punch of Supplies' 'high-water mark' interventionism. Lemass's apologetic tone in his 1944 trade association speech should not, however, be read as confirmation that Supplies dealt rather lightly with businesses acting against the state's moral economic principles. Rather, it had much to do with the continuation of prosecutions of businessmen for rationing offences and unfair market practices towards the *end* of the Emergency. Similarly, rather than an admission of defeat to business interests, the Survey's downbeat tone demonstrates the difficulties which Supplies faced when its interventionism reached a point uncomfortable to most traders, corporations and corner shops alike.[111]

The bulk of such prosecutions took place long after the 'cold, clammy fear' of 1940 when Ireland faced a real threat of invasion,[112] or the introduction of full rationing in 1942, when the country's shortages appeared most pressing. Indeed, by the time Lemass had made the speech in November 1944, Fianna Fáil's June re-election had coincided with the successful Allied landings in Normandy, and Adolf Hitler had already retreated to his Berlin bunker. The Allied position, and consequently Ireland's medium-term supply situation, looked altogether more positive. In these more assured circumstances, the businessmen who assembled to hear Lemass were expecting the government to relax its interventionism. On the contrary, Supplies secured several white collar convictions during the Emergency's long dénouement.

Supplies confirmed its tough and haughty reputation by refusing as a matter of policy 'to recommend any mitigation of penalties when petitions from the offenders were referred to it by the Department of Justice'.[113] This stance had a suitable backdrop, too, in the veritable moral panic surrounding the increase in crime since Emergency shortages had really taken hold. Supplies' resolute attitude resulted in the prosecution of 'men of standing' such as Arthur Hamilton Whiteside, Secretary of eight Irish trade associations including the Chocolate Manufacturers Association and the Food Manufacturers' Federation. Whiteside was jailed for insider trading on sugar supplies in November 1943.[114] The following month Supplies secured substantial fines at the Special Criminal Court against five large Dublin firms dealing in sugar without licences.[115]

With scant chemical supplies to augment the country's agro-industry and with the Battle of the Atlantic consistently unsettling imports, Ireland's farmers were under pressure to produce alternative foodstuffs. Due to this situation, in July 1941, Imperial Chemical Industries Ltd, the main importer and distributor of Ireland's supply of industrial chemicals, was ordered to set aside reserve stocks and cease all Irish sales of sodium carbonate – a key component in potato sprays.[116] In November of the same year, Supplies ordered Imperial to do the same with bicarbonate of soda, a commodity subject to an Emergency Powers Order due to its widespread use in home baking.[117] In both cases, Imperial's board members protested to Lemass but were informed that they had no option but to oblige.

These examples illustrate that Supplies' reliance on private enterprise was balanced by a harder attitude towards illegal enterprise. During the Emergency, native businessmen were initially pleased by the fact that the number of licences granted to foreign companies had slowed to a trickle. For native businesses this seemed like an improvement from the previous decade, when the Control of Manufactures Acts had been practically circumvented due to the lack of native expertise.[118] But the determination of Supplies to establish and enforce an altered economic order soon ensured that it clashed with native capital. Indeed, the *Report of the Commission on Vocational Organisation* (1943) registered complaints by various trade organisations against Supplies and the Department of Industry and Commerce.[119]

These actions contrasted with the department's toothlessness in other instances, proving that its power, if 'cannibalistic', as one commentator has described it,[120] was not consummate. For instance, in 1941, the Drogheda firm Irish Oil and Cake Supplies incited the wrath of the department by refusing to take on Ireland's import of vitamin D as central importing agent.[121] This refusal was, once again, due to Lemass's refusal to grant the firm a guarantee against any loss. This was a recurrent theme in the relationship between the department and industry. Oil and Cake's attitude was matched by Charles Tennant Ltd, a British firm who between 1938 and 1940 repeatedly refused Supplies' orders that they build up reserves of copper sulphate because the Irish state would not guarantee against any loss.[122] In both these instances, the profit motive powerfully overrode the access of the wider community. Significantly, though, although both firms faced censure from Supplies, neither faced prosecution.

This was a symptom of the state's practical reliance on private enterprise. As a critic of the saturation of Fianna Fáil by big business and an admirer of German and Soviet state-driven developmentalism,[123] Todd Andrews certainly overstates Leydon's agency in the combating of illicit business practice.[124] In fact, there are several examples where, confronted with unacceptable commercial behaviour, the department proved powerless. In 1944, for instance, it merely reprimanded a leading clothes manufacturer for the illegal purchase of much-needed surgical lint for use in the production of children's clothes.[125] Similarly, in 1945, a businessman who had supplied milk so contaminated that it made hundreds of Dublin schoolchildren ill successfully appealed against conviction because the relevant Act did not provide for the sampling of milk distributed in one-third pint bottles.[126]

If the above example indicates that Lemass's department was engaged in a war against the sort of cruel racketeering documented in Graham Greene's *The Third Man* (1949), more honest firms felt harshly done by Supplies. Dermot Findlater, proprietor of the prominent Dublin food retail business Findlaters', railed against what he perceived as Lemass's headstrong refusal to avail of his trade expertise in the management of food supplies. Findlater, who joined the Local Defence Force (LDF) and possessed a civic conscience wanting in some of his peers, offered his assistance as a trade expert to the department a day before war was declared. Lemass, however, refused to recruit him in the management of food supply.[127] Findlater began to feel persecuted by Lemass after his request for permission to increase the amount of butter held in cold storage was refused in late 1941, only for Lemass to blame the retail trade for not laying in enough stocks when shortages occurred a few months later. To his further chagrin, the firm also incurred a fine in November 1942 after an assistant overcharged an inspector for lard by a quarter of a penny. This fine stood, despite Findlater's protestations that he had issued over 400 circulars to staff since the Emergency had begun detailing the frequent changes in Lemass's price orders.[128] Findlater, like many grocers, perceived himself caught in a bureaucratic cobweb woven by Lemass. In 1942, the grocery trade formed a protesting association, the Retail Grocery Dairy and Allied Trades Association (RGDATA), after a Kimmage trader was jailed for two weeks for selling flakemeal at a penny over the controlled price. Relations between Lemass and the trade remained tempestuous, and by the end of the Emergency, RGDATA could count 12,000 members.[129] This contrasted markedly with the vocational British approach, where Lord Woolton – a private retailer – was made state food supremo by Neville Chamberlain.

With flour supplies receding fast after the fall of France, one of the department's most prominent tasks was the regulation of wheat extraction. This began in October 1940, leading to the infamous black loaf by February 1942. The following month, Supplies closed an entire Limerick flour mill because white flour was found on the premises by inspectors. 'Is the Minister aware that these two mills have been in operation for more than a couple of hundred years?' asked Fine Gael's George Bennett. 'That does not entitle them to break the law', replied Lemass.[130] The closure of the mill provides an example of the redoubtable determination of Lemass and Leydon to tackle the nation's industrialists head-on if necessary. Interestingly, however, Lemass's curt reply to Bennett on the historical entitlement of the mill to stay open contrasts with his defence of another firm two years later. In 1944, a question of patronage arose when it was revealed that Lemass had issued licences for the export of prune wine to a company inherited by Leydon. Defending his departmental secretary in the Dáil, Lemass referred to the historical entitlement of the company to the licence, stating 'it is true that the secretary of my department has some interest in that firm, but that firm has been in existence for 75 years'.[131]

If the number of firms that refused to meet Supplies' demands represented 'a relatively small minority', as the Historical Survey claims,[132] there was widespread middle-class resentment against the department's decision to ration petrol and ban private motoring. In October 1939, Lemass introduced a partial petrol rationing scheme.[133] As mentioned above, the department failed to secure adequate petrol stocks before the war. Consequently, in January 1941, Lemass announced that petrol consumption was to be radically reduced. Although leeway was granted to owners of commercial vehicles supplying outlying rural areas, 'public service vehicles' and clergymen, the use of private cars was eliminated.[134] In April 1942, Lemass somewhat casually announced to the Dáil that small farmers and fruit and vegetable traders should convert their private cars into commercial trucks.[135] By May 1942, Supplies restricted commercial drivers to fifty miles per week; in August of the same year, it eliminated the use of commercial trucks altogether.[136]

Lemass's directives reflected the massive shortfall in supply. National monthly petrol consumption in Ireland fell from just under three million gallons in 1940 to around a million gallons in 1942 and three quarters of a million in 1943.[137] The measures drew strong protests from the Society of Irish Motor Traders, who presented the department with a survey revealing that employment in garages had fallen by over 1,500 as a result.[138] Faced with such stark statistics, civil servants within Supplies privately conceded that its imposition of rationing had hitherto been 'far too drastic'.[139] Typically, however, Lemass refused requests from the petrol trade that an advisory committee composed of trade representatives be set up to liaise with Supplies.[140]

Resistance to seemingly knee-jerk decisions by Lemass occurred in other industries. In a typically sweeping move, clothes rationing was introduced by Lemass in June 1942 without any consultation with the drapery trade.[141] Employers and unions marched together to oppose the extension of rationing, a protest which Lemass, displaying little sympathy for his family trade, denounced as 'unnecessary and foolish'.[142] The drapery trade protested every time margins were controlled by government order and baulked at the introduction of maximum yardage restrictions for jackets, skirts and dresses: an idea borrowed from the British system. Nonetheless, the drapery trade found that government restrictions aimed at ensuring goods that were more reasonably priced resulted in an increase in business. Arnott's 'Emergency Sales' and gift tokens grew in popularity, and the company recorded net profits for the war years that were double pre-war figures.[143]

As usual, and despite Lemass's ostensibly secret decision to introduce clothes rationing, there was a rush on the drapery trade in the weeks prior to clothes rationing as rumours spread of its impending introduction.[144] Throughout the Emergency, Lemass strove to prevent the disruption to a fragile market that panic-buying wrought. This determination to avert panic-buying helps to explain Lemass's negative attitude towards Dermot Findlater. He had been irked by Findlater in late August 1939 when the retailer had posted bills advising 'all citizens of Éire to have at least one full week's food supply in their homes in case hostilities break out'.[145] Dermot's son Alex's insistence that this was an act borne solely of philanthropy is unconvincing. In the context of efforts to establish tenets of moral economy through the elimination of hoarding, it was an irresponsible act, and it is little surprise that relations between the two men suffered as a result.

Supplies did not manage to secure the legislation that would have given Lemass, the 'economic overlord', full autocratic powers over business. Nonetheless, native companies and businessmen who chose not to cooperate with the department almost always did so to their detriment. The tension between Supplies' moral interventionism and trade expertise was encapsulated in a Dáil debate of 1947 over Lemass's Industrial Efficiency and Prices Bill, a never-realised piece of legislation that aimed to punish profiteering in the protected industries. Defending the Bill, Lemass argued that 'where an industry receives help in that form from the community it must be prepared to give to the community reasonable safeguards that it is not unduly exploiting that position for the private benefit of individuals'. Fine Gael's James Dillon responded by branding Lemass 'the Moses from Merrion Street',[146] a put-down which conveyed the anger that many captains of Irish industry harboured towards Lemass's stewardship of the Emergency economy. Lemass, however, remained unapologetic, regarding himself as chief superintendant in the policing of the moral economy, as discussed in the following chapter.

The failures

On the one hand, the Department of Supplies was at the mercy of the bullying efforts of Britain to recruit Ireland to the Allied cause. On the other, domestically, the department exerted an at times sweeping and inhibiting agency over Irish capitalism. In both lights, Lemass's department appears dynamic, resourceful and possessive of a moral economic imperative, yet ultimately frustrated by structures and interests often outside its control.

A third reading of the department's activities demonstrates that Ireland's supply situation was significantly aggravated by the department's relative indolence in the initial stages of the Emergency. The department's exploits before the changes forced upon it by the supply squeeze in 1941 therefore deserve scrutiny. At the outbreak of the Emergency, Ireland had the second highest consumption rate of tea in the world.[147] Tea, a most coveted commodity at the time, for which – according to the Historical Survey – 'neither coffee nor cocoa provides a suitable substitute',[148] was reduced to a meagre half ounce ration for much of the Emergency. This situation arose because of the unwillingness of the tea trade to lay in supplies unless the government gave a guarantee against loss. The department blamed this and many other factors for Ireland's inadequate supply of tea, such as the 'false optimism' that followed the Munich Agreement, the intensification of the war at sea and in the Far East and Britain's curtailment of supplies between January and April 1941.[149] But Lemass was clearly responsible, in this case, for the failure to implement a single, centrally directed import agency earlier.[150] The attitude of the Irish Wholesale Tea Dealers Association was, if ungenerous, unsurprising. Importers, as the department was aware, were naturally concerned about incurring losses.

The refusal of Supplies to provide a guarantee to the trade against losses that their greater capital outlay threatened was a recurrent theme in Ireland's supply situation. The department's bullishness on this matter resulted in many firms simply refusing to import extra stocks. When this happened, officials from the department were frequently sluggish in taking their own steps to secure existing stocks. In the case of tea, it meant that when war broke out in 1939, Ireland had only fourteen weeks' supply left, based on normal consumption patterns of two and a half ounces per person per week.[151] This left Ireland reliant on Britain: 77% of Ireland's tea originated in British India and nearly all tea came through London.[152] When Britain decreased supplies to 85% in January 1941, 60% in February, 50% in March and 25% in April, the Irish ration fell accordingly. The development of the war in the East ensured that when Lemass did establish the importing firm Tea Importers (Éire) Ltd in June 1941, it proved ineffective, eventually being forced by authorities in India to dispose of much of its accumulated stock by sale in Calcutta.[153] This situation ensured a boom in prices on the Irish black market, as demand for tea well surpassed supply.

The department's generous appraisal of its own performance is rightly toned down in some passages in its Historical Survey. For instance, the survey concedes that the department pursued a 'short-sighted' and 'dangerous' policy of allowing the export of machinery and plant to Britain in the first fourteen months of the Emergency.[154] Similarly, shortly after the outbreak of war, Lemass announced strict supervision on the usage of timber.[155] He continued, however, to grant export licences for timber freely up to the end of 1940. This, too, is acknowledged in the Historical Survey as a critical mistake.[156] In a Dáil debate of December 1940, when the consequences of the fall of France were beginning to be properly felt, Fine Gael's Patrick Belton asked: 'Why was not £10,000,000 worth of timber brought in?' The government had not shown proper foresight, he claimed; 'surely it did not take a prophet to see that war was coming after Munich. Why were the necessary raw materials not brought in in bulk and stored here to enable us to carry on?'[157]

In Lemass's defence, securing supplies of machinery and timber was overshadowed by the turf drive. Turf production took on a greater impetus at this juncture because supplies were aggravated by a wet summer in 1940, which rendered much turf useless.[158] Nevertheless, in several other instances, the department's ineptitude is clearly exposed and Belton's point about timing substantiated. Chemicals essential to wheat production provide a case in point. Through the semi-state Grain Importers (Éire), Supplies liaised regularly with the Cereals Import Branch of the British Ministry of Food to try and secure supplies,[159] but, as in other countries, domestic production remained paramount if the population was to have enough bread to survive. With this forced increase in the production of cereals and grains came an increase in the rat population. Rats posed a great threat to productivity because 'Red Squills', the most effective rat poison available at the time, was produced in the East Indies and by the end of 1941, there was none available in Ireland.[160] In this and in countless other areas, Supplies failed to accumulate stocks early and relied instead upon its scientific wing, the Emergency Scientific Research Bureau (ESRB). Where Supplies failed to secure imports of certain commodities, the Bureau stepped in: 'Red Squills' was replaced by a hastily concocted substitute. Similarly, when carbon dioxide imports ran low, the demand of Ireland's dairy creameries for the gas was met by the ESRB, which adapted a plant in University College Dublin to produce it.[161] The piecemeal nature of some of these substitutes was a source of some amusement, with the satirical *Dublin Opinion* depicting soap substitutes that corroded the skin and people gagging to death on tea substitutes.[162] As much as demonstrating the ESRB's talent in providing makeshift solutions, the reliance on this wing again exposes Supplies' short-sightedness in failing to stockpile essential supplies.

As mentioned, despite its tough approach, Lemass's department displayed a reluctance to supersede private enterprise entirely, particularly when the businesses concerned held expert knowledge.[163] During the Emergency, businesses were required to give Lemass a written undertaking that they would maintain an agreed rate of profit, but the department allowed firms 'a reasonable tolerance or margin of error' based on the understanding that 'even with the best intentions', a firm might depart from the strict terms of its promise.[164] Such leeway was not always forthcoming from Lemass, though, and in several cases, clumsy interventionism prevailed. For example, the department effectively ruined the fairly successful small industry in scrap metal export based on the west coast through maladroit intervention. Although the British Board of Trade was unwilling to barter with Supplies and release finished metal in return for scrap, its officials were glad to receive scrap in return for money. Haulbowline Industries Ltd, a large scrap merchants based in

Passage West, County Cork, exported 25% of Ireland's scrap to the British Iron and Steel Corporation Ltd and also provided valuable local employment. But the company was effectively ruined by the annual delay in the granting of a licence from Supplies.[165] There followed a similar stop–start approach to scrap merchants Western Supply Co. Ltd of Achill, Mayo.[166] In each case, the local industries faced near ruin, having to periodically shut down completely and lay off all staff. Even the granting of a licence to Haulbowline in 1943 appears to have been an ad hoc response to a shortage of shoeing iron for horses, through its substitution with scrap iron.[167] From 1941, Ireland's scrap merchants were forced by the department to hold supplies and halt production, while the government dithered over the establishment of Irish Steel. Eventually allowed to export freely again in 1945, these business were for the duration of the Emergency, as the Survey acknowledges, at the whim of the lumbering Irish Steel and its 'financial embarrassments'.[168]

Conclusion

Although Lemass's priority was always a material one, his remit as Minister for Supplies became strongly influenced by moral considerations of equitable distribution and fair price. Civil servants at Lemass's department regarded themselves as the policemen of a moral economy, as discussed in the next chapter. It was a self-image imbued in them by their chief and was admirably wielded against profiteers. While conflict with well-established pre-independence concerns was predictable, the department also clashed with newer businesses built up under the protectionist policies of the 1930s. Such a stance was necessary as a last resort to ensure equitable distribution, but it was rarely tempered by a willingness to cooperate with trade expertise. Although Lemass and Leydon relied on the participation of Irish capitalists in the management of the Emergency economy, these captains of industry were effectively sidelined in several instances. In this crucial regard, it seems that a statist approach was often foisted on businessmen to their chagrin and, in some cases, to the country's detriment. In Switzerland, for example, the state obliged businesses to lay in six months of supplies for storage in the Alpine valleys and to rent land to their employees to cultivate. In return, business experts were consulted at every stage of the planning process.[169]

Leydon and Lemass were very much at the mercy of geopolitical and economic currents that placed a very high premium on Ireland's steadfast maintenance of neutrality. Britain and America regularly used food as a weapon of war. People in neutral countries suffered as a result. In late 1942, Churchill promised to 'enrich the economic life of the Iberian peninsula',[170] a statement less benevolent than it appears: a year earlier, he had admitted to Roosevelt that much of neutral Spain was at 'starvation point' due to the Allied economic blockade.[171] Both Lemass and Leydon displayed an understandable wariness of British 'gentleman's agreements', and their suspicious stance was justified in certain cases.

Unfortunately, it seems that neither Lemass nor Leydon foresaw the extent of the British trade squeeze of early 1941. Britain's pursuit of *economic warfare* was clearly signalled: between 1939 and 1945, there was an entire Whitehall Ministry devoted to just that. In such a volatile trading environment, it is surprising that Lemass did not oversee greater stockpiling of chemicals and machinery vital to Ireland's agricultural economy. In defending himself against charges in the Dáil that he had misled the country, Lemass revealed just how unstable trade relations with Britain were and just how subservient Ireland was in this relationship but omitted to mention the department's errors as well.[172] It is obvious that in the interests of supply, Lemass was obliged to withhold certain information from the public. It is equally obvious, despite his claim in the Dáil to the contrary, that when it came to supplies, Lemass had been painting far too rosy a picture.[173] This was also the case when it came to the supervision of the domestic economy, as the next chapter reveals.

Notes

1 Supplies, 'Record of Activities'. NAI, IND/EHR 3/15, p. 2.
2 Memorandum on interdepartmental committees on essential materials, NAI, Department of the Taoiseach (DT)/S 8203.
3 Memorandum from H. French, Head of British Food Department, November 1937. Irish Military Archives of Ireland (MA), Secret Files (S)/49.
4 For the interpersonal relationships of the Fianna Fáil elite in this period, see Bryce Evans, *Seán Lemass; Democratic Dictator* (Cork, 2011).
5 Department of Supplies, 'Tea – Maintenance of Supplies and Equitable Distribution during the Emergency'. NAI, IND/EHR 3/13, p. 3.
6 Emergency Powers Act (Dublin, 1939), 29/39.
7 *Dáil Debates*, vol. 77, col. 7, 2 September 1939.
8 'Record of Activities'. NAI, IND/EHR/3/15, p. 2.
9 'Record of Activities'. NAI, IND/EHR/3/15, appendix I.
10 Ronan Fanning, *Independent Ireland* (Dublin, 1983), 148.
11 'Record of Activities'. NAI, IND/EHR/3/15, p. 11. A corporation may be either *aggregate*, comprising many individuals, or *sole*, consisting of only one person and his or her successors preserving powers in perpetual succession, like a monarch.
12 'Record of Activities'. NAI, IND/EHR/3/15, p. 1.
13 NAI, Department of Finance (FIN)/S53/12/39.
14 Department of Supplies. 'Historical Survey of Work Dealing with Rationing, Miscellaneous Supplies and Control of Exports, 1938–1945'. NAI, IND/EHR/3/C1.
15 'Record of Activities'. NAI, IND/EHR/3/15, appendix III.
16 'Record of Activities'. NAI, IND/EHR/3/15, p. 7.
17 'Record of Activities'. NAI, IND/EHR/3/15, p. 9.
18 See *Irish Independent*, 29 July 1935; *The Times*, 1 December 1936. See Frank Forde, *The Long Watch: The History of the Irish Mercantile Marine in World War Two* (Dublin, 1981) and Hazel P. Smyth, *The B&I Line* (Dublin, 1984).
19 James Meenan, *The Irish Economy Since 1922* (Liverpool, 1970), 164.

20 *Irish Press*, 28 June 1939.
21 Basil Peterson, *Turn of the Tide, an Outline of Irish Maritime History* (Dublin 1962), p. 119.
22 Memorandum on Dependence on Other Countries in Connection with Essential Imports, Exports and Shipping, 15 February 1939. NAI, IND/EMR/8/89.
23 Memorandum on Dependence. NAI, IND/EMR/8/89.
24 Leydon memo, 13 April 1939. NAI, INDC/EMR/8/89.
25 The National Archives of the United Kingdom (NAUK), Ministry of War Transport (MW)/5937/1939. Shipping Defence Advisory Committee, T 02828.
26 'Record of Activities'. NAI, IND/EHR/3/15, p. 89.
27 *Report of Meeting at the Dominions Office*, 30 April 1940. UCDA, de Valera papers, P150/2571.
28 Leathers to Churchill, 12 August 1940. NAUK, Cabinet files (CAB)/67/8/13. See also Rigney, *Trains*, 87–93.
29 Leathers to Churchill, 12 August 1940. NAUK, CAB/67/8/13.
30 For the British appraisal of German pressure on Swedish shipping, see NAUK, Eden papers, FO/954/23B (30 September 1941). See also Paul A. Levine, 'Swedish Neutrality during the Second World War: Tactical Success or Moral Compromise?', in Wylie ed., *European Neutrals*, 304–330.
31 See Lizzie Collingham, *The Taste of War; World War Two and the Battle for Food* (London, 2011), 35.
32 Navicert regulations ensured that Irish ships now had to call in at Fishguard, Wales, when homeward bound from Lisbon for inspection by the Royal Navy.
33 'Record of Activities', NAI, IND/EHR/3/15, p. 66.
34 Fisk, *In Time of War*, 250–259.
35 Eric Lyde Hargreaves and Margaret Gowing, *History of the Second World War: Civil Industry and Trade* (London, 1952), 283.
36 'Record of Activities'. NAI, IND/EHR/3/15, p. 27.
37 'Record of Activities'. NAI, IND/EHR/3/15, p. 101.
38 'Record of Activities'. NAI, IND/EHR/3/15, p. 86. See Michael Kennedy, *Guarding Neutral Ireland: The Coast Watching Service and Military Intelligence, 1939–1945* (Dublin, 2008), 120–128.
39 'Record of Activities'. NAI, IND/EHR/3/15, p. 31.
40 Peterson, *Turn of the Tide*, 131.
41 Leydon to Coyne, 14 May 1941. MA, Office of the Controller of Censorship (OCC)/2/90.
42 Coyne to Leydon, 15 May 1941. MA, OCC/2/90.
43 Leydon to Coyne, 26 April 1944. MA, OCC/2/90.
44 Coyne to Knightly, 26 April 1944. MA, OCC/2/90.
45 'Historical Survey'. NAI, IND/EHR/3/C1, part I, p. 9.
46 'Historical Survey'. NAI, IND/EHR/3/C4, part XI, p. 601.
47 'Historical Survey'. NAI, IND/EHR/3/C4, part XI, pp. 593–601.
48 Lord Granard, memorandum on Ireland, 26 July 1941. NAI, FA/P23.
49 'Record of Activities'. NAI, IND/EHR/3/15, p. 66.
50 'Record of Activities'. NAI, IND/EHR/3/15, p. 148.
51 'Historical Survey'. NAI, IND/EHR/3/C1, part I, p. 21.

52 'Record of Activities'. NAI, IND/EHR/3/15, p. 39.
53 See Harold L. Smith, *War and Social Change: British Society in the Second World War* (Manchester, 1986), 248–252.
54 'Historical Survey'. NAI, IND/EHR/3/C1, part III, pp. 103–104.
55 'Tea – Maintenance of Supplies'. NAI, IND/EHR 3/13, p. 19.
56 'Historical Survey'. NAI, IND/EHR/3/C4, part XI, p. 501.
57 'Historical Survey'. NAI, IND/EHR/3/C1, part III, p. 67.
58 'Historical Survey'. NAI, IND/EHR/3/C3, part IX, p. 311.
59 'Historical Survey'. NAI, IND/EHR/3/C4, part XI, p. 633.
60 'Historical Survey'. NAI, IND/EHR/3/C2, part VI, p. 254.
61 'Historical Survey'. NAI, IND/EHR/3/C4, part XI, p. 535.
62 'Historical Survey'. NAI, IND/EHR/3/C3, part IX, pp. 401–402. The emphasis is my own.
63 'Historical Survey'. NAI, IND/EHR/3/C4, part XI, p. 606.
64 Leydon memo, 12 March 1942. NAI, FA/P58.
65 Leydon memo, 6 May 1942. NAI, FA/P58.
66 Leydon, Report on discussions in London, 17–19 November 1942. NAI, FA/P58.
67 Leydon memo, 28 November 1942. The ostensibly principled British stance against barter arrangements was bunk. See NAI, FA/P23 (i) for British attempts to secure Irish labour on a plant in Wales considered too 'dirty' for British workers in exchange for briquettes.
68 Report of meeting at Department of Supplies, 11 March 1943. NAI, FA/P58.
69 'Historical Survey'. NAI, IND/EHR/3/C4, part XI, p. 607.
70 'Historical Survey'. NAI, IND/EHR/3/C4, part XI, p. 476.
71 'Historical Survey'. NAI, IND/EHR/3/C4, part XI, p. 544.
72 See James Ryan to Leydon, 22 June 1943. NAI, FA/P58.
73 Department of Supplies memorandum to Cabinet, 22 September 1943. NAI, FA/P58.
74 Supplies memorandum to Cabinet, 22 September 1943. NAI, FA/P58.
75 Urs Schwarz, *The Eye of the Hurricane: Switzerland in World War Two* (Boulder, 1980), 68.
76 R.A. Butler, 'Ships under Swiss flag', 11 April 1943. NAUK, Eden papers, FO/954/28A.
77 See memo 'Swiss trade with Germany', 5 May 1943 at NAUK, Eden papers, FO/954/28A.
78 Anglo-Swedish shipping agreements are detailed in British cabinet minutes of 2 November 1939. See NAUK, CAB/65/2/2. Later Allied economic pressure on Sweden in July 1944 is outlined in NAUK, Eden papers, FO/954/23B. See also W.M. Carlgren, *Swedish Foreign Policy during World War Two* (London, 1977), 72–138.
79 Wayne H. Bowen, *Spain during World War II* (Missouri, 2006), 108.
80 Hugh Kay, *Salazar and Modern Portugal* (New York, 1970), 120.
81 'Historical Survey'. part I, pp. 1–3.
82 'Historical Survey'. NAI, IND/EHR/3/C1, part I, p. 2.
83 Richard Dunphy, *The Making of Fianna Fáil Power in Ireland, 1923–1948* (Oxford, 1995), 218.
84 'Record of Activities'. NAI, IND/EHR/3/15, p. 33.

85 'Record of Activities'. NAI, IND/EHR/3/15, p. 85.

86 'Historical Survey'. NAI, IND/EHR/3/C3, part IX, p. 387.

87 'Historical Survey'. NAI, IND/EHR/3/C1, part I, p. 24

88 'Historical Survey'. NAI, IND/EHR/3/C1, part I, p. 5–7.

89 Mary E. Daly, *Industrial Development and Irish National Identity, 1922–1939* (New York, 1992), 173–179. See also Daly, *Social and Economic History*,145–153.

90 'Historical Survey'. NAI, IND/EHR/3/C3, part IX, p. 352.

91 'Historical Survey'. NAI, IND/EHR/3/C3, part IX, p. 354.

92 Horgan, *Enigmatic Patriot*, 108.

93 Department of Supplies, 'Memorandum Relative to Proposals to Enact Legislation for the Imposition of Special Penalties on Traders in Cases of Breach of Orders or Direction Made or Given by the Minister for Supplies in Regard to the Control of Profits and Prices'. p. 1. NAI, DT/S13545.

94 Supplies, Memorandum on Control of Profits and Prices' p. 1. NAI, DT/S13545. Prices and profits were chiefly controlled under Emergency Powers Orders 224 (1939) and 166 and 173 (1942).

95 Supplies, Memorandum on Control of Profits and Prices', p. 1. NAI, DT/S13545.

96 Tom Garvin, *Judging Lemass: The Measure of the Man* (Dublin, 2009), 50.

97 Wylie, 'Switzerland', 341.

98 'Historical Survey'. NAI, IND/EHR/3/C1, part I, p. 6.

99 'Tea – Maintenance of Supplies'. NAI, IND/EHR 3/13, p. 15.

100 Horgan, *Enigmatic Patriot*, 110.

101 P.L. MacEvoy to Lemass, 1946. UCDA, Liam Skinner, unpublished biography of SeánLemass, P161, 97–99.

102 C.S. Andrews, *Man of No Property* (Dublin, 2001), 173.

103 John Leydon to Eamon de Valera, 1 September 1943. NAI, DT/RA 103/44.

104 *Irish Times*, 13 December 1941.

105 Horgan, *Enigmatic Patriot*, 95.

106 Horgan, *Enigmatic Patriot*, 101.

107 Lemass was associated with the base materialism of the sort associated with the planned economies of the Soviet Union. See Garvin, *Preventing*, 145.

108 Seán Lemass to the National Convention of Retail, Grocery, Dairy and Allied Trades' Associations, 29 November, 1944. NAI, Tweedy Papers, 98/17/5/5/43.

109 'Historical Survey'. NAI, IND/EHR/3/C1, part I, p. 24.

110 'Historical Survey'. NAI, IND/EHR/3/C1, part I, p. 5.

111 'Historical Survey'. NAI, IND/EHR/3/C1, part II, p. 26.

112 Quote from Lee, *Ireland 1912–1985*, 250. See also Eunan O'Halpin, *MI5 and Ireland, 1939–1945: The Official History* (Dublin, 2003), 30.

113 'Historical Survey'. NAI, IND/EHR/3/C1, part II, 43.

114 *Evening Herald*, 18 November 1943.

115 *Irish Independent*, 4 December 1943.

116 'Historical Survey'. NAI, IND/EHR/3/C2, part V, pp. 237–239.

117 'Historical Survey'. NAI, IND/EHR/3/C2, part V, p. 235.

118 Mary E. Daly, 'An Irish-Ireland for Business?: The Control of Manufactures Acts, 1932 and 1934', *Irish Historical Studies*, 24, 94 (November 1984), 259–272.

119 J.H. Whyte, *Church and State in Modern Ireland* (Dublin, 1980), 97.

120 Horgan, *Enigmatic Patriot*, 101.

121 'Historical Survey'. NAI, IND/EHR/3/C1, part III, p. 88.

122 'Historical Survey'. NAI, IND/EHR/3/C2, part V, p. 235.

123 Garvin, *Preventing*, 107.

124 Andrews, *Man of No Property*, 173.

125 'Historical Survey'. NAI, IND/EHR/3/C1, part III, p. 137.

126 'Evidence of the Irish Housewives before the Milk Tribunal', NAI, Tweedy papers, JUS/98/17/5/1/6.

127 Alex Findlater, *Findlaters: The Story of a Dublin Merchant Family, 1774–2001* (Dublin, 2001), 405.

128 Findlater, *Findlaters*, 412.

129 RGDATA stood for the Retail Grocery Dairy and Allied Trades Association.

130 *Dáil Debates*, vol. 87, col. 13, 26 May 1942.

131 *Irish Press*, 16 March 1944.

132 Supplies, Memorandum on Control of Profits and Prices', p. 2. NAI, DT/S13545.

133 Department of Supplies Memorandum on Petrol, November 1939. NAI, SS/99/50/39.

134 'Historical Survey'. NAI, IND/EHR/3/C1, 'Petrol Rationing' appendix.

135 *Dáil Debates*, vol. 86, col. 445, 15 April 1942.

136 'Historical Survey'. NAI, IND/EHR/3/C1, 'Petrol Rationing' appendix.

137 'Historical Survey'. NAI, IND/EHR/3/C1, 'Petrol Rationing' appendix.

138 Representation from the Society of Irish Motor Traders for Revision of Petrol Rationing Scheme, 6 November 1939. NAI, IND/EHR/3/C1.

139 Memorandum on Petrol. NAI, Supply Series (SS)/99/50/39.

140 *Irish Independent*, 28 September 1939.

141 *Dáil Debates*, vol. 87, col. 1002, 16 June 1942. See also Ronald Nesbitt, *At Arnott's of Dublin* (Dublin, 1993), 114.

142 *Irish Press*, 25 June 1942.

143 Nesbitt, *At Arnott's*, 119.

144 *Dáil Debates*, vol. 87, col. 1003, 16 June 1942.

145 Findlater, *Findlaters*, 405.

146 *Dáil Debates*, vol. 108, col. 750, 22 October 1947.

147 Wills, *Neutral Island*, 239.

148 'Tea – Maintenance of Supplies'. NAI, IND/EHR 3/13, p. 32.

149 'Tea – Maintenance of Supplies'. NAI, IND/EHR 3/13, pp. 5–28.

150 'Tea – Maintenance of Supplies'. NAI, IND/EHR 3/13, p. 32.

151 'Tea – Maintenance of Supplies'. NAI, IND/EHR 3/13, p. 7.

152 'Tea – Maintenance of Supplies'. NAI, IND/EHR 3/13, p. 3.

153 'Tea – Maintenance of Supplies'. NAI, IND/EHR 3/13, p. 19.

154 'Historical Survey'. NAI, IND/EHR/3/C4, part XI, p. 556.

155 *Irish Independent*, 19 October 1939.

156 'Historical Survey'. NAI, IND/EHR/3/C4, part XI, p. 562.

157 *Dáil Debates*, vol. 81, col. 1263, 12 December 1940.

158 S. Quinn, in T. Coillte ed., *A Social History of Forestry in Ireland: Essays and Recollections on Social Aspects of Forestry in the 20ᵗʰ Century* (Castlemorris, Kilkenny, 2000), 201.

159 *Dáil Debates*, vol. 82, col. 1366, 3 April 1941.
160 'Historical Survey'. NAI, IND/EHR/3/C2, part V, p. 201.
161 'Historical Survey'. NAI, IND/EHR/3/C2, part V, p. 194.
162 *Dublin Opinion*, September 1941.
163 'Record of Activities'. NAI, IND/EHR/3/15, p. 4.
164 Supplies, Memorandum on Control of Profits and Prices', p. 2. NAI, DT/S13545.
165 'Historical Survey'. NAI, IND/EHR/3/C4, part XI, pp. 530–535.
166 'Historical Survey'. NAI, IND/EHR/3/C4, part XI, p. 534.
167 *Dáil Debates*, vol. 89, col. 804, 3 March 1943.
168 'Historical Survey'. NAI, IND/EHR/3/C4, part XI, p. 536.
169 See Schwarz, *Hurricane*, 67–85.
170 Churchill, 'A Gleam of Victory', Mansion House, London, 10 November 1942, in Charles Eade ed., *Winston Churchill. The Wartime Speeches*, two volumes (London, 1952), 344.
171 Elena Hernández-Sandoica and Enrique Moradiello, 'Spain and the Second World War, 1939–1945', in Wylie ed., *European Neutrals*, 248.
172 *Irish Press*, 17 January 1941.
173 *Dáil Debates*, vol. 81, col. 1362, 16 January 1941.

3

Moral policemen of the domestic economy

Guinness good. Sherry good. No wine. No coal. No petrol. No gas. No electric. No paraffin.

John Betjeman, 27 March 1943

From 'voluntary measures of economy' to full rationing

The shortages John Betjeman grumpily recorded to friends in England highlight the gaps in the Irish supply system. While Betjeman's government bore much responsibility for the shortages, the role of the Department of Supplies also demands scrutiny. It is surprising that firmer steps were not taken by Minister for Supplies Seán Lemass to establish a comprehensive rationing system before war broke out in September 1939. Given the heavy reliance on Britain for trade and the frequency of movement between the two territories, the restriction of trade that hit Ireland with such rude force in 1941 was, although unexpected, not astonishing. As discussed in the last chapter, Britain had announced in no uncertain terms as early as 1937 that heavy market restrictions would apply domestically. The repercussions on trade with Ireland, and the likelihood that Ireland would have to develop similarly wide-ranging domestic controls, should have been fairly obvious. However, the committees established in 1936 did not report to the government until the summer of 1939, by which time conflict was only months away.[1]

In neutral Ireland, the effects of Britain's declaration of war on Germany on 3 September 1939 were immediate. Irish people resident in Britain crammed on to boats home.[2] Anxiety about wartime shortages caused a surge of panic buying and forced prices up considerably. As the month progressed, prices continued to rise. Lemass was forced to respond by introducing rationing for essential commodities undergoing the most serious price inflation, such as sugar, tea and fuel. Significantly, though, he stated that he did not want to introduce a full rationing system.[3] Asserting the need for the public to practise frugality, Lemass stated that the government had neither the resources nor the organisation to overcome the supply crisis without voluntary cooperation.[4] 'Voluntary measures of economy' were preferable to full rationing, he asserted, asking for the 'voluntary assistance of every housewife' in reducing consumption.[5]

Under this early and incomplete form of rationing and price control, newspapers were obliged to frequently publish a long list of goods detailing the maximum retail price allowed.[6] Maximum price orders were constantly revised due to the frequent trade fluctuations that accompanied the European state of nervousness. This led to the constant addition and removal of price orders and regulatory measures on certain goods. This, in turn, led to accusations of complacency.[7] In these early stages of the Emergency, the censorship of articles relating to supply was relatively weak. Adverts soon appeared, placed by profiteers, offering the sought-after goods at prices well above the retail price dictated by Lemass. Lemass was tied to the moral imperative of protecting the consumer from black market prices under the Prices Standstill Order. But he faced huge fluctuations in the price and supply of goods. The trade situation was dictated by large British importing firms and Lemass was powerless. Despite these conditions, Lemass refused calls for a full rationing system in Ireland to protect the most needy.[8]

As the initial frenzy surrounding prices died down, Minister for Finance Seán MacEntee stated that the Minister for Supplies had been much more successful than he had anticipated he would be four months ago and that as long as Lemass's success in managing shortages continued, the position was not likely to get much worse.[9] Illustrating MacEntee's uncanny ability to confound his colleagues by pledging them his support, the supply situation was to get much worse in the months to come.

When France fell in June 1940, the war swung in favour of Germany. As discussed in the previous chapter, in early 1941 Ireland started to feel the effects of a British trade squeeze that was intended to pressure Ireland into joining the Allied war effort. With the consequent decline in diplomatic and trade relations, there was a sharp curtailment of supplies and an increase in domestic state regulation. Shortly afterwards, Lemass informed the Irish public that they had been 'lucky' on the economic front for the past fifteen months and that the effects of the war were now going to become worse.[10] In 1941, coal (January), fuel oil (March), kerosene (April) and turf (August) became rationed goods.[11] It was not long before Lemass announced that a full rationing system would be implemented.

Comprehensive rationing was a different matter altogether from the price controls which Supplies periodically imposed on certain goods. Full rationing necessitated the taking of a mini-census and the mass issuing of ration books. On 'Registration Night', 16 November 1941, the department issued ration books to three million people.[12] A complete system of rationing was in place by May 1942. The country adjusted to a more complete system of regulation of economic activity and consumption. Bread, clothes and footwear were added to the list of controlled articles, followed by butter (September) and soap (October).[13] Private motoring and the sale of cooking and heating appliances were banned later in the year.

'Registration Night' was an immense effort and one in which the Department of Supplies was instrumental. Supplies claimed that 99% of people resident in the state received books in May 1942. This figure increased to 99.86% after a second

'Registration Night' was carried out in December 1943.[14] Although these figures are undoubtedly exaggerated, the energetic implementation of the scheme is impressive. It was a formidable undertaking which involved great organisation and mobilisation of people and the use of a considerable quantity of paper, a commodity in very short supply at the time.

Formal rationing did not come without its problems, though. Those born after, who had arrived in the country after, or who had changed address since 'Registration Night' did not initially receive ration books.[15] There was also great confusion over the eligibility of returning migrants for ration books. Officially, ration books were only issued to those who could prove that they would be staying in Ireland for a year or more.[16] The department held a high regard for its own efforts in the establishment and policing of rationing. This is encapsulated in the Survey, which omits to mention the numerous oversights and exceptions that are bound to have occurred. While acknowledging the help of the Gardaí in sharing the burden of the rationing effort, the Survey nonetheless lamented the devolution of some of Supplies' functions to other departments. In a future Emergency, Lemass's officials envisaged *their* department's growth at the expense of other branches of government: numerous centrally directed 'local offices' would form the outposts of its empire.[17]

The Department of Supplies did not make the same effective use of radio and cinema as the British Ministry of Food,[18] but at intervals, Lemass did address the public over the airwaves. His radio broadcast following the fall of France was addressed to 'all citizens', informing them that 'trade with the continent of Europe has been almost entirely cut off' and 'it is possibly only a matter of days when the full fury of the storm of war will rage around our coasts'. 'On the brighter side', he listed Ireland's stocks of food, warning that any waste was 'inexcusable' but urging people not to panic as Ireland had six months' worth of supplies.[19] His tone was invariably instructive rather than condescending, as demonstrated in a broadcast on clothes rationing in 1942: 'anyone who uses up all his coupons this summer will find himself in a difficult position next winter and he will only have to put up with it'.[20] Lemass has been described as exhibiting 'superlatively good public relations' during the Emergency.[21]

And yet the Irish public were confused by the transition from partial rationing, with the emphasis on voluntary curtailment of consumption, to full rationing. Lemass's pronouncements on the flour supply provide a good example of why. In June 1942, he urged 'all citizens who can afford to purchase flour' to do so, assuring listeners that 'some people may have been reluctant to do so for fear that they might leave short other less fortunately circumstanced people' but that 'supplies are more than adequate'.[22] This assurance sounded like the 'on the brighter side' message of 1940; similarly, it was somewhat misleading. By early 1942, flour was very scarce and available in very small amounts on a strictly ration-only basis. 'The poor are like hunted rats looking for bread', remarked Richard Mulcahy of the bread queues which had developed as flour dwindled.[23] The insouciance of Lemass's 1940 speech, although exuding much-needed composure in a time of uncertainty, did little to encourage a frugal approach to flour.

The desperation caused by tea rationing, the subject of much contemporary satire, provides a similar example of Lemass's complacency. Months after the collapse of negotiations with tea importers, tea was finally rationed. It was placed on the ration without the comprehensive registration or issue of books seen in 'Registration Night' and the full ration system of 1941/1942. Instead, tea was subject to its own mini 'Registration Night' in March 1941, where members of the Local Security Force (LSF) delivered registration cards to households. The black market grew as demand intensified. The supply of tea quickly became the realm of 'the professional smuggler, the unscrupulous trader and the dishonest speculator', as departmental officials put it.[24] For many poor families, tea was the 'principal item of food'.[25] Due to the high price of black market tea and the restriction of consumption through the ration, poorer families would often dry tea leaves and reuse them several times.[26]

This desperation of consumers was greatly aggravated by the uneven regulation which Supplies applied to the commodity. Difficulties arose immediately after rationing was introduced. Lemass envisaged a simple system where people would voluntarily register with local retailers, who would exchange tea for coupons. These retailers would procure all their tea from a single wholesaler and keep a sales record. In reality, voluntary registration did not work smoothly. Wholesalers were not punctual in supplying monthly returns to Supplies. Many grocers maintained several wholesale suppliers, served more than their 'fair share' of customers, engrossed measurements or simply did not bother to obtain a licence.[27] These licences, as a Labour Party deputy pointed out, were 'very heavy on small shops which are a great convenience to the poor'.[28]

Neither did the public behave in accordance with the economic principles Supplies urged. Because many small shops did not obtain licences, many people tried to get tea from shops outside their local area. The sick or the elderly were frequently physically unable to voluntarily register. Most significantly, when they needed more tea than they could legally procure, people spurned Lemass's moral economic urgings and turned to the black market.[29]

Unlike with tea, Lemass did not subject other commodities to a comprehensive registration system until the imposition of full rationing in 1942. Instead, as mentioned, single consumer items were often subject to the abrupt announcement and then suspension of rationing. Consequently, the black market in those goods underwent a mini-boom. Officials from Supplies were consistently disappointed by the public's illegal procurement of goods, but the Survey does not acknowledge that this behaviour was partially the result of the department's approach. Whereas the collective regulation of a host of commodities under the comprehensive rationing system of 1942 did not eradicate the black market, it at least provided a system based on a book. Naturally, there were many instances of people disposing of coupons to others, motivated both by need and greed.[30] Nevertheless, this system was clear, providing a number of coupons for different commodities in one coherent document. Backed up by a mature bureaucratic operation, this system made the regulation of trade readily intelligible for the public and ensured abuses could be policed more easily.[31]

The overriding point is that Ireland's full rationing system was instituted *so late* that the cultural and economic practice of black market trade was already well established. Rationing was not implemented as late in other neutral states. Spain's Minister for Industry and Commerce introduced rationing as early as May 1939 in anticipation of wartime shortages.[32] After the outbreak of war, neutral Sweden's Minister for Supply soon followed suit.[33] In every canton of Switzerland, the poor were issued with a 'blue card' two months prior to war, and every household in the country had a rationing card by October 1939.[34] Significantly Portugal, like Ireland, implemented a full rationing system very late (1943). Like Lemass, Salazar placed too much faith in the adherence of his population to Catholic moral practices regulating production and distribution. Although Portugal's *Estado Novo* was widely admired in Ireland as a functioning corporatist alternative to parliamentary democracy, Irish diplomats based in Lisbon during the war noted the poverty and profiteering that lurked beneath the Salazarian veneer of social order and criticised the absence of a full rationing system.[35] For those reading their reports back in Iveagh House, the parallel with Irish domestic conditions would have been obvious.

An inspector calls

The congratulatory tone of the Department of Supplies' Survey is dampened by the fact that its own expansion was accompanied by the attendant growth of its counterpoint – the black market. In continental Europe during the war, the black market became an established method of allocation of supply and, in some countries, was as active as the official food markets.[36] In neutral Spain, the black market, dubbed the *estraperlo* (rigged roulette machine), boomed and aggravated inflation. In neutral Portugal, wartime village-level profiteers in the wolfram (tungsten) trade became identified through the neologism *wolframista*.[37] As in Ireland, warnings appeared in daily newspapers, accompanied by notices of prison sentences, but did little to deter the illicit trade.

Black market activity was not specific to Emergency controls but its intensification certainly was. Shortages and ration restrictions forced many consumers to turn to the black market for everyday foodstuffs. Black market traders would charge 'a huge amount', but 'when the war was over and the rationing stopped their business disappeared'.[38] The vastly inflated prices of black market goods contributed strongly to the rise in the cost of living. Black market activity, both real and imagined, also provided justification for the expansion of the punitive power of the state in the economic realm. The beginning of concerted government effort to suppress the black trade coincided with the period of greatest material hardship and most extreme shortages – 1941 – when the 'supply position had become critical in every regard'.[39] This suggests that if the enforced hardship of the Emergency had excited in Fianna Fáil's elite the image of an Ireland 'pious, disciplined and folksy',[40] such daydreams were at least tempered by an awareness of the seriousness of the black trade and the material conditions that underpinned it.

Although dependent on the help of Gardaí in ration book registration and the punishment of black marketers, on the Registrar General for lists of deaths, and on Customs to record those leaving the state without ration books, there is little doubt that Supplies' officials viewed themselves as the 'real' policemen of the Emergency moral economy. Such aspirations were typical of Supplies under Lemass and Leydon. This ambitious duo soon set about expanding the role of their new department within the state's bureaucratic apparatus. With posts filled by officers headhunted from other departments, its capacity rose dramatically. There were 169 people working for the department in 1940. This figure increased to 1,069 by 1944.[41]

The bureaucratic expansion of Supplies was signalled most clearly by the emergence of the department's Inspection Branch. The branch was established in March 1941 when the department recruited twenty customs officers. Lemass now charged these men with visiting traders to ensure they were complying with their 'statutory obligations of equitable distribution at fair price'.[42] By March 1943, the Inspection Branch boasted sixty-three customs officers and seven temporary inspectors. There were stations in Cork, Waterford, Limerick, Galway, Sligo and Dundalk as well as Dublin. By October 1943, there were 106 Department of Supplies Inspectors, five Deputy Senior Inspectors, one Senior Inspector and six clerical staff. Supplies had additional inspection centres in Fenit, Westport, Mullingar and Letterkenny and had divided the Dublin operation into seven sub-areas.[43]

The men and women of the Inspection Branch operated at the sharp interface of public engagement with the black market rather than from the comfort of Supplies' Ballsbridge offices. They were subject to fairly rigorous internal checks and controls to guard against corruption. Money was saved on travel expenses as the branch grew because the expansion of regional centres reduced the distances travelled, yet it was often necessary to concentrate a large number of inspectors in a certain area over a short period of time if 'large scale black market operations' were detected.[44] These internal checks reflected the fact that in those uniquely hard times, the inflated state bureaucracy operated on strictly frugal lines, a culture of thrift parodied in *Dublin Opinion*, whose cartoonists pictured government committees resorting to feats of frugality such as sharing a single pen and a chair.[45]

A 'scattered staff' was given uniformity by close adherence to fresh Emergency Powers Orders and branch circulars,[46] but individual inspectors also wielded great power. According to one source, black market activity was most prevalent 'under the counter' of local shops.[47] And it was at the local shop counter that inspectors carried out their war on the black market. Most visits were carried out on a surprise basis as the result of tip-offs from members of the public. A high proportion of these were 'well founded', according to a memorandum on the branch.[48] When in-store, inspectors could order the trader to produce stock and books for inspection and had the power to prohibit the sale or movement of goods. Inspectors worked in pairs and after a fruitful visit, each submitted a report to the state solicitor. When cases were brought to court, the Minister for Supplies was named as the plaintiff and proceedings rested on evidence given by the inspectors. When necessary, inspectors could call on the Gardaí for help, but they did not require police authorisation to seize documents and could hold them for up to a month.[49]

As well as former Customs men, there were also a number of inspectorate staff recruited through interview. 'Established civil servants of proved integrity' were favoured in this means of recruitment. A mostly male staff was complemented by a small female contingent who proved particularly effective in making detections where male staff were 'unsuited', for instance, in the 'irregular sale of ladies' underclothing' as the record of the branch rather awkwardly puts it.[50] As well as visits to businesses, the branch also ran administrative checks from its Dublin headquarters requesting traders to send returns. The visit remained the preferred means of inspection, though, after suspicions arose that some firms were sending books accompanied by fake auditors' certificates.[51]

As well as the visit to the country store, inspectors intervened in auctions. At these auctions, the department suspected, rationed goods were sold in illegal quantities and unrationed goods were sold above the market price.[52] On 6 March 1942, the Wholesale Fruit Traders Association sent a delegation to Leydon to complain about the action of officials from Supplies at a citrus fruits auction the previous evening. Pushing aside the auctioneer, an official from Supplies had mounted the rostrum declaring the event cancelled and that the prices of oranges, lemon and grapefruit would now be controlled to ensure a fair margin of profit.[53] As he spoke, inspectors seized the fruit.

Countrywide records of District Court prosecutions brought in the name of the Minister for Supplies reveal that small shopkeepers were summoned for a number of offences. The most common were selling goods at prices in excess of that fixed by Lemass, selling goods to people not registered as local customers, and the failure to keep records of transactions. These records are too numerous to discuss by district in any depth. Instead, Ballyhaunis, County Mayo, provides a random case study of prosecutions brought by Supplies against retailers in a small country town. Records reveal that offenders were either reported by members of the public or inspectors posing as members of the public. Cases were usually heard consecutively on the same day. Complainants reporting pricing and rationing offences were typically married women. This points to the paramount diligence of women in ensuring that Lemass's list of retail prices for domestic goods was adhered to.[54] Viewed in an unfavourable light, inspectors' reliance on local informants indicates that the maintenance of the state's version moral economy at times resembled little more than the indulgence of gossip. On the other hand, local knowledge was invaluable.

The Ballyhaunis records also show that inspectors typically operated on a day-by-day, town-by-town basis. On 22 September 1942, an inspector was sold goods at excess price by no fewer than five different retailers in Ballyhaunis.[55] That an individual inspector was overcharged in five different shops in a small town on the same day underscores just how widespread the flouting of Lemass's price orders was.

The majority of fines issued by Supplies were relatively small, reflecting the fact that the black market in consumer goods was often based around overcharging for a mere quarter pound of tea or coffee or a single candle. Many Irish people would have been aware of how seriously black market activity was punished in occupied Europe.[56] In Ireland, by contrast, relatively few black marketers even faced prison. Typically, Ballyhaunis's offending retailers were charged ten shillings with the threat of seven days in Sligo jail if they failed to pay.[57] Fines increased according to the nature and quantity of goods. Selling four and a half ounces of tea to an undercover inspector warranted a £1 fine.[58] Selling half a pound of drinking chocolate warranted the usual ten shillings fine.[59] Receiving single bicycle parts usually brought a substantial fine, as did the sale of any type of fuel (from firewood to kerosene) on the black market.[60]

Significantly, records show that inspectors proved meticulous in pursuing prosecutions against *every* member of staff involved in any element of the black transaction for 'aiding and abetting', including shop owners, their spouses and even shop boys or girls. A hefty fine handed down by a judge at an inspector's urging could seriously damage a small business. In late 1943, for example, a County Galway grocer declared himself 'finished' after Supplies successfully won £520 worth of fines for offences under the Emergency Powers Orders.[61] Defending the stringency of his department's approach in the Dáil, Lemass argued that 'failure to keep records or the keeping of inaccurate records is not and should not be regarded as a trivial offence' but was integral to 'the aim of rationing'. This aim was articulated in unequivocally moral economic language: 'to ensure that every person in the community will get an equal right to a fair share of the available supplies'.[62]

The Inspectorate was aided by thorough Emergency press censorship. Radio and press publicity urged the public to come forward and report ration violations by their neighbours or local retailers. Official announcements on shortages and rationing dominated Irish newspapers.[63] On Lemass's instruction, shortly after the start of formal rationing, Supplies launched an advertising campaign in the press encouraging people to 'break the backbone' of the illegal trade by informing.[64] Supplies kept censorship officials under Chief Press Censor Michael Knightly regularly updated with goods added to the list of rationed items and commodities subject to price control. Officials from Supplies, most notably Assistant Secretary of the department John Williams, liaised regularly with the top censorship officials, Coyne and Knightly, to ensure that certain advertisements and articles were never published. After receiving the list from Supplies, Knightly issued circulars to all the newspaper editors in the country asking them to exclude any small advertisements offering restricted goods for sale or auction. A typical circular from Knightly to Ireland's

newspaper editors would contain little more than the description of the heterogeneous list of goods now deemed unacceptable for advertisement by Supplies: 'jams,
marmalades, wheaten meal, soda crystals, copper sulphate'; 'twine, shotgun car-
tridges, thread'; and 'clothes, peas, sausages, black and white pudding'.[65] Any news
items on the food position likely to cause public disorder or panic were censored.
Advertisements offering goods for sale at prices in excess of the maximum retail
price fixed by Supplies or above the ration allowance were banned and, as far as was
possible, the advertisers investigated. Examples of such banned advertisements
were 'Highest Prices Paid, Ladies and Gents' Clothes'; 'Diamonds, old gold. Highest Prices Paid'; and '100 gallons of white spirit, what offers?'.[66]

Bolstered by press censorship and the Inspectorate, Lemass's power rose as Emergency conditions worsened and his department expanded. The number of Orders he
issued leapt from 56 in 1939 to 148 in 1941, 189 in 1942 and 160 in 1943.[67] This
enforcement of the ration was ostensibly successful. In August 1942, the department
revealed that in nine months, it had prosecuted 700 people for rationing offences.[68]
The illegal use of ration books of people who had died or gone abroad gave rise to 'a
considerable number of prosecutions' and, according to the Survey, the public
proved diligent in informing officials of the misuse of ration books by neighbours.[69]

On the one hand, Supplies' determination to prosecute had gathered momentum
over the Emergency due to the seriousness of the supply situation and black market
activity. On the other, the department was quite simply able to redouble its efforts
as the police force of a moral economy because its bureaucratic capacity had
expanded so dramatically.[70]

Despite the volume of prosecutions, there were 'very few complaints' about inspectors who, so it was claimed, enjoyed a 'good relationship with the community'.[71] Lemass
was also capable of a pragmatism which cut through red tape. While Lemass and other
senior officials had wanted people to surrender their ration books prior to leaving the
state, the continuous traffic over the land and sea borders with the United Kingdom
convinced them that such a scheme was unworkable; so, when formal rationing was
introduced, everyone was allowed to take their ration book with them.[72]

It is uncertain, though, whether the professionalisation and growth of the Inspections Branch resulted in a greater proportion of detections for overcharging. There
were 2,078 detections of excessive pricing (January to April 1944) when the Branch
was in its stride.[73] The figure of 2,078 pricing detections in four months in 1944
alone demonstrates the gargantuan scale of both the assault on the black market and
the flouting of controls. Remarkably, due to a backlog of paperwork, this figure represented only 6% of the total number of pricing cases ongoing in early 1944.

As the war on the Irish black market escalated, Lemass demanded that those
flouting regulations faced tough justice. Cases against those alleged to be middle- to
large-scale black marketers were commonly heard at the Special Criminal Court.
Frequently, these individuals received large fines or prison sentences. For example,
in late 1942, a Dublin man who attempted to sell an inspector a large quantity of

tyres, candles and flour was sentenced to three years imprisonment by a Special Criminal Court judge.[74] Those accused of black market activity on a smaller scale appeared at District Court hearings. In some District Courts, fines were harsh and in others petty. According to the department, 'the practice of the courts in different areas has been found to vary in cases of an exactly similar nature'.[75]

In contrast to major cases, there are examples from every county in Ireland of district justices dismissing summons altogether. Instead of a pliant judiciary willing to impose harsh penalties for infringement of the moral economy, the department was frustrated by justices' 'uneven applications of justice'.[76] Frequently, cases were taken on merit, and the imposition of mandatory fines or prison sentences, which Supplies insisted were a necessary deterrent to black market activity, were refused. Throwing out a prosecution for the overcharging of tea in 1943, a Dublin justice declared that he did not pretend to keep track of price orders and that there were so many of them that he felt 'baffled' by them.[77] Often, officials from Supplies were frustrated when penalties imposed for irregular market activity were 'most trivial'.[78] A state-appointed solicitor in Mayo complained that 90% of his time was taken up with pricing and rationing offences but that district justices issued only nominal fines when these cases reached court.[79]

Ruminating on the matter, the anonymous civil servant who authored the Department of Supplies' report on its inspection branch proposed that 'judicial functions be usurped by officials' with Supplies acting as 'prosecutor, judge and jury'. Instead of the status quo (where an offence was committed only when a price control order was clearly contravened), the assumption of judicial functions by Supplies would give the department the power to impose sentences. Anticipating legal challenges, the department would mitigate sentences on its terms, rather than the court's, and 'only if it saw fit'. The author was frustrated by the one-month restriction on the holding of seized documents. Because investigations often took longer, officials had to secure immediate summonses for 'token charges' in order to arrange for cases to be adjourned each time they were due for hearing. The author advocated the end of this 'cumbersome' practice by allowing Supplies to hold papers 'indefinitely'.[80] This self-righteous approach to the sentencing of black marketers provides a fine example of the 'cannibalism' which distinguished the department's approach. The assault on the black market was becoming a dirty war.

White hope versus black market: the moral economy of the Department of Supplies in critical perspective

The Historical Survey omits criticism of Supplies' record in policing the Emergency black market in two key regards. Firstly, it ignores the popular disdain for the department's zealous pursuit of a moral economy. Secondly, it downplays the internal contradictions and shortcomings of the department's mission to ensure equitable distribution.

As mentioned, the press's take on the department's attempts to quell the black market was nearly unanimous. All mainstream newspapers condemned the illegal trade, frequently in outraged moral economic terms. 'It is a crime against the whole community and the customers should be punished with the unscrupulous rogues', fumed the *Connacht Sentinel* in January 1940.[81] The government's activity was not, according to an *Irish Times* article of 1942, 'like prohibition-era U.S.A.', but was rather 'an act of simple justice'.[82] 'Their malpractices are not only an injustice to the consumer, but are a grave menace to the nation's standards of commercial morality' raged a typical attack on black marketers in the *Irish Independent*. The latter piece was tempered, though, by the growing realisation that a sense of proportion was being lost in the severe sentences which Supplies were pressing for. It sagely warned that 'officials should not delude themselves that they are in this way getting after the real culprits - the people behind the scenes who manipulate the black market on the grand scale'.[83]

The wisdom of this sentiment is borne out by the large number of women who appeared in court for using coupons from ration books that were not their own but who claimed (quite honestly, it seems) that they had a large number of children to feed and were not aware that they were committing an offence by using a friend or relative's coupons.[84] Supplies' remit, to 'control supplies and services essential to the life of the community', was essentially material but contained strong ethical over-tones. In the department's war on the black market, the pursuit of social justice was to increasingly become an elusive end justifying sometimes dubious means.

The full force of Lemass's weighty department often bore down disproportion-ately on small shopkeepers because they administered food and clothing coupons and were at the forefront of black market involvement. Bigger businesses, on the other hand, often evaded censure. As Jonathan Swift wrote, 'Laws are like cobwebs, which may catch small flies but let wasps and hornets break through'. Large firms, whose crimes were harder to see than those of the shopkeeper, often broke through the cobwebs. The Historical Survey conceded that, despite their efforts, 'the pri-mary object of any trader is to make profits and most traders made higher profits in the war period than they had ever found attainable in days of plenty'.[85]

The proportion of petty offences recorded by the print media outweigh convic-tions for serious corporate fraud. The *Waterford News* reported in November 1943 that three Waterford businesses were charged a combined total of £1,090 for supplying surplus tea, sugar and coal at inflated prices.[86] This story was exceptional. It stands out because the newspaper's regular coverage of court proceedings was dominated by the prosecution of individuals for small-time offences such as the sieving of brown flour to make it white and, in March 1943, the sale of turf mould as tea.[87] Supplies often fined small retailers for overcharging on the most sought-after commodities such as tea and cigarettes or for watering down milk. Most frequently, it was these shopkeepers who appeared in court to receive nominal fines for incidents of overcharging, brought to book by inspectors who had been tipped off by locals.

Some of the more petty prosecutions pursued by Supplies included the fining of a sixteen-year-old Limerick girl for overcharging for a packet of cigarettes[88] and a £10 fine on a Dublin woman for selling eight cigarettes to an inspector at the price of ten.[89] In another case, a Dundalk trader was entrapped by two inspectors posing as man and wife into selling a lady's cardigan to them without coupons.[90] In an example of how Supplies' enthusiastic offensive against the black market could lead to disproportionate punishment, the department successfully pressed for the imprisonment of Nora Barnes, a Waterford shopkeeper, who was sentenced to two months in July 1944 for receiving a stolen coat.[91]

Supplies' hard-nosed attitude in pursuing prosecutions provides further explanation of the comparatively poor return for its activities. Lemass admitted in early 1942 that the government could not suppress the black market unless the public helped 'and the public aren't helping'. This situation, he claimed, was jeopardising the very 'institutions of state'.[92] The superiority of black marketers in their war with Supplies' inspectors was parodied brilliantly in the 1942 *Dublin Opinion* boxing skit 'White Hope versus Black Market'[93] in which Lemass was portrayed as the archetypal 'White Hope' boxer confronting the beefy, lumbering presence of 'Black Market', the more impressive-looking African pugilist. White Hope, skinny but plucky, determinedly pursues his opponent. 'Black Market', in the opposite corner of the ring, is a 'slippery, elusive' opponent who concentrates on evading the punches of White Hope and thus 'keeping out of trouble'. As the fight ensues, White Hope's attack is thwarted by the excessive amount of *red tape* his trainer has applied to his fists and his obedience to the rules. White Hope 'chases his man round the ring without inflicting much punishment'. Finally, when White Hope has Black Market against the ropes and is about to deliver the killer blow, there is a power cut and the ring is plunged into darkness, resulting in the postponement of the match. Black Market not only successfully evades his opponent, but during the bout his team manages to steal several items and when the power is cut even offers to provide candles at an extortionate price so that the fight can continue.

This satiric broadside against Lemass reflected the fact that the malodour of unnecessary and abrupt state intervention during the Emergency was most commonly associated with his department. Although their activities were undoubtedly geared towards the welfare of the community, the actions of the officials of the Department of Supplies also embodied a bureaucratic expansion of the state's role. This bred exasperation and resentment. For example, Supplies was accused of agent provocateur tactics in confiscating the petrol ration from six doctors after recruiting another doctor to offer them black market petrol at work.[94] In a 1941 Dáil debate on pricing, Fianna Fáil TD Cornelius Meaney encapsulated a growing anti-apparatchik sentiment by contending 'you will require an inspector at every cross-roads, probably a committee inspecting him, and even an inspector inspecting the inspectors'.[95]

The negative popular image of the department was not dispelled by the well-intentioned but rather sudden measures Lemass introduced alongside the hundreds of continuously fluctuating price orders. In 1941, he unexpectedly discontinued the sale of cooking appliances and announced that electricity and gas were to be rationed. Prior to this move, the government introduced that embodiment of Emergency petty officialdom, the 'glimmer man', an inspector who regulated gas and electricity use and who was the subject of much derision.[96] Shortly afterwards, the ranks of an increasingly absurd-sounding officialdom were epitomised by Lemass's appointment of a new much-needed but mean-sounding flour controller.[97] Reacting against these and similar measures, *The Standard* complained that 'The People Have a Right to be Told Government Plans'.[98]

Lemass's strident interventionism often manifested itself in a clumsy approach to complex issues. The boom in the black trade in bicycles provides a good example. Rather naively, neither the bicycle industry nor the government had anticipated any real difficulties in obtaining supplies at the outbreak of war.[99] In 1939, Supplies had urged Irish Dunlop Ltd to lay in extra stocks. As in other cases, without a financial guarantee against loss from the government, Dunlop refused. As the war continued, the supply position deteriorated seriously until by 1941, with the outbreak of war in the Far East and the commencement of British export prohibitions, Ireland's rubber supplies were cut off completely.[100] The import of bicycles and bicycle parts from Britain fell to 12.5% of normal imports by 1941, a figure which was halved the following year.[101]

With a dearth of petrol and the prohibition on private motoring in early 1942, bicycles became essential to transport needs, both commercial and personal. Although the bicycle black market may appear a trifling matter, the importance of bicycles in Emergency Ireland cannot be understated. It provided much-needed mobility in rural Ireland, a situation best parodied in Flann O'Brien's *The Third Policeman* where, continuously perched on bicycle seats, men slowly become their machines through the transfer of atoms. In urban areas, the bicycle provided a bulwark of livelihood and liberty against the worst excesses of poverty. The demand for bicycles and, in particular, rubber tyres was enormous, aggravated by the Defence Forces' operational demands. Petrol restrictions also meant that the better off were no longer able to have food delivered to them and they, too, took to the bicycle to do their weekly shop.[102] The theft of a bicycle, therefore, could seriously compromise one's standard of living. Lemass dealt with the black market in bicycles and bicycle parts in a forthright manner which again demonstrated the department's encouragement of Report Thy Neighbour. In early 1943, he publicly urged people to inform Supplies or the Gardaí of black market prices being offered for bicycle parts. Anyone doing so qualified for a permit enabling them to obtain their desired article at the price fixed by the government.[103] Few availed of this offer, however.

The previous year, Supplies had taken a number of measures which all failed to regulate the market effectively. The number of inspections of cycle dealers' premises and the number of licences revoked for overcharging were both increased. Additionally, in 1942 Lemass appointed eight regional 'tyre inspectors' with full control over distribution.[104] By that year, reflecting the fact that rubber supplies had by then entirely ceased, the government had issued no fewer than nine Emergency Powers Orders specific to this commodity.[105] Despite the extraordinary number of orders, 'the cooperation of the public was not as good as it could have been', and 'sales continued in the black market'. Tyres were obtained across the border, and to the chagrin of Supplies and their tyre inspectors, 'even tyres supplied by Dunlop to registered cycle dealers found their way into the black market'.[106]

Lemass, then, was in the unhappy position of losing the fight against the black market and simultaneously exciting popular criticism for the forthright measures he took to increase his chances of winning.

In Britain, disdain for excessive bureaucracy was a common theme in the wartime experience as well. Reacting to a 1944 case in which a baker had been fined for decorating doughnuts with sugar that he had saved from the batter mix, Prime Minister Winston Churchill was moved to write to his Minister for Food stating 'You will gain much credit by stamping on these trashy little prosecutions, and also by purging the regulations from petty, meticulous arrogant officialism.'[107] In early 1942, Lemass made it illegal to serve bread – even the new black loaf – at any social events, and self-denial was strongly urged. Lemass asked 'all those who can afford other foods' to practise self-imposed frugality and 'cut out bread almost entirely'.[108] Bread was never added to the ration by Lemass, despite calls for him to do so detailing how, in Dublin, after queuing for hours women could only get one loaf despite having seven or eight children to feed.[109] Lemass did secure hefty subsidies from the public purse in order to subsidise its price.[110] Nonetheless, the new black loaf was roundly detested by Ireland's inhabitants, who were generally unconvinced of the health benefits of it and for many years retained a prejudice towards 'that old bran bread an' all'.[111]

If Lemass gained further unpopularity by introducing the 'black loaf', this move also provides an example of the development of voluntary movements in support of the government's moral economic goal. The *Irish Times* reacted by starting a 'No Bread For Breakfast League' (NBBL or 'Nibble')[112] in an effort to help the government overcome supply difficulties. Another example of voluntary efforts to curb black market activity, and no less peculiar than 'Nibble', was General Eoin O'Duffy's establishment of a 'new Dublin movement' against bicycle thefts in 1942. O'Duffy, a former Garda Commissioner, leader of Fine Gael and head of the quasi-fascist 'Blueshirt' movement, had formally retired from politics after spearheading the Irish Brigade's abortive entry into the Spanish Civil War to fight for General Francisco Franco. Speaking at the movement's initial meeting in early 1942, O'Duffy claimed '410 machines were stolen during the last month' in a trend that was becoming 'a menace to the public' orchestrated by a 'sophisticated operation' which used vans and cars to transport the bikes.[113]

O'Duffy's 'movement' (which has more than a hint of Flann O'Brienesque farce to it) fared little more successfully than his Irish Brigade of a few years previously.

But its foundation reflected a trend in the establishment of non-governmental bodies to try and curb the steep rise in black market activity. Lemass consistently encouraged such initiatives. The punitive measures used by Supplies to police the
Emergency moral economy differed from the tone Lemass struck in his public
addresses on the supply situation, where voluntarism was stressed. Yet the development of such voluntary groups also threatened to expose the shortcomings of
Lemass's management of the Emergency. While individual or small-scale voluntary
efforts were welcome, larger movements were a different matter altogether.

In this regard, both 'Nibble' and O'Duffy's 'movement' pale in significance to the
most prominent Emergency non-state group aimed at eradicating unfair market
practices: the Irish Housewives Association (IHA).[114] Intent on rescuing a moral
economy from the teeth of the black economy in Ireland's urban centres, the IHA
developed to become a thorn in Lemass's side during the Emergency. Seeing urban
poverty and malnutrition during the Emergency as the direct result of government
inaction, ex-teacher Hilda Tweedy founded the IHA in 1941, claiming 'Women are
apt to grumble about high prices and food scarcities but [are] too slow to realise
their duty to try to remedy these social evils.'[115]

The IHA's well-publicised 1941 memorandum exhibited some markedly socialist
tendencies, calling on the government to institute a fair price for producers and consumers, a minimum wage for workers, greater market regulation, communal feeding
centres and 'the suppression of all black markets'.[116] The Irish Housewives publicly
pressed for the government to enforce a moral economy more fully, declaring themselves 'For the Community, Not for Profit'.[117] Its members marched through Dublin
in March 1942 with placards that read 'The Children Must be Fed' and 'Fair Prices'.[118]
In 1945, the organisation complained that the government was not only too lenient
on profiteers but had taken too long to enforce the necessary restrictions on a
domestic market squeezed by shortages.[119] Some measures the IHA lobbied for
were obviously heeded by government. For example, the IHA campaigned for free
milk for children and price control on cooking fats: both calls were answered by
legislation in 1944.[120]

The IHA's May 1941 memorandum, or the 'Housewives' Petition' as the press
dubbed it, was its most famous act. It was a landmark document in both its vision of
a comprehensive and state-directed moral economy, its exposure of urban squalor,
and its impact on the government. Significantly, the IHA challenged the partial
rationing system instituted by Lemass whereby people registered at their local shop
to exchange coupons for certain items. The organisation questioned whether 'a voluntary curtailment of consumption' was working and called instead for a comprehensive system of rationing.[121] It pointed to Britain's formal rationing as a model and
contended that the poorest and largest families could not survive on the government's meagre food and clothing allowances.

The influence of this pressure on Lemass's policy was greater than has been
acknowledged. The submission of the 'Housewives' Petition' coincided with

Lemass's decision to introduce formal rationing. The timing implies that as a document of consumer dissatisfaction it acted, alongside material factors, as the sort of firm stimulus needed by a Fianna Fáil regime dithering over the introduction of coherent social and economic measures to deal with the crisis of supplies and black marketing. The IHA is not mentioned in the Historical Survey, however. Lemass did not announce the introduction of comprehensive rationing of essential foodstuffs until January 1942, and ration books were not delivered until May of that year. This was a delayed reaction to a situation which had been getting progressively worse since the fall of France in June 1940. The IHA, by contrast, had called for such a move since its establishment in early 1941.

Despite the conspicuous omission of its influence in the surviving records of the Department of Supplies, the IHA was the most active and radical voluntary organisation to combat the effects of shortages in urban Ireland. And yet, for all its good work, the group's anti-black market views were not representative of Irish society during the Emergency. While the Irish Housewives tapped into the popular mood of resentment towards excessive profiteering, their abstinence from more modest involvement with the black market was exceptional. A senior figure in the state hierarchy, Todd Andrews, relates how his wife Mary (a member of the IHA) broke off social relations with friends who had treated her to bread and cakes made from black market white flour.[122] While laudable, it is important to note that Mrs Andrews had the luxury to take this decision, whereas poor and working-class mothers in Ireland's towns and cities relied on the black market to feed their families. Despite campaigning on their behalf, the IHA was typically not composed of the mothers of the poorest and largest families. By Tweedy's own admission, it was a 'predominately Protestant, middle class venture'.[123] While the IHA possessed many middle-class members of similar conviction to Tweedy, many other members of the middle class used their relatively strong purchasing power to stock up in advance of scarcity.

Nonetheless, as a pressure group rather than as a non-political voluntary effort, the IHA struck a nerve at the Department of Supplies. The IHA's activities certainly influenced the government's decision to implement full rationing, even if 'the preparation and issue of three million ration books was certain to be a difficult task and the decision to undertake it was postponed as long as possible' as the Historical Survey claims.[124] Departmental records omit the IHA's role, falsely claiming that 'at no point did any serious volume of complaint from householders arise'.[125] It is clear, nevertheless, that the pressure the organisation put on the government to realise a moral economy through the extension of rationing and price regulation to all goods was decisive. This dilutes the image of the Department of Supplies as confidently interventionist on its own initiative.

As mentioned, the war on the black market was not the sole preserve of Supplies. The department was aided by censorship officials, who monitored commercial output in the press. The relationship between Supplies and censorship system was not symbiotically smooth, though, as Leydon's spat with censorship officials

over shipping information illustrates. Occasionally, the enforcement of the government's version of the Emergency moral economy through censorship foundered.
As with all aspects of Supplies' activities, these tensions emerged as problems in the
wake of the British economic squeeze of 1941.

In combating black market advertisements, Supplies found itself in the familiar
role of dictating to another department. The Chief Censor's Office – otherwise
renowned for its rigour during the Emergency – failed to meet Supplies' very high
standards. Advertisements diverging from the moral neutrality line, depicting soldiers, sailors or pilots or with messages to the consumer such as 'Blitz that Cough!',
were straightforward for the Censor, as Assistant Controller of Censorship T.J.
Coyne explained to Leydon.[126] On the other hand, getting the press to refuse 'for
sale' and 'wanted' advertisements was, as Coyne argued, difficult, particularly
with newspapers like the *Evening Mail* 'to which the small ad is the breath of life'.[127]
Censorship officials favoured maintaining the system of self-regulation that had
operated since the start of the Emergency because the alternative – having newspapers submit a full list of small advertisements to the Censor for approval –
would have created a great burden on the already busy civil servants under
Knightly and Coyne.[128]

The problem with the system of self-regulation lay with the fact that many newspapers carried a disclaimer beside the 'buy and sell' section. Supplies' Assistant Secretary John Williams tried to establish that newspapers which carried banned
advertisements were liable to be prosecuted under section five of the Emergency
Powers Act (1939), which held corporate bodies responsible by consent or approval
if an offence had been made under the act.[129] The Attorney General, however,
advised that newspapers which carried such advertisements were not guilty of an
offence.[130] Officials from Supplies had to content themselves with writing letters to
the Censor, pointing out black market advertisements that had been overlooked. In
1941, Lemass successfully proposed an amendment to the Emergency Powers
(Control of Prices) Order (1939) which was intended to make prosecution easier.
Introduced in an effort to broaden the scope of black market offences, it changed
articles 'sold' to 'sold or agreed, or offered to be sold or made the subject of an invitation of an offer to buy'.[131] To Lemass and Leydon's disappointment, though, it proved
very difficult for Supplies to elicit details from newspapers of black market advertisers, many of whom seem to have had plenty of money to pay for advertisements but
were unsurprisingly reluctant to leave personal details.

If Lemass was frustrated by the limits of the censor's powers, the evidence con-
cerning his own attitude to those who committed rationing offences is somewhat
contradictory. Brian Farrell cites Lemass's 'grim satisfaction in the fact that
acquaintances of his own were prosecuted in the special court set up to deal with
offences under the rationing legislation'.[132] Yet Kevin O'Doherty, Lemass's private
secretary from 1944 to 1946, praised Lemass's 'human streak' when it came to
policing the moral economy, recalling an occasion when Lemass – won over by a

letter from a schoolboy pleading him not to revoke his father's taxi licence for illegally conveying passengers to a 'non-essential' engagement (a golf match) – tore up
the prosecution.[133]

This account provides a rare glimpse of Lemass's compassionate side. As demonstrated, when it came to wider ranging attempts to influence consumer activity,
Lemass could appear similarly contradictory, his advice ranging from urging self-
help to insisting on obedience to state control. His somewhat contradictory stance
on flour supplies was matched by Leydon's. In mid-1941, a Censorship official wrote
to the Ministerial Secretary expressing concern over Supplies' instruction to censor
an article from the May edition of the *Bakery Trades Journal*. In the article, the author
had expressed his anger at Supplies' lack of action in ensuring the fair distribution of
the steady stream of white flour that was coming over the border and being sold via
the black market. The high price of white flour, contended the author, ensured that
the masses had to make do with 'ordinary flour', while white flour 'swelled the dump-
lings of the idle rich'.[134] The obviously sympathetic censorship official went on to
argue that censorship of the article would be construed as 'smothering legitimate
criticism of the government'.[135] Leydon replied that Supplies was ensuring the fair
distribution of tea and petrol by banning advertisements because they were rationed
goods. White flour, on the other hand, was a different matter:

> In so far as the rich can afford to buy white flour, their consumption of the ordinary
> flour is correspondingly reduced ... those who cannot afford to buy the white flour
> should be glad that somebody else is able to buy it and so reduce the risk of an eventual
> shortage ... *most of the profit is taken by the people who are taking the risks and if anybody
> thinks that white flour is too dear he should simply refrain from buying it* ... it is quite
> impossible for the government to take any steps to ration white flour or regulate its
> distribution.[136]

As mentioned, just a few months later, Supplies was taking tough action against anyone found using white flour and had made it a rationed commodity. More startling
than Leydon's hubris in this case is the incongruity of this statement with his public
and private stance on the black market. Leydon belonged to the careful Whitehall
tradition, having worked for the Ministry of Pensions in London in the 1920s. He
was, to quote Garvin, 'a small man in a black suit, vaguely clerical in manner'.[137]
Despite feeling 'betrayed' by British economic bullying during the Emergency,[138] he
remained the consummate civil servant. In private correspondence in 1943, he had
urged de Valera that even 'people of standing' should be prosecuted for black market
activities.[139] Yet in this letter, Leydon implied disdain for those unable to afford
white flour and admiration for the 'risk-takers' of the trade.

Whether the 'risk-takers' to whom Leydon referred were smugglers or commercial risk-takers is somewhat ambiguous. Either way, his sentiments do not sit comfortably with the moral economic effort which Supplies was pursuing in the media.
Connolly, the Censorship official, evidently disliked what he perceived as Leydon's

hypocrisy and, unsatisfied with his reply, wrote back informing him that the Censor's Office was 'bound to allow any reasonable criticism'.[140] Leydon's views on the matter reflect frustration at the supply situation but also, conceivably, the influence of Lemass. Leydon held his minister in the highest esteem, a respect reciprocated by Lemass, who regarded him as the most able man he had ever met. But by contrast to Leydon, Lemass was a gambler who regarded the Irish people as regrettably devoid of the spirit of 'risk-taking' enterprise.[141] Leydon's remarks to Connolly possess all the hallmarks of Lemassian brusqueness. Perhaps, given the supply desperation of 1941, Lemass's attitude was starting to rub off on Leydon.

In Leydon's defence, Supplies' somewhat contradictory attitude towards flour reflected Ireland's differing supply needs at different points in the Emergency. Hidden within Leydon's flippancy was his prime concern: to 'reduce the risk of an eventual shortage'. This overriding goal allowed both Leydon and Lemass to turn a blind eye to the inequitable distribution of white flour in May 1941 but to pursue convictions when the flour supply worsened in 1942. In general terms, too, Leydon was more scrupulous than Lemass when it came to upholding the rules.

Nonetheless, such means-to-an-end rationalisation smacks of double standards. More importantly, Supplies' failure to establish a comprehensive rationing system earlier in the Emergency meant that its somersaults on issues like flour supply did little to instill and encourage a much-needed culture of moral economy in the wider population. Leydon's cynicism highlights the chimeral status of the Emergency moral economy. The government failed to harness this sentiment early in the Emergency through instituting a consistent system of market regulation. In Britain, by contrast, market controls were vertically and horizontally integrated from the earliest stages of war, the state controlling a product at all stages from import and restricting production to a limited range of commodities. Lemass's wide-ranging economic powers camouflaged the fact that the state possessed relatively little muscle when it came to combating profiteers who operated on a plane above that of both the Bill Sykeses and the pompous, respectable citizens.

Conclusion

Jonathan Swift's reflection on the freedom of wasps and hornets, written in the early eighteenth century, when modern money markets were being founded and where the concept of moral economy had its broadest application, rang true in mid-twentieth-century Ireland where Supplies failed to stymie the worst excesses of profiteering and small shopkeepers received by far the greatest number of convictions for unfair pricing. In the public interest, Lemass's department pursued an admirably tough line on black market offences, yet in its uneven rationing, regulation of trade and rash expansionism, it caught more small flies than hornets.

This, of course, is not conveyed in Supplies' Historical Survey. Taken on face value, it provides a glowing portrayal of the department.[142] On closer examination,

Supplies' dynamism is counterpoised elsewhere by ineptitude. Despite the imposition of the trade squeeze, Britain was not solely responsible for Ireland's supply situation during the Emergency. As Gerard Fee claims, state intervention during the
Emergency unsurely navigated a way between the twin peaks of Beveridgism and
Catholic Social Teaching. Hence, it was 'gradualist and never to be all-encompassing',
a last resort rather than the product of radical social thinking.[143] Due to many factors, both within and outside its control – its early failure to safeguard supplies, its
own arrogance, widespread non-compliance with regulations, wartime shortages
and the British squeeze – the Department of Supplies conforms to this model and
does not quite match the stridently interventionist image described in its departmental 'history'.

In the department's self-image, instilled by its chief, Supplies was the defender of the
lowly citizen, whose economic and social environment during the Emergency is discussed in the following chapter. Lemass rejected the recommendations of the *Report of
the Commission on Vocational Organisation* (1943) because of the danger that under a
vocationalist order workers and employers would connive at the expense of the community at large. After all, his department was looking after that.[144] In reality, the department's strident interventionism – exhibited most strongly in the implementation and
management of full rationing – was as much the product of institutional expansion as
of its success in establishing a moral economy based on meaningful interaction with
the nation's citizens. Significantly, in Northern Ireland, the Ministry of Food's administrative structure was less punitive than that of Supplies. Regionally, there were divisional food offices rather than inspection centres and organisation extended to the
parish level where Local Food Control Committees met regularly to compile lists of
licensed retailers and suspend or revoke licences for black market activity.[145] These
bodies resembled those propounded by Irish vocationalists in that they had a mixed
membership of three or more local retailers (including a grocer and a butcher) and six
or more consumer representatives (including at least one woman).[146]

In Sweden and Switzerland, wartime market regulation was based around the
meetings of voluntary committees and councils, including women, at local level.[147]
The British Ministry of Food succeeded in dealing with the public with sensitivity,
recognising that overtly didactic propaganda measures would alienate people, dam-
aging the message of social unity it promoted.[148] Supplies' organisation was, by
comparison, authoritarian and in this regard, as James Dillon claimed, Lemass was
'the father and mother of the black market'.[149] In a post-war Dáil debate, Lemass
even argued that rationing and price control offences should have been scheduled
for the military court: large-scale black marketers should have been hanged.[150]
While Lemass's desire for the death penalty for Irish black marketers was not realised, in Franco's neutral Spain the most egregious offenders were indeed executed.[151]
But if the hard-line approach was sometimes necessary with British officials when
conducting essential yet highly volatile trade talks, it was clearly less suited to the
domestic sphere. Even in occupied Europe, the threat of death if found trading on

the black market did not result in a reduction of the black trade but rather an increase in prices due to the high risks involved.[152]

Unsurprisingly, then, with fines the common penalty for black market activity, the department's disciplinary approach to the Irish black market was not very successful. A localised, consultative approach – supported by a full rationing structure and therefore a pro-rationing culture – would have proved more popular and, in all likelihood, more effective. Lemass's early reluctance to institute the wide-ranging regulatory features of a war economy meant that his department's zeal for its own version of moral economy was not matched by traders, the general public or judges. A 1944 article describing Irish drinking culture in the literary journal *The Bell* depicted a pub radio blaring 'dreary news items', including price orders, completely ignored by the clientele.[153] As this image demonstrates, ministerial orders continued to be treated 'rather lightly' by the Irish public, as Lemass's civil servants complained.[154] Black market had prevailed over white hope.

Notes

1 Memorandum on interdepartmental committees on essential materials, NAI, DT/S8203.
2 *Statistical Abstracts*, 1938–1946.
3 *Munster Express*, 15 November 1940.
4 *Meath Chronicle*, 13 July 1940.
5 *Irish Independent*, 12 October 1940.
6 Ó Drisceoil, *Censorship in Ireland*, 105.
7 Editorial, *Southern Star*, 18 November 1939.
8 *Dáil Debates*, vol. 77, col. 203, 27 September 1939.
9 *Irish Press*, 20 October 1939.
10 *Irish Press*, 17 January 1941.
11 'Record of Activities'. NAI, IND/EHR/3/15, p. 26.
12 'Historical Survey'. NAI, IND/EHR/3/C1, part II, p. 27.
13 'Record of Activities'. NAI, IND/EHR/3/15, p. 29.
14 'Historical Survey'. NAI, IND/EHR/3/C1, part II, pp. 32–35.
15 'Historical Survey'. NAI, IND/EHR/3/C1, part II, p. 26.
16 *Irish Independent*, 20 October 1942.
17 'Historical Survey'. NAI, IND/EHR/3/C1, part II, pp. 47–48.
18 See Richard Farmer, *The Food Companions: Cinema and Consumption in Wartime Britain, 1939–45* (Manchester, 2011).
19 Lemass, radio broadcast, 21 June 1940. 'Record of Activities'. NAI, IND/EHR/3/15, appendix VI.
20 Lemass, radio broadcast, 8 June 1942. 'Record of Activities'. NAI, IND/EHR/3/15, appendix VIII.
21 Meenan, 'The Irish Economy during the War', 31.
22 Lemass, 8 June 1942. 'Record of Activities'. NAI, IND/EHR/3/15, appendix VIII.
23 Wills, *Neutral Island*, 241.
24 'Tea – Maintenance of Supplies'. NAI, IND/EHR/3/13, p. 27.

25 Alfie Byrne junior, *Dáil Debates*, vol. 83, col. 356, 14 May 1941.
26 Mary Immaculate College Limerick Oral History Archive (MIOA), Christy Hennessy, b. 1932, Waterford City. Interviewed 8 April 2000, p. 5.
27 'Tea – Maintenance of Supplies'. NAI, IND/EHR/3/13, p. 11.
28 Richard Corish, *Dáil Debates*, vol. 82, col. 445, 12 March 1941.
29 'Tea – Maintenance of Supplies'. NAI, IND/EHR/3/13, pp. 10–16.
30 *Munster Express*, 11 September 1942.
31 *Irish Independent*, 10 July 1942.
32 Bowen, *Spain*, 122.
33 Lars Magnusson, *An Economic History of Sweden* (London, 2000), 202.
34 Schwarz, *Hurricane*, 69.
35 See Filipe Ribeiro de Meneses, 'Investigating Portugal, Salazar and the New State: The Work of the Irish Legation in Lisbon, 1942–1945', *Contemporary European History*, 11, 3 (2002), 399–408.
36 Milward, *War, Economy and Society*, 282.
37 Neill Lochery, *Lisbon: War in the Shadows of the City of Light, 1939–1945* (New york, 2011), 118.
38 MIOA, Father Matt Turby, b. 1933, Nenagh, co. Tipperary. Interviewed 29 April 2002.
39 'Historical Survey'. NAI, IND/EHR/3/C1, part I, p. 5.
40 Garvin, *Preventing*, 63.
41 'Record of Activities'. NAI, IND/EHR/3/15, p. 50.
42 Department of Supplies, 'History and Organisation of the Inspection Branch'. NAI, IND/EHR/3/4, p. 1.
43 'Inspection Branch'. NAI, IND/EHR/3/4, p. 4.
44 'Inspection Branch'. NAI, IND/EHR/3/4, p. 13.
45 *Dublin Opinion*, April 1940.
46 'Inspection Branch'. NAI, IND/EHR/3/4, p. 7.
47 MIOA, Christy Hennessy, b. 1932, Waterford City. Interviewed 8 April 2000, p. 6.
48 'Inspection Branch'. NAI, IND/EHR/3/4, p. 4.
49 'Inspection Branch'. NAI, IND/EHR/3/4, p. 12.
50 'Inspection Branch'. NAI, IND/EHR/3/4, p. 10.
51 'Inspection Branch'. NAI, IND/EHR/3/4, p. 9.
52 'Historical Survey'. NAI, IND/EHR/3/C4, part XI, p. 613.
53 *Irish Press*, 4 March 1942.
54 See NAI, District Court records (DC)/MO/2004/85/37.
55 Justice's Notes, 13 November 1942. NAI, DC/MO/2004/85/37.
56 See, for example, the report in the *Irish Times* of 26 May 1942 on six German black marketers being sentenced to death. Similarly, on 4 August 1941, the newspaper carried a story about how the Vichy regime had sent seventeen people to concentration camps for food hoarding and illegally forcing up prices on the black market.
57 Justice's Notes, 15 April, 13 November 1942; 29 December 1944; 27 July 1945. NAI, DC/MO/2004/85/37.
58 Justice's Notes, 29 December 1944. NAI, DC/MO/2004/85/37.
59 Justice's Notes, 13 November 1942. NAI, DC/MO/2004/85/37.
60 See, for instance, Justice's Notes, 5 May 1942, 7 July 1942, 1 September 1942. NAI, DC/DN/2001/138/4.

61 *Connacht Sentinel*, 30 November 1943.
62 *Dáil Debates*, vol. 91, col. 574, 9 July 1943.
63 Ó Drisceoil, *Censorship in Ireland*, 104.
64 See *Irish Times* and *Irish Independent*, 11 August 1942.
65 Michael Knightly to newspaper editors, 8 May 1942; 17 July 1942; 11 June 1943. MA, OCC/2/57, 'Control of Advertisements offering rationed commodities for sale'.
66 *Irish Examiner*, 14 November 1941; *Irish Press*, 6 November 1941; *Irish Press*, 16 June 1943.
67 'Record of Activities'. NAI, IND/EHR/3/15, p. 46.
68 *Leitrim Observer*, 15 August 1942.
69 'Historical Survey'. NAI, IND/EHR/3/C1, part II, p. 42.
70 'Inspection Branch'. NAI, IND/EHR/3/4, appendix III.
71 'Inspection Branch'. NAI, IND/EHR/3/4, p. 8.
72 'Historical Survey'. NAI, IND/EHR/3/C1, part II, p. 39.
73 'Inspection Branch'. NAI, IND/EHR/3/4, appendix III.
74 *Irish Independent*, 19 December 1942.
75 'Inspection Branch'. NAI, IND/EHR/3/4, p. 11.
76 'Inspection Branch'. NAI, IND/EHR/3/4, p. 11.
77 *Irish Independent*, 16 January 1943.
78 'Record of Activities'. NAI, IND/EHR/3/15, p. 52.
79 Alfred Thornton to M.A. Corrigan, 14 September 1943. NAI, Attorney General's Office (AGO)/48/38.
80 'Inspection Branch'. NAI, IND/EHR/3/4, p. 11.
81 *Connacht Sentinel*, 26 January 1940.
82 *Irish Times*, 10 November 1942.
83 *Irish Independent*, 19 November 1942.
84 See, for instance, *Munster Express*, 11 September 1942.
85 'Historical Survey'. NAI, IND/EHR/3/C1, part I, p. 24.
86 *Waterford News*, 19 November 1943.
87 *Waterford News*, 5 March 1943.
88 *Munster Express*, 25 September 1942.
89 *Irish Independent*, 16 October 1942.
90 *Irish Independent*, 4 February 1944.
91 *Munster Express*, 14 July 1944.
92 *Irish Independent*, 8 May 1942.
93 *Dublin Opinion*, February 1942.
94 *Irish Press*, 26 June 1942.
95 Cornelius Meaney, 'Cereal Prices', *Dáil Debates*, vol. 84, col. 2360, 23 July 1941.
96 Wills, *Neutral Island*, 247.
97 *Irish Press*, 27 September 1939.
98 *The Standard*, 15 August 1941.
99 'Historical Survey'. NAI, IND/EHR/3/C3, part IX, p. 315.
100 'Historical Survey'. NAI, IND/EHR/3/C3, part IX, p. 387.
101 'Historical Survey'. NAI, IND/EHR/3/C3, part IX, p. 316.
102 Findlater, *Findlaters*, 409.
103 'Historical Survey'. NAI, IND/EHR/3/C3, part IX, p. 395.

104 'Historical Survey'. NAI, IND/EHR/3/C3, part IX, p. 391.

105 'Historical Survey'. NAI, IND/EHR/3/C3, part IX, pp. 406–408.

106 'Historical Survey'. NAI, IND/EHR/3/C3, part IX, p. 394.

107 Ina Zweiniger-Bargielowska, *Austerity in Britain: Rationing, Controls, and Consumption, 1939–1955* (Oxford, 2000), 176.

108 *Irish Times*, 20 February 1942.

109 Alfie Byrne, *Dáil Debates*, vol. 86, col. 7, 24 March 1942.

110 *Dáil Debates*, vol. 86, col. 1164, 29 April 1942.

111 MIOA, Patrick J. Baily, b. 1932, Ballymacelligot, co. Kerry. Interviewed 2 April 2002.

112 Gray, *The Lost Years*, 185.

113 *Irish Times*, 13 May 1942.

114 See Bryce Evans, 'The IHA and the Introduction of Rationing in Ireland', in Alan Hayes ed., *Hilda Tweedy and the Irish Housewives' Association: Links in the Chain* (Dublin, 2012), 95–103.

115 Hilda Tweedy to Women's Social and Progressive League, 11 November 1943. NAI, Tweedy Papers, Department of Justice (JUS)/98/17/5/1/2.

116 Irish Housewives Association, 'Memorandum on the Food and Fuel Emergency', 5 May 1941. NAI, Tweedy Papers, JUS/98/17/5/1/1.

117 NAI, Tweedy Papers, 98/17/5/1/2.

118 'Irish Housewives Protest', 13 March 1942. NAI, Tweedy Papers, JUS/98/17/5/1/3.

119 'Evidence of the Irish Housewives before the Milk Tribunal', NAI, Tweedy Papers, JUS/98/17/5/1/6.

120 NAI, Tweedy Papers, 98/17/5/1/2.

121 *Irish Times*, 22 February 1942.

122 Andrews, *Man of No Property*, 329.

123 Hilda Tweedy, *A Link in the Chain* (Dublin, 1992), 15.

124 'Historical Survey'. NAI, IND/EHR/3/C1, part II, p. 26.

125 'Tea – Maintenance of Supplies'. NAI, IND/EHR 3/13, p. 30.

126 Coyne to Leydon, 31 May 1941, MA, OCC/2/57. Coyne was promoted from Assistant Controller to Controller of Censorship in September 1941.

127 Coyne to J. Williams, 21 April 1942, MA, OCC/2/57.

128 Coyne to Leydon, 31 May 1941, MA, OCC/2/57.

129 Dáil Eireann, Acts. http://acts.oireachtas.ie/zza28y1939.1.html. Accessed 1 March 2009.

130 Attorney General to J. Williams, 16 April 1944. MA, OCC/2/98.

131 Amendments to Emergency Powers (Control of Prices) Order (1939). MA, OCC/2/57.

132 Brain Farrell, *Seán Lemass* (Dublin, 1991), 59.

133 Kevin O'Doherty, cited in Horgan, *Enigmatic Patriot*, 105–106.

134 J. Connolly to Leydon, 19 May 1941. MA, OCC/2/57, 'Control of Advertisements Offering Rationed Commodities for Sale'.

135 Connolly to Leydon, 19 May 1941. MA, OCC/2/57.

136 Leydon to Connolly, 24 May 1941, MA, OCC/2/57. The italics are my own.

137 Garvin, *Judging Lemass*, 129.

138 Andrews, *Man of No Property*, 173.

139 Leydon to de Valera, 1 September 1943. NAI, DT, RA 103/44.

140 Connolly to Leydon, 30 May 1941. MA, OCC/2/57.

141 Garvin, *Judging Lemass*, 133.
142 Farrell, *Lemass*, 51–63.
143 Fee, 'The Effects', 237.
144 *Report of the Commission on Vocational Organisation: Observations of the Department of Supplies*, NAI, DT/S13552.
145 John W. Blake, *Northern Ireland in the Second World War* (Belfast, 1956), 101.
146 Blake, *Northern Ireland*, 102.
147 See Magnusson, *Economic History of Sweden*, 207; Schwarz, *Hurricane*, 68.
148 Farmer, *Food Companions*, 84.
149 *Irish Times*, 13 May 1942.
150 Lemass, cited in *Irish Independent*, 27 June 1946.
151 Michael Richards, *A Time of Silence: Civil War and the Culture of Repression in Franco's Spain, 1936–1945* (Cambridge, 1998), 140.
152 Milward, *War, Economy and Society*, 282.
153 Philip Rooney, 'dhrink!', *The Bell*, 8, 4 (July 1944), 290–297.
154 'Record of Activities'. NAI, IND/EHR/3/15, p. 52.

4

Conditions in town and country

No petrol at all – public buses to go everywhere and walks through suburbs. It feels like St John's Wood in Leicester.

John Betjeman, 17 March 1941

Conditions in Ireland's towns and cities

Writing after the war, the British Minister for Food, Lord Woolton, claimed that the black market in wartime Britain was relatively insignificant. This, he claimed, was largely due to the superiority of the British national character: 'the British public disapproves of black markets', 'a tribute to the British people which I hope the historians of this period will proudly record'.[1] Historians critical of this narrative of heroic national sacrifice have demonstrated that the black market in wartime Britain was more extensive than Woolton assumed.[2] Similarly, the existence of black market activity in Ireland – where the message of shared sacrifice was pegged to a less coherent rationing structure – casts doubt on the Irish public's adherence to the government line.

Although admitting, in places, to the 'serious proportions'[3] of the black market, the historical retrospectives churned out by Supplies and Industry and Commerce tend to underplay the significance of black market trade: activity which seriously undermined state efforts to establish a theme of moral economy. As 1945's *Statistical Abstract* noted, 'criminal proceedings have shown a very serious increase generally since the outbreak of the war'.[4] In early 1943, Minister for Justice Gerald Boland expressed concern at the increase in theft linked to black market activity. Lamenting the rise in convictions, he went on to explain 'People are short of commodities and I am afraid our morality is not as deep-seated as it ought to be.'[5] Boland's reflection was moralistic, but not merely rhetorical. Official statistics show a notable upsurge in crime during the Emergency compared to the preceding decade.[6] His comments demonstrate a real concern that the materialism created by shortages was threatening the very fabric of Irish life.

In 1943, de Valera claimed 'there is no one who is not getting proper food in this country'.[7] In the same year, though, a United States intelligence agent posted to Ireland, who had the luxury of ample financial support from his government, recorded a loss in weight of twenty pounds after living in Dublin for a month.[8] In a 1944 article in *The Bell*, columnist Sheila May recounted a visit to two slums on either side of the Liffey. In the first, she found some inhabitants who had never eaten fruit or vegetables, and in the second, she observed that when inhabitants defecated, it was from a third floor window into the street below.[9]

Decaying Georgian Dublin mirrored the shabbiness of the once-grand capitals of the Iberian neutrals, Lisbon and Madrid, with their peeling plasterwork and cracked tiles. Brothels, another feature of the Iberian capitals, were to be found in Dublin as well. The criminal 'D.83222', who wrote about Irish prison life in *The Bell*, recalled staying overnight in Dublin for a District Court appearance. That evening, he came across a 'Mister and Missus Joint' on the Quays and a prostitute called 'Sadie', who instead of payment requested soap and clean towels.[10] The sheer dirtiness of Dublin was noted. 'The children ran around in droves', wrote another *Bell* contributor, of the Dublin tenements: 'closed up in this dark alley, all in torn clothes', 'women sitting on doorsteps with sickly little children close to their bosom, trying to enjoy the sun that broke through the gap on the opposite side of the street'.[11] Unlike in Ireland, house building continued in Spain and Portugal during the war. But while property was being destroyed in the Spanish Civil War in the late 1930s, Fianna Fáil had been building houses. This ensured that Dublin did not develop the vast diseased wartime shanty towns of Madrid, populated by hundreds of thousands of people.[12]

Relocation from the slums was not a guarantee of better social conditions. Writing in the Jesuit journal *Studies* in 1945, Medical Professor T.W.T. Dillon bemoaned the absence of social amenities in new Dublin settlements such as Crumlin and Drimnagh. To Dillon, building 'row upon row of houses' offered only slight material improvement; the urban poor remained 'the last to be employed, and the first to be discharged'; 'they leave school at 14 in a state of incredible ignorance'; 'dressed in rags, inarticulate, dirty and often dishonest they drift into the street corner gangs which are the despair of social workers and the police'.[13]

Dillon's comments exhibited a widely held social concern about the debilitating effects of urbanisation. During the Emergency, Ireland's towns and cities experienced lower net migration than rural areas. Dublin and Dun Laoghaire actually registered an increase in population between 1941 and 1943. Cork, Limerick and Waterford suffered a small but insignificant population decrease.[14] Outlying rural areas, on the other hand, suffered greater proportional population decline during the Emergency as the flight from the land continued. Although most emigrants went overseas, there was also significant internal migration to Ireland's urban centres.[15]

This population drift was accompanied by fears over the declining status of farming and rural life. They were accentuated by the political and literary tendency to define Ireland against industrial England. Writing in 1940, Cornelius Lucey, Bishop of Cork, denounced 'foolish expenditure' on tobacco, drink and cinema but articulated these leisure pursuits as particularly urban vices.[16] These vices were commonly associated with gangs of young male 'corner boys' who congregated in

cinema foyers and made a living from crime.[17] To a great extent, this popular sentiment rested on the rural essentialism and anti-materialism noticeable in both
church and state thinking on public morality during the Emergency. There was a
penchant in official Irish political culture for the frugal, rural idyll, one which
shared the communitarian tenets of the German *Volksgemeinschaft*.[18] The conspic-
uousness of the urban black market tied in neatly with the political ruralism that
held the agrarian smallholder aloof and pitied those described by one Catholic
commentator as 'city dwellers with harassed minds and dejected hearts'.[19]

Unlike the rural population, city dwellers of all classes had less opportunity to
exploit their environment to overcome shortages. From 1941, Dublin Corporation
allocated residents plots throughout the city and in the Phoenix Park to grow their
own food.[20] Tony Gray's tale of how many Dubliners got their first taste of venison
during the Emergency (due to the culling of the Phoenix Park deer when they
threatened the vegetable plots) is, if not apocryphal, certainly misleading.[21] The
majority of the urban poor still subsisted on a diet of little nutritional value. 'A diet
of tea, bread and factory-made jam is far too prevalent', a government pamphlet of
1942 complained.[22] To these people, tea and white bread – low in nutritional value
but high in black market price – were not happily substituted for other foodstuffs.

Instead, the Dublin poor continued to rely on the numerous tiny, dim-lit huxter
shops that nestled in areas like the Coombe. The huxter shop was typically no honestly run *Old Curiosity Shop*. During the Emergency, owners would keep books for
customers who would pay for their goods 'on tick'. Although this provided a vital
extension of credit to the urban poor and working class, there was often little chance
of ever clearing the debt.[23] The scarcity and poor quality of bread in the shops during
the Emergency provided an archetypal historical problem. In 1942, North Dublin
TD Alfie Byrne told the Dáil of a queue outside a bread shop in Wexford Street 300
people long, complaining that they had queued for four hours.[24] While riding his
bicycle around North Dublin, Byrne was said to have been called over by a Mrs
Gleeson of Summerhill; showing him a small black loaf of bread, she informed him
'that loaf is for meself, me husband, and eleven children'.[25] From other sources, there
were reports of Dublin women fainting in bread queues. There were consequences
for public health, too. The 100% black loaf introduced by the government in 1942
due to the wheat shortage caused calcium deficiency. Dublin hospitals consequently
reported an increase in the incidence of rickets in children.[26] A 1943 report found
that in Dublin, just under half of all children aged between eighteen months and two
years had the disease. Remarkably, this was double the pre-war figure.[27]

As a Waterford City resident recalled, 'things were bad before the war but they
were to get worse. Between '39 and '46 life wasn't good at all, especially for the
working class people.'[28] It is illustrative of the deprivation in urban areas that
government orders could focus on relatively specific urban areas in an effort to
overcome the worst effects of shortages. A good example is the increase of the butter ration in Bray and Dublin only in 1943.[29] The urban poor were certainly the

most reliant on government efforts to counter unfair economic practice, and the 'middleman' black marketer, the exploiter of the poor, was a favourite demon of *Dáil Debates*. Responding to Lemass's claim that 'the national larder was well-stocked', an independent TD claimed that 'the only larder well-stocked is the black market larder, as the poor of Dublin know to their bitter cost'.[30] Most working-class housewives' larders were too small to stock food in bulk in any case. A 1943 survey of a local authority housing estate in Dublin concluded that inadequate storage space, along with the unavailability of transport and overpriced shops, prevented working-class housewives from buying wisely and amply.[31]

Garda records show that the theft of all sorts of food was commonplace in Dublin at the time.[32] It is likely that the perpetrators of a number of these thefts justified their actions by the very perception that it was the common bogey – the 'middleman' – and not they, the small-time crooks, who were responsible for shortages. Although the role of this folk devil was exaggerated, the law of supply and demand itself invariably acted to the detriment of the urban poor. In a June 1940 debate, the claim that fish were being dumped at sea was repeated by a Cork TD, who informed Minister for Agriculture James Ryan that 25,000 mackerel had been dumped into the sea at Kinsale because the fishermen were unable to obtain high enough prices for their catch.[33] As with similar incidents outside Dublin, dumping forced prices in Cork City's fish market so high that the poor of the city were unable to buy fish.

Environmental factors – most notably Ireland's cold, wet winters – added to hardship. In February 1940, the Dáil heard that the increase in the price of cotton since the start of the Emergency was forcing the urban poor to endure the cold because they could not afford clothes.[34] Unfortunately for the urban dweller, there was a dearth of fuel as well. Crisis shortages of domestic fuel – coal, turf and firewood – occurred in the winter of 1940/1941 as the British economic squeeze took hold. Fortunately, the harvest was not as bad as that year's in neutral Spain, where grave food shortages coincided with the disruption of trade caused by the fall of France. Nonetheless, Irish city dwellers were reduced to scavenging for timber in corporation refuse dumps and elsewhere.[35] In a desperate drive for fuel, Supplies instructed forestry officials to carry out a national survey of firewood. Foresters recall how such activity could prove embarrassing because it provided country people with the amusing spectacle of a team of trainee foresters overseen by an inspector walking the hedgerows and fastidiously recording every single stem of firewood.[36] The desperate shortage of fuel and the painstaking attempts to combat it was lampooned in a *Dublin Opinion* cartoon of 1942, depicting a nervous Macbeth as the witches' prophecy is fulfilled and Birnam Wood comes to Dunsinane Hill – in the form of people collecting wood for fuel.[37]

Firewood identified through the survey was felled by foresters, sent to Dublin by train and taken by trucks to a great fuel pyramid in the Phoenix Park. Even this most obviously communal of fuel reserves was regularly pillaged. Almost all inhabitants of Ireland during the Emergency experienced fuel poverty. Sawdust, procured from the sawmill on Thomas Street, was used as fuel for Dublin fires.[38] Supplies' Inspection Branch identified the sale of wood and turf at excess prices as particularly prevalent aspects of Dublin's black market.[39] Turf, it was claimed in a 1941 article, was 'sold by the sackful at the canalside by merchants at anything they dare' above Lemass's controlled price of forty-five shillings per ton and fetching as much as £3 per ton.[40] Garda records show that turf was so sought after that it was regularly stolen by members of the force from Garda stations.[41] Children were often sent to collect fuel from corporation depots. In autumn 1942 one of these thousands of child fuel scavengers was tragically buried alive in Inchicore.[42] Because people had to bring their own bags, jute bags became another highly sought-after commodity and were sold on the black market for 'an absolute fortune'.[43] As well as making for miserably cold winters, fuel shortages had a negative effect on urban mobility: by 1943, all evening bus services were suspended in Dublin due to the shortage of fuel and tyres.[44] Due to the dearth of petrol, the Liffey ferry service was seriously curtailed as well, resulting in workers losing their jobs because they could not get from one side to the other in reasonable time.[45]

Writing to a British counterpart to request more coal in October 1940, John Leydon cited the negative effect on urban dwellers of the exorbitant black market prices caused by fuel shortages. He revealed the 'steep increase' in coal prices since the start of the Emergency. Dublin and Sligo had witnessed a 30% increase, Cork 40% and Tralee almost 50%. The average increase in price across the country was 37%.[46] However, the Irish government continued to prioritise the supply of British coal to industry,[47] and the British repeatedly refused export licences for extra coal to be used for household supply. 'This situation is not peculiar to Eire', one British official stated, claiming that in Argentina, people were resorting to using maize as fuel, even in powering railway locomotives.[48] Leydon's pleas to the British highlighting 'the hardships of the domestic consumer'[49] often met with British belligerence. 'This fuel will be used to provide light and heat to the German and Italian legations in Dublin' it was claimed in a Commons debate on the export of coal to Ireland.[50]

Ireland's damp climate combined with shortages and regulation to increase demand for clothes. From 1940, clothes production for civilian use was only allowed by permit, and most clothing manufacture was directed to the military.[51] In mid-1942, Lemass added clothes to the ration. Coupled with the expansion in the number of men in the armed forces, these restrictions resulted in a black market in army clothing. New recruits immediately received a number of items which they would normally have to save up coupons to obtain. Whereas the Local Defence Force (LDF) was distinguished by its poor uniform,[52] army recruits received a full uniform. At the end of the war, G2 estimated that approximately 5,000 non-commissioned officers and men of the Defence Forces were absent without leave, and many had been since the early stages of the Emergency.[53] Discharged soldiers were permitted to take with them a number of articles, including braces, shirts, socks, towels and boots; soldiers on temporary release for agricultural work or for other reasons were also permitted to bring kit with them.[54]

A Dublin woman working as a tailor's assistant at the time recalls that an army 'contact' would surreptitiously enter the shop with army grey blankets which the tailor bought to turn into overcoats.[55] By 1942, it was apparent to the government that a significant amount of army property was going missing and being traded on the black market. On the instruction of the Department of Finance, a survey of the four main Commands was carried out for the year 1941. It revealed that the greatest deficiency in store items occurred in the Cork garrison. There, in one year, the losses included 79 tunics, 144 pairs of socks, 237 enamel mugs and 33 pullovers.[56] Chemists' accounts from the four Commands show that medical and transit supplies were stolen and traded on the black market. In the Curragh command alone, thirty-seven bicycles were unaccounted for in one year.[57] Although the Department of Finance looked askance at all losses, the army did not consider the figures excessive 'when taking into account the emergency period, the volume of material handled, the numbers of men equipped and the inadequate and untrained staff dealing with the situation'.[58] The Quartermaster General, however, reprimanded the stocktaking boards of the Commands for neglect of duty.[59]

Army kit made up a sizeable proportion of the urban black market in clothes. Children's clothes coupons would also often be used by mothers and aunts to obtain stockings and other items that restrictions denied them.[60] Admitting that 'a regular traffic' in rationed articles developed, the Historical Survey nonetheless asserted that 'no case of fraudulent application [for a ration book] ever came to light'.[61] Although fraud, theft, forgery or trafficking of rationing books themselves was relatively rare, this boast attests to the failure of the department in detecting such fraud rather than pointing to its absence. In fact, there was a major traffic in clothes coupons centred around Amiens Street Station in Dublin.[62]

The urban experience of hardship was not without qualification, then, with the black market providing a livelihood for some. As one urban slum dweller of the era recalled, 'the only thing that seemed to be thriving was the black market'.[63] The urban poor were not always merely the passive, emaciated victims of Emergency shortages, and black market resourcefulness took many forms. When a British plane crashed outside Waterford City, for instance, the scarcity of metal ensured 'everything was taken', 'half of the back wing and all number of other pieces'.[64] On seeing any queue, a child was expected to enquire what it was for before running home to tell mother. Then, the child was usually sent running back to join the queue with strict instructions on what to purchase and how much to pay for it.[65] The urban poor and working class were at times able to negotiate their own economy between maximum price orders, on the one hand, and black market prices, on the other. Significantly, their conception of what constituted a fair price was constructed from conversations and hearsay rather than studied adherence to Lemass's list of maximum retail prices published periodically in newspapers. Black market goods would be purchased, but not at prices considered too inflated.

Neither did the black market always operate to the detriment of the most needy. In an effort to combat the poverty and shortages of the Emergency, Limerick Dispensary officials and nuns were involved in a significant underground network in the recycling of medicine and materials to the city's poor. On the appeal of a poor mother, staff would provide extra cotton wool for her child's 'bad shoulder', material that would actually be used to fill cushions.[66] Such activity illustrates that 'black market' activity in urban areas was not confined to petty theft or exorbitant pricing and neither was it confined to the criminal fraternity.

Conditions in the countryside

By contrast to urban centres, economic and social life in rural Ireland was distinguished by the primacy of the local and the diversity of communities. Local issues predominated in market practices, reinforced by a rationing system based around the local shop and a rural economy based around the farm and the local creamery. The localism of food distribution, coupled with fuel shortages, ensured that the common rural experience of the Emergency rested on the decline in mobility. This condition had two major effects in the Irish countryside. On the one hand, if they turned their back against the government's moral economy, country people were generally at greater liberty to carry out black market activity due to a lack of surveillance. On the other, outlying rural areas suffered a severe restriction in supplies. Productivity and living standards were negatively affected by this isolation.

On the first point, Ireland conformed to the common experience in countries occupied during the war, where people in rural areas had better access to food than urban dwellers.[67] Many Irish country-dwellers grew their own fruit and vegetables and, in season, would eat nuts and berries. Farmers often raised pigs and hens in the house and slaughtered them at home. By contrast to urban Ireland, there is a narrative of plenty surrounding rural life during the Emergency. A County Limerick woman recalls 'Everybody grew their own food and everyone had their own pig', 'we'd eat bacon and cabbage all week and have a roast at the weekend' and 'my grandmother always laid a big pot of potatoes on the window-sill for people to take'.[68] A County Leitrim woman remembers 'we churned our own butter and milk and always had plenty of vegetables and chicken, turkey and geese'.[69] Although these women also told of poverty and social division, relative to the queues for food in Ireland's cities, these are narratives of abundance. They convey the ability to live off the land portrayed in the preceding decade by the American anthropologists Conrad Arensberg and Solon T. Kimball who recorded that the County Clare smallholder typically had 'a garden in potatoes and cabbage with a few oats and turnips' and 'a large flock of ducks, geese, hens and several pigs'.[70]

Instead of food, many remember the lack of tea and tobacco as 'the worst hardship' in rural Ireland.[71] Tea was rationed at two ounces per week in January 1941. In April, this was reduced to one ounce and shortly thereafter to half an ounce.

For men, the break-time cup of tea was keenly anticipated in the course of the work day. In many workplaces, even this little luxury was curtailed because of shortages. A woman from County Kerry cites her first recollection of the Emergency as the short-age of tea.[72] The poor standard of the cup of tea during the Emergency, often made from reused tea leaves, is renowned, and people went to great lengths and paid a great amount to procure tea from the black market. Contemporary commentators from Ireland's concerned middle class may have perceived the urban environment as fostering the subterranean black trade, but the Irish countryside was not the urban environment's idyllic pastoral antithesis. To quote a Connemara man, 'there was an awful lot of racketeering and marketeering going on' during the Emergency.[73]

Arensberg and Kimball recorded that in the 1930s, the motor car was used by country people generally only in time of 'crisis and high ceremony'.[74] During the Emergency, too, the only three cars at mass were likely to be those of the priest, the schoolteacher and the large farmer.[75] But while class divisions persisted, Emer-gency petrol restrictions meant that an even greater number of people across social strata walked, cycled or travelled by horse and cart. The disappearance of cars from the Irish countryside had one very noticeable criminal consequence: the decrease in the number of people apprehended for poaching, although such activity definitely increased.[76] Even P.J. Ruttledge, Minister for Local Government and Public Health, suffered the theft of fowl from his residence in 1941.[77] Poachers benefited from the restriction on petrol supplies as the official regulation of rivers and estates lapsed and the motorised activities of gamekeepers of Ireland's rivers and estates were curtailed.[78] Poaching was cat-and-mouse stuff, as an article in *The Bell* showed: 'we had called our hut The Black Watch', 'the name cut both ways because the river bailiffs had other ideas about that hut, they watched it as an Irish terrier would watch a hole where he has got the rat-scent'.[79] Pursuits between out-raged gamekeepers and poachers now took place almost exclusively on foot. As well as illegal fishing, there is evidence of a roaring black market in rabbits during the Emergency. Rabbits could provide food or fetch ready cash from middlemen, who exported their carcasses to Britain to sell as meat or fur to line servicemen's jackets.[80] Similarly, poached turkeys were frequently smuggled to Britain and Northern Ireland.[81]

Country towns and villages also sporadically hosted events that attracted black market activity. The number of 'fit-up' shows touring Ireland increased during this period because many of their performers had left England due to the commercialisa-tion of music halls in the 1930s and bombing during the war. These shows were usually highly melodramatic versions of Shakespearean tragedies or popular anti-colonial tales performed in village halls or ramshackle sheds. 'Fit-ups' were unpopu-lar with priests and Gardaí for a number of reasons: their bawdy themes, the subversive dialect, the association of travelling people with petty criminality and raffles which offered prizes likely to have been acquired on the black market, such as tobacco and utensils.[82]

Although viewed as a separate social group, travellers do not appear to have suffered as much popular dislike for their alternative economic practices as Ireland's Jewish community at the time, as is discussed later. 'To see these uncouth, unshaven ruffians beating their women in drunken rows on fair day, one would believe they were illiterate morons', wrote 'D.83222' in his account of Irish life during the Emergency, but 'they have an intimate, intelligent knowledge of every corner of Ireland and are a fund of folklore'.[83] Nonetheless, their transitory economic lifestyle was viewed as sufficient reason for Limerick County Council to vote in favour of their internment, while the foot-and-mouth outbreak of 1941 lasted and travellers were also subject to restrictions on movement (due to concerns about the spread of typhus) in 1940.[84]

Similar to the ribaldry of the 'fit-up' was the carnival atmosphere of market day in the small Irish town. Sylvia Couturié, a French girl from an aristocratic background forced to spend her teenage years with her Irish nanny as a refugee in County Waterford, provides an account of rural Ireland that is at times Dickensian in conveying the unfamiliar and the deviant through the eyes of a child. She learnt not to mix with Protestants and to 'make the sign of the cross before crossing each street, in the improbable case of a mortal car accident'. Market days fascinated her. The streets would be covered in straw and cow dung, full of men 'leaning against the walls of local pubs…thick tweed caps sitting on their heads',[85] fights breaking out in pubs between rival farmers.[86] Black market traders were frequently present at these rural cattle marts and fairs as well. Although such gatherings centred on the barter for cattle, barter for clothes and food also took place. Traders of second-hand clothes would be present, for instance, 'asking for exorbitant prices like five pounds for a coat'.[87]

Access to black markets and the fat of the land was mitigated, however, by enhanced isolation, the overriding condition of rural life during this period. Remote areas were particularly vulnerable to the depredation caused by high prices and poor transport. The low density of commercial food stores in rural areas also restricted access to supplies. The number of people per shopkeeper was lowest in the west: counties Leitrim, Roscommon, Mayo, Donegal, Galway and Clare had an average of sixty-six people per shop, compared to forty-three in Carlow or Tipperary (or twenty-six in Dublin). While most urban areas had the benefits of electrification by the time of the Emergency, most rural settlements did not.[88] Deputies brought the government's attention to the acute shortage of paraffin oil and other fuel along the western seaboard. Unlike the special measures taken in urban areas, these appeals were nearly always met with the insistence that exceptions could not be made by increasing the ration to the poor of the west.[89]

Yet the threat of starvation due to Emergency shortages was certainly greatest in Ireland's remotest western reaches. In correspondence written over two decades, Eibhlís Ní Shúilleabháin, a resident of the Great Blasket Island, conveyed how wartime inflation had affected life. In 1931, she described the island as a place where one might marry and raise a family. By November 1939, two months into the war, her family was living on five shillings a week. Of this money, two shillings were prioritised for her husband Seán's tobacco. In February 1940, she complained 'meat and food and flour are all gone up in prices and they with other hardships of Islands together leave no hope at all for islanders'. In June 1940, she reported that 'shillings are far and scarce at the moment' and that rabbit meat was their staple. By April 1942, she revealed how Emergency shortages had tipped the balance in favour of migration to the mainland. Islanders' trips to the mainland and back had become unfruitful: 'no sugar is there, no soap, no tea, no tobacco and the worst of all no flour nor bread nor biscuits nor paraffin oil for light nor a candle'; 'men could not light their pipes after a hard day's ordeal as they did not get a pipe of tobacco in town'.[90]

Ní Shúilleabháin's correspondence demonstrates that rationing based on the release of small quantities from the local shop proved unsuitable to people in the most remote areas. In outlying communities in the west, men were expected to return laden with supplies for the community as a whole. León Ó Broin, one of seven regional commissioners established by Supplies amid the panic of July 1940, vividly detailed the effect of such scarcity. Hurried to a remote Irish-speaking area in west Mayo by an aide, Ó Broin recalled the eerie spectacle of emaciated people moving down from the hills towards his car, carrying sacks. It became clear that the villagers expected the sacks to be filled with flour. Disappointed men and women harangued Ó Broin in Irish, angry that telegram messages to Dublin officials complaining of near starvation had gone unanswered and claiming that they feared a recurrence of the Famine.[91] Ó Broin's recollection is supported by comparable contemporary reports. In May, the Dáil heard that in parishes in West Cork, there were eight ounces of flour per head – the people there were 'practically on a black fast'.[92] In Connemara, also in early 1942, there were reports of a 'three week bread famine' in Clifden because the local trader had had his petrol allowance cut.[93] A rare entry in de Valera's 1943 pocket diary reads simply 'Kilrush: no bacon, no potatoes, no butter, no work'.[94]

The relationship between island dwellers and the mainland could be similar to the relationship between peripheral areas and market towns. Kerry County Committee of Agriculture repeatedly passed resolutions calling on the government and Great Southern Railways to reverse public transport cuts 'hindering all sections of the community, cattle traders, farmers, schoolchildren and the general public'.[95] Dislocation was aggravated by low wages. Notwithstanding the higher cost of living in urban areas, wages were low in country towns and villages, particularly in the west: a Dublin road labourer earned forty-eight shillings a week, whereas a Galway road labourer earned just thirty.[96] In December 1941, the government decided it would not extend the food vouchers scheme – a precursor to ration books – to unemployed single men and widows in rural areas, despite its availability to these groups in urban areas.[97] An unemployed County Limerick man recalled 'them were hard times, fellas were like sows that time, eating anything'.[98] This was due to government efforts to control prices for the sake of the urban poor and in recognition of the extra costs in transit incurred by traders located outside the port towns. It was also an example of central intrusion upon local autonomy, particularly hard to stomach for local authorities, which lost the power both to determine works and fix wage rates. Local authorities' preference for long-term projects also clashed markedly with the decisions of the cabinet emergency committee, which possessed a more knee-jerk style.

The price of goods was also generally higher in provincial towns and rural areas than in Ireland's major towns and cities. In 1943, flour was reportedly selling for an average price of three shillings and ten pence per stone in the Irish countryside, while in Dublin, Dun Laoghaire, Cork, Limerick and Waterford, it was three shillings and six pence per stone.[99] According to the records of Supplies' Inspection Branch, the evasion of pricing orders by shopkeepers was 'more extensive and more systematic in rural areas'. The report identified counties Louth, Galway, Mayo, Westmeath, Waterford and Monaghan as particular hotspots.[100] Although the new black loaf was endorsed by the government, it was never popular with the people: 'You could kick it around like a football, it was that hard.'[101] So great was people's desire for white flour that women 'would sieve the brown flour through a stocking to try and get the white bits out'.[102]

Small shopkeepers in rural areas justified charging relatively high prices because their businesses had suffered due to supply shortages and government restrictions on consumption. In small towns and rural areas without electricity, many shops had to close earlier during the winter months of the Emergency due to the shortage of kerosene.[103] Candles, an alternative light source, were also in very short supply from 1941 onwards.[104] Until the legislation was reviewed in 1942, shopkeepers who had charged reasonable prices for goods which were not covered by price control orders were obliged to sell these same goods at the same prices even after later orders had increased the maximum price. This was due to a proviso intended by Lemass to keep prices down. In practice, it affected country retailers worst because there was generally less price inflation than in towns and cities.[105]

For some grocers and small shopkeepers, justification for engaging in activity that contradicted the state's line took on markedly moral dimensions *in defiance* of the moral economic measures the government were attempting to enforce. A County Leitrim grocer inverted the state's vision of moral economy. He recalled that the Gardaí of the time 'weren't too bad as long as they got a drink from me and you and everyone else', but sneered at the 'efficiency' of inspectors from Supplies, claiming to have delighted in defying their scrupulousness by engrossing the rations of the poorer, larger families at the expense of wealthier families.[106] Similarly, a letter from a 'Gombeen man' to the *Irish Times* reveals the power of *An Béal Bocht* in opposing Lemass's directives: 'A short time ago a respectable looking man offered me 50% more than my retail price for any quantity of tea that I could give him, if I had a large young family to provide for, I would probably have unloaded my stock at these fantastic offers'.[107]

Most rural dwellers relied on the local shop for fuel. As in the towns, the scarcity of fuel in these small country retailers frequently resulted in children being sent to scavenge for fuel. Similarly, this resulted in tragically premature deaths such as that of a ten-year-old County Tipperary boy whose father had sent him to gather turf but who fell to his death down a bog hole.[108] With fuel scarce, Sylvia Couturié, the French girl living in Waterford, recalled her astonishment that most Irish children went barefoot and unwashed and her revulsion for being reduced to going out 'every single day in search of driftwood and cow dung' alongside them.[109]

Child labour was not unique to Ireland during the war and was performed de facto, whereas in other countries, it became compulsory.[110] Nonetheless, there was a growth in child labour in the Irish agricultural sphere. This was due to the increased workload demanded by compulsory tillage quotas, which are discussed later. Emigration to the British war economy also drove the decline in the regular male workforce, pushing children out of the classroom and into the field. Most of the wartime neutrals relied on the war economies of their larger industrial neighbours for employment, and the Irish government acquiesced in the movement of these workers to Britain. For the workers themselves, employment in Britain was chance to 'get their fingers on money needed for clothing and food which the farm does not grow', as the republican writer Peadar O'Donnell described it.[111]

The small number of women in the workforce was also a factor in the increase in child labour. In the Irish countryside, women commonly worked as butter makers in creameries or carried out unpaid work at home.[112] Although important work, in terms of the output of the agricultural economy, it was insignificant compared to the mobilisation of women as workers in the United Kingdom where between 1939 and 1943, 80% of the total addition to the workforce was female.[113] Demographically, young women emigrated in the largest numbers. Apart from concerns over social disruption, there was also the issue of male unemployment. These twin considerations were articulated, according to his memoir, by Frank McCourt's parents: 'Dad says a factory is no place for a woman. Mam says sitting on your arse by the fire is no place for a man.'[114]

Case study: cooperative creameries, an alternative to the 'gombeen'

The operation of the nation's cooperative creameries provides a case study of the structure and practices of rural Irish communities at this time and their relationship to Emergency state interventionism, notions of moral economy and the black market. The dairy sector benefited little from the 1938 Anglo-Irish Trade Agreement, where the main Irish gain was the lifting of restrictions on cattle.[115] Dairy output remained poor during the Emergency (another result of compulsory tillage, discussed later). Milk yields fell due to a poor hay crop, but the government refused to increase the price of butter.[116] The supply of milk and butter to Ireland's urban centres suffered as a result.

The cooperative movement was the largest Irish agricultural organisation at this time, consisting of over 400 societies and just under 100,000 members.[117] Dairying was the main focus and legacy of Horace Plunkett (1854–1932), the pioneer of agricultural cooperation in Ireland, who sought to develop a patronage network consisting of benign paternalist landlords. During the Emergency, dairy farming remained the largest sector of agricultural cooperative activity in the country.[118] Ostensibly, the principles of the cooperative movement challenged the 'gombeenism' of the rural economy. Wealthier farmers availed of banks, but most small farmers and farm labourers used the 'gombeen man' as a source of credit. The rough equivalent of the urban moneylender, the 'gombeen' dealt in a wide variety of goods and services. Arensberg and Kimball identified the credit obtained by small farmers as based on a benign system of mutual obligation, an assertion which overlooked the progressively more severe exactions placed on debtors, often aggravating their impoverishment.[119]

By contrast, cooperative creameries provided an uncomplicated economic contract based around community ties. When a farmer bought shares, he was obliged to supply milk to the creamery. The creamery was obliged to sell the finished product. Commonly, the creamery bought milk from local farmers and manufactured it into butter and cream. Small stores stood alongside the creamery and sold its produce. In the Irish countryside, then, the cooperative dairy creamery ostensibly provided an alternative and non-exploitative source of credit for small farmers, a market for their produce, ownership through shares and a source of employment for the farm worker. The great majority of transactions were carried out between local men, and committee membership was likewise restricted to locals, a communal structure that ostensibly bound cooperative creameries to look after their members' welfare as well as their livelihoods.[120] Expressing this communal spirit at a speech in Cavan in 1939, Charlie Riddell, the Assistant Secretary of the Irish Agricultural Organisation Society (IAOS), described cooperative creameries as operating on a basis of 'each for all and all for each' which allowed 'no room for selfishness'. 'In other days' he continued 'the creamery business was owned and controlled by outsiders, capitalists who came in to enrich themselves at the expense of the farmers'. By contrast, he stressed, cooperative creameries were opposed to 'speculative business' and united farmers in common cause.[121]

On face value, the more equitable economy pursued by the government during the Emergency sat well with this cooperative ethic. Riddell's sentiments were mirrored in the government's efforts to prevent speculation and profiteering. In contrast to the slick finance of other industries, many cooperative creameries were characterised by rather primitive accounting. Farmers took their produce to the creamery for weighing and were regularly paid, by cheque, at the end of every month.[122] Shares were often transferred on death without deeds of transfer, and many creameries did not keep comprehensive financial records. 'Very few of the managers have any proper training in regard to matters of the kind', Riddell confided to an associate in 1940.[123] Commonly, cooperatives were marked by an intense localism and a reluctance to engage with the law. In a County Leitrim creamery, a committee member avoided sanction for seriously defrauding the society because the issue was 'unpleasant' and 'embarrassing' for the other committee members, despite the insistence of IAOS lawyers that 'the law is the law' and he be prosecuted.[124] These were small-scale businesses. Cooperative society financial records show that during the Emergency the majority did not qualify for the government's corporation tax threshold of £1,000 profit. Moreover, their professed communalist emphasis was similar not only to that of government propaganda which sought to legitimate the restricted market conditions of the Emergency but also, according to some Catholic commentators of the time, to the status of Catholicism as antithetical to Protestant 'individualism'.[125]

Creameries, the state and the black market

Creameries were audited and administered by the IAOS, a body set up by Plunkett which liaised regularly with the Department of Agriculture and provided coordination and guidance for local cooperatives. During the Emergency, the IAOS was headed by Dr Henry Kennedy, who had been head of the organisation since 1926.[126] In a 1943 speech at University College Cork, Kennedy frankly warned of the 'dangerous cleavage between town and country' that had developed during the Emergency.[127] These remarks reflected how shortages had aggravated the country's rural/urban divide but also indicated his desire for modernisation. Kennedy did not believe in the creamery at every crossroads and, like Lemass, had little time for agrarian communities if they were based around uneconomic units. Kennedy backed a rationalisation process, which involved the closure of a number of creameries during the 1930s, causing a predictable degree of parochial discontent against central intervention.[128] A crucial consideration in the assessment of farmers' attitudes to state intervention during the Emergency is that such resentment was commonly reserved for the *government* (rather than the IAOS or Dr Kennedy) because despite the IAOS's involvement, it was the Department of Agriculture that carried out the closures.

In his support for rationalisation, then, Kennedy had more to do with causing the 'dangerous cleavage' than most cooperative farmers realised. Nonetheless, anger towards the state hardened for a number of other reasons as well. The dislike of the small farming community for the red tape of state incursion was embedded in the experience of dealing with the Congested Districts Board (established in 1891).[129] Also, critically, by 1939, it is evident that the IAOS and the Department of Agriculture were no longer cosy bedfellows. In 1944, the IAOS Conference passed resolutions that encapsulated their complaints against the government's behaviour during the Emergency: firstly, the government should give better prices for their produce, and, secondly, the dairying industry should be better represented at official level.[130] As was common during the Emergency, the industry thought that the government was directing too much and consulting too little.

Dairy farmers and cooperative creameries had a tough Emergency. There was a serious scarcity of feed and other supplies, British restrictions stymied trade, fuel shortages restricted rural mobility, the foot-and-mouth outbreak of 1941 destroyed herds, butter was rationed and prices controlled, and the official focus on tillage proved time-consuming. It is evident that the collective response of the cooperative creameries' management was not always to bow their heads and extend their spirit of cooperative toil to the national effort.

Matching the unwillingness of some big commercial concerns to cooperate with Supplies, Drinagh Cooperative Creamery, County Cork, repeatedly flouted orders. In late 1942, the state successfully brought charges against the creamery, which was heavily fined for selling sugar equivalent to the weekly ration of some fifteen thousand people to a sole businessman in Sligo.[131] After unsuccessfully appealing against the fine, Michael McNamara, the manager of the cooperative, came to regard the Department of Supplies with little more than contempt. A year after the case, the department published an order that eggs be sold at a maximum price in Cork City so that the urban poor would receive a fair share. McNamara wrote to Kennedy scoffing at the order. 'A Dublin man is anxious to get some eggs for himself and his pals', he wrote, revealing that the Dublin black market price was more lucrative than the maximum price in Cork. 'Naturally we shall endeavour to sell all our eggs in Dublin and if we succeed in doing so then Dublin will have plenty of eggs and everyone else [the poor of Cork City] can whistle for them.'[132] In common with others who engaged in black market activity during the Emergency, McNamara inverted the moral economic principles which the government claimed to be enforcing. Refuting the maximum prices fixed by Supplies, McNamara argued that 'fair distribution' – in other words a freer market – had been impeded by such government orders.[133]

IAOS records show that McNamara's relations with neighbouring cooperatives centred around 'jealousy and the desire to grow bigger'[134] and despite denying involvement in 'outrageous black marketing',[135] his creamery was later fined for petrol rationing offences as well.[136] McNamara was obviously an unscrupulous individual, then, and his flagrant engagement with the black market was exceptional for a creamery manager. In his 1939 speech extolling the virtues of cooperative creameries as based on the policy of 'each for all and all for each', Riddell had omitted those cooperatives, generally bigger operations, that engaged in egg poultry sales (like Drinagh) because these were, he contended, 'speculative concerns', whereas dairy was a more honest undertaking.[137]

Nevertheless, McNamara's open admission of black market activity suggests that he expected a sympathetic ear from the IAOS. This is illustrative of how far relations between farmers, managers and the IAOS, on the one hand, and government, on the other, had deteriorated during the Emergency. Emergency shortages and restrictions exacerbated the former camp's scorn for Dublin centralism. In late 1944, Lemass instructed that milk deliveries to creameries were to be reduced by half that of the previous year due to the national supply situation. The manager of a County

Tipperary cooperative wrote to Kennedy complaining that such restrictions would 'ruin the society'.[138] Kennedy wrote back, informing him that despite bringing the issue up in a meeting, Lemass had maintained that they could not modify the rules for any one society. Anything else, Lemass told Kennedy, would do 'injustice to the ordinary household consumers in towns'.[139] The response that this is likely to have elicited in the creamery manager is encapsulated in a letter to the editor of the *Irish Times* in 1944, incidentally published on the same date that Kennedy's letter was written. A Kildare reader alleged that 'a small minority inside the New Pale assume that outside the Pale there is a land flowing with milk and honey. This is absurd!'.[140]

During the Emergency, the departments of Supplies and Agriculture kept a close watch on production and distribution, together dictating the distribution of stock, prices and wages. These heightened restrictions applied in addition to normal control procedures whereby inspectors from Agriculture visited cooperatives periodically to take samples for testing. In certain cases, the overlap between Supplies and Agriculture resulted in bureaucratic overkill. The management of a Monaghan creamery, for instance, received a summons to the Department of Supplies for exceeding a milk quota based on figures previously recorded by Agriculture which, the latter department had since conceded, were completely inaccurate.[141]

Some cooperative societies were ruined by Emergency restrictions. When the supply situation became severe in 1941, Supplies instructed Achonry cooperative, County Sligo, to cut back deliveries. Under Lemass's restriction of petrol consumption, announced in January 1941, leeway was granted to owners of commercial vehicles supplying outlying rural areas. Nonetheless, after discussions with Supplies, Riddell wrote to the manager of Achonry cooperative informing him that 'as matters stand at the moment there is not much prospect of supplies for you for February'.[142] The restriction of petrol supplies presented a crushing blow to the creamery, but worse was to follow. In October, Agriculture imposed a 50% quota on the cooperative's slaughter figures. 'The imposition of this quota means that we cannot kill pigs even for our own shareholders', wrote the disconsolate manager to Kennedy.[143] Kennedy personally appealed the decision to Minister James Ryan; nonetheless, the decision stood.[144]

In contrast to the management of Drinagh, the board at Achonry appear to have been honest men who were dealt a harsh blow on several occasions by the dictates of central government. In 1943, they were reprimanded again, this time by the Department of Industry and Commerce (at this point under Lemass's auspices again), for granting unauthorised wage increases.[145] An IAOS inspector illustrated the society's decline in its fortunes over the Emergency in a report of his visit to Achonry in February 1944. Eight thousand pigs were slaughtered there in 1941. The following year, quota restrictions had seen this total fall to 3,000. By 1943, this figure stood at just under 1,800 pigs.[146] He noted that, predictably enough, farmers had turned to the black market to satisfy demand: 'the quotas fixed for sales of bacon have had the effect of encouraging the killing of pigs by farmers at home and the selling of bacon in the black market'.[147]

Cooperative creameries do not fit quite so easily into the Emergency narrative of hardship, however. Nor does Riddell's dichotomy between capitalist exploitation and cooperative spirit, as the activities of the brazen McNamara illustrate. Oral accounts detail how rigid social hierarchies operated within creameries. One creamery worker recalled how the creamery manager 'was domineering. They laid down the law and we were like slaves under them.'[148] Underlining the subtle class differences that marked these professedly egalitarian bodies, much correspondence between worried management and the IAOS concerned liability for incidents such as injury to carters and factory workers and disputes over the ownership of shares. There are examples of carters attempting to blackmail creameries to secure wage increases,[149] but, generally, the more significant 'black' behaviour was carried out by managers and large shareholders. A Cork creamery worker claimed that when 'the bosses' weighed farmers' milk on the scales at the creamery, they would often deduct money from each weighing.[150] This was exactly the same dishonest market behaviour ('engrossing') identified by E.P. Thompson in his study of the moral economic justification for crowd violence in eighteenth-century England.[151] While there is no evidence of *riots* during the Emergency due to popular anger against unfair market behaviour, there is abundant evidence of fights involving several men at the gates of rural creameries.[152] These altercations were caused by disputes over the weight and price creameries paid farmers for milk.

IAOS audits during the Emergency reveal that managerial dishonesty was not confined to Cork creameries like the one described above and the one in Drinagh. In 1948, an IAOS official wrote to Kennedy reporting 'a devastating fire' at a creamery in Cahir, County Tipperary, claiming 'all rationed goods are lost and many locals had ration books deposited with the society which are also now lost'.[153] Kennedy struck a suspicious tone: 'This seems to be the fourth society having such unfortunate occurrences so far this year'.[154] Aside from the locals who lost their precious ration books and the loss of a focal point for the community, the fire does not seem to have been quite so 'devastating' for many people. Farmers who supplied milk to the creamery were able to avail of the higher prices offered at another society; the damages were considerable and, on their receipt, the shareholders voted the creamery into voluntary liquidation.[155] Disgusted, the manager of another Tipperary creamery wrote to the creamery's manager, attacking his 'lack of regard for your members, suppliers and staff'.[156]

Conclusion

The rising cost of living and the stasis in wages mark the Emergency as a period of greater material deprivation than the 1930s. The boom in the black market only intensified the effect of these unhealthy trends upon the mass of the Irish people. The urban poor were guaranteed at least subsistence by the state and were often pointed to by representatives of the church and state as a justification of moral economic measures to regulate price, production and consumption. Nonetheless, their diet, life patterns and access to goods remained pitifully poor. The majority of people resident in Ireland during the Emergency did not have the ability to hoard goods or to pay exorbitant amounts for luxury items as some members of the urban middle class did.

Reflecting the priorities of the age, however, even the poorest would aggravate their situation by buying greater amounts of tea or white bread on the black market. The urban working class would do so also, despite the fact that their wages remained constant while the cost of living skyrocketed. Urban dwellers benefited from the concentration of black market activity in centres of population but had to put up with the higher prices foisted on them by urban commerce. In contrast to their rural counterparts, they also had little access – if any – to natural resources.

Shortages were acute in the rural context as well. The great advantage to rural living was the perks afforded by nature and its great disadvantage remoteness from jobs and markets, exacerbated by the collapse of modern transport links. The collective rural idyll was non-existent: the 'common table' at which farmer and farmhand sat to eat together is not evident. Small dairy farmers often experienced subaltern status within cooperatives. A striking proportion of these enterprises were characterised by dishonest management. Rural shopkeepers, farmers and traders felt unfairly prejudiced by Emergency regulation, an all too common emotion for interest groups during the Emergency as state direction of the economy took on new proportions. By virtue of their remote position, those who lived along the western seaboard and on the Atlantic islands were impacted hardest by the common experience of food and fuel scarcity. Shortages, then, impacted across the state. But for those that lived in Ireland's border region, cross-border smuggling provided opportunities to overcome want. This colourful phenomenon is discussed in the following chapter.

Notes

1   Lord Woolton, *The Memoirs of the Rt. Hon. The Earl of Woolton* (London, 1959), 230.
2   Zweiniger-Bargielowska, *Austerity in Britain*, 151.
3   'Tea – Maintenance of Supplies'. NAI, IND/EHR/3/13, p. 27.
4   *Statistical Abstract*, 1945, 168.
5   *Dáil Debates*, vol. 89, col. 1834, 8 April 1943.
6   *Statistical Abstract*, 1945, 162.
7   *Irish Times*, 7 June 1943.
8   Martin S. Quigley, *A U.S. Spy in Ireland* (Dublin, 1999), p. 63.
9   Sheila May, 'Two Dublin Slums', *The Bell*, 7, 4 (January 1944), 351–356.
10 D.83222 (Walter Mahon-Smith), *I Did Penal Servitude* (Dublin, 1945), 14.
11 John Sharkey, 'What I Saw in Dublin', *The Bell*, 9, 2 (November 1944), 149–154.
12 Bowen, *Spain*, 113.

13 T.W.T. Dillon, 'Slum Clearance: Past and Future', *Studies*, 34 (1945), 13–20.
14 *Statistical Abstract*, 1945, 19.
15 Daly, *Slow Failure*, 22.
16 Cornelius Lucey, 'The Spending of the Living Wage', *Irish Ecclesiastical Record*, 55 (January–June 1940), 151.
17 See Bryce Evans, 'The Construction Corps, 1940–48', *Saothar*, 32 (2007), 19–31.
18 See, for example, Hugo Flinn to de Valera, 9 December 1938. NAI, DT/S10927.
19 Aloisius J. Muench, 'Farmer Is Collaborator with the Creator', *Irish Monthly*, 70 (1942), 25–26.
20 Wills, *Neutral Island*, 239–249.
21 Tony Gray, *Ireland This Century* (Dublin, 1994), 156.
22 Department of Local Government and Public Health, *A Simple Guide to Wholesome Diet* (Dublin, 1941), cited in *Irish Press*, 23 June 1942.
23 Phil O'Keeffe, *Standing at the Crossroads* (Dingle, 1997), 36.
24 *Dáil Debates*, vol. 87, col. 6, 26 May 1942.
25 Share, *The Emergency: Neutral Ireland*, 38.
26 Mary E. Daly, *The First Department: A History of the Department of Agriculture* (Dublin, 2002), 231.
27 *Nenagh Guardian*, 12 June 1943.
28 MIOA, Christy Hennessy, b. 1932, Waterford City. Interviewed 8 April 2000, p. 2.
29 *Dáil Debates*, vol. 89, col. 2230, 5 May 1943.
30 *Irish Times*, 10 June 1943.
31 Catriona Clear, *Women of the House: Women's Household Work in Ireland, 1922–1961* (Dublin, 2000), 32.
32 Dublin Garda Index to Special Files, 1929–1945.
33 James Hickey, *Dáil Debates*, vol. 80, col. 1481, 5 June 1940.
34 James Dillon, *Dáil Debates*, vol.78, col. 1826, 22 February 1940.
35 Fee, 'The Effects', 133.
36 Quinn in *Forestry*, 203.
37 *Dublin Opinion*, January 1942.
38 Phil O'Keefe, b. Dublin, 1928. Interviewed 18 March 2009.
39 'Inspection Branch'. NAI, IND/EHR/3/4, p. 8.
40 Barney Heron, 'Winning the Turf', *The Bell*, 2, 6 (September 1941), 35.
41 332 (23 November 1943), Dublin Garda Index to Special Files, 1929–1945.
42 Fee, 'The Effects', 133.
43 MIOA, Christy Hennessy, b. 1932, Waterford City. Interviewed 8 April 2000, p. 8.
44 Seán Lemass, *Dáil Debates*, vol. 89, col. 2234, 5 May 1943.
45 Alfie Byrne junior, *Dáil Debates*, vol. 87, col. 290, 28 May 1942.
46 John Leydon to L.G. Lowry, 14 October 1940. NAI, FA/P23 (i).
47 This coal was of an inferior quality and was often responsible for explosions. See W.J. Grey to Leydon, 22 May 1941. NAI, FA/P23 (i).
48 L.G. Lowry to Leydon, 8 November 1940. NAI, FA/P23 (i).
49 Leydon's report on discussions in London, 17–19 November 1942. NAI, FA/P23.
50 Viscount Castlereagh, extract from British House of Commons debate, 16 March 1943. NAI, FA/P23.

51 *Dáil Debates*, vol. 87, col. 1002, 16 June 1942.

52 Alfie Byrne, *Dáil Debates*, vol. 81, col. 2339, 20 February 1941.

53 Wills, *Neutral Island*, 225.

54 'Regulations – Consolidated Clothing and Necessaries'. MA, CRF/2/59986.

55 Phil O'Keefe, b. Dublin, 1928. Interviewed 18 March 2009.

56 Memorandum on 'Army Stores – Stocktaking Deficiencies', 28 April 1943. NAI, FIN/S8/25/39.

57 J.K. Ryan to Quartermaster General, 24 November 1943. NAI, FIN/S8/25/39.

58 Memorandum on army stores, 28 April 1943. NAI, FIN/S8/25/39.

59 L. Egan to Heads of Commands, 16 July 1946. NAI, FIN/S8/25/39.

60 Tom Conlon, b. 1932, Dublin. Interviewed 6 November 2009.

61 'Historical Survey'. NAI, IND/EHR/3/C1, part II, p. 38.

62 'Historical Survey'. NAI, IND/HER/3/C1, part II, p. 42.

63 Márín Johnston, *Around the Banks of Pimlico* (Dublin, 1985), 122.

64 MIOA, Christy Hennessy, b. 1932, Waterford City. Interviewed 8 April 2000, p. 12–13.

65 Phil O'Keefe, b. Dublin, 1928. Interviewed 18 March 2009.

66 Maura Cronin, 'Status, Respectability and Small Places, the Limerick Dispensary 1940–1970'. UCD, 25 September 2008.

67 Milward, *War, Economy and Society*, 282.

68 Margaret MacLellan, b. 1926, Galbally, co. Limerick. Interviewed 28 September 2008.

69 Mary Gilbane, b. 1926, Jamestown, co. Leitrim. Interviewed 17 July 2008.

70 Conrad M. Arensberg and Solon T. Kimball, *Family and Community in Ireland* (2nd edition, Cambridge, 1968), 7.

71 Caitlin Ui Mhurchú, in Ní Shúilleabháin ed. *Bibeanna*, 192.

72 Peig Uí Chuinn, in Ní Shúilleabháin ed. *Bibeanna*, 140.

73 Raymonde Standún and Bill Long, *Singing Stone, Whispering Wind* (Dublin, 2001), 80.

74 Arensberg and Kimball, *Family*, 280.

75 Jack Magill, b. 1927, Saul, co. Down. Interviewed 16 April 2000, p. 7.

76 John Marcus O'Sullivan, *Dáil Debates*, vol. 83, col. 353, 14 May 1941.

77 185 (31 March 1941). Dublin Garda Index to Special Files, 1929–1945.

78 George Bennett, *Dáil Debates*, vol. 85, col. 2363, 11 March 1942.

79 Seán MacEamuinn, 'Poachers', *The Bell*, 1, 4 (January 1941), 18–22.

80 Wills, *Neutral Island*, 252.

81 726 (16 December 1941), Dublin Garda Index to Special Files, 1929–1945.

82 Mícheal Ó Aodha, 'Socializing in the 1940s: The Role of the Fit-Ups in Rural Ireland', Trinity College Dublin, 4 February 2009.

83 D.83222, *I Did Penal Servitude*, 56.

84 Carroll, *Ireland in the War Years*, 86.

85 Sylvia Couturié, *No Tears in Ireland* (Ballivor, co. Meath, 1999), 64.

86 MIOA, Patrick Heneghan, b. 1926, Kilmaine, co. Mayo. Interviewed 2 April 2000, p. 7.

87 MIOA, Weeshie Corless, b. 1920, Kinvarra, co. Limerick. Interviewed 7 April 2000, p. 5.

88 Daly, *Slow Failure*, 53.

89 Lemass, *Dáil Debates*, vol. 82, col. 1159, 2 April 1941; Hugo Flinn, *Dáil Debates*, vol. 88, col. 1494, 28 October 1942.

90 Eibhlís Ní Shúilleabháin to George Chambers, 19 November 1939, in Eibhlís Ní Shúilleabháin *Letters from the Great Blasket* (Cork, 1988), 81–89.

91 León Ó Broin, *Just Like Yesterday, an Autobiography* (Dublin, 1986), 142.

92 Joseph O'Donovan, *Dáil Debates*, vol. 87, col. 407, 28 May 1942.

93 *Connacht Tribune*, 7 February 1942.

94 Diary entry, 26 June 1943. UCDA, Eamon de Valera papers, P150/2571.

95 Kerry County Committee of Agriculture, Minutes, 25 November 1943.

96 Diarmaid Ferriter, *'Lovers of Liberty?' Local Government in 20th Century Ireland* (Dublin, 2001), 168.

97 Lemass, *Dáil Debates*, vol. 85, col. 1321, 10 December 1941.

98 MIOA, Edmund Carey, b. 1920, Galbally, co. Limerick. Interviewed 8 April 2000.

99 John O'Leary, *Dáil Debates*, vol. 91, col. 1429, 3 November 1943.

100 'Inspection Branch'. NAI, IND/EHR/3/4, p. 7.

101 James Kelly, b. 1924, Drumshambo, co. Leitrim. Interviewed 17 July 2008.

102 John James Gunning, b.1927, Kilclare, co. Leitrim. Interviewed 17 July 2008.

103 Patrick Browne, *Dáil Debates*, vol. 92, col. 8, 23 November 1943.

104 Lemass, *Dáil Debates*, vol. 91, col. 2076, 16 November 1943.

105 James Dillon, *Dáil Debates*, vol. 85, col. 1043, 3 December 1941.

106 Pat Masterson, b. 1922, Carigallen, co. Leitrim. Interviewed 17 July 2008.

107 *Irish Times*, 8 September 1941.

108 *Nenagh Guardian*, 11 September 1943.

109 Couturié, *No Tears*, 54–138.

110 Milward, *War, Economy and Society*, 221.

111 Peadar O'Donnell, 'Migration Is a Way of Keeping a Grip', *The Bell*, 3, 2 (November 1941), 115–119.

112 MIOA, Mairéad Dwyer, b. 1929, Gooldscross, co. Tipperary. Interviewed 7 April 2000, p. 3.

113 Milward, *War, Economy and Society*, 219.

114 McCourt, *Angela's Ashes*, 248.

115 Kevin B. Nowlan, 'On the Eve of War', in Nowlan and Williams ed., *Ireland in the War Years*, 3.

116 Daly, *Agriculture*, 248–250.

117 *Report of the Commission on Vocational Organisation* (Dublin, 1943), 131.

118 *Commission on Vocational Organisation*, 131–135.

119 Arensberg and Kimball, *Family*, 138.

120 Patrick Bolger, *The Irish Co-operative Movement, Its History and Development* (Dublin, 1977), 183.

121 *Anglo-Celt*, April 8 1939.

122 MIOA, Edmund Carey, b. 1920, Galbally, co. Limerick, p. 4.

123 Riddell to R.A. Maccauley, 28 May 1940. NAI, Irish Co-Operative Organisation Society records (ICOS)/1088/646/16.

124 Arthur Cox to Riddell, 5 June 1940. NAI, ICOS/1088/413/2.

125 Denis O'Keefe, 'Catholic Political Theory', *Studies* 30 (1941), 485; Don O'Leary, *Vocationalism and Social Catholicism in Twentieth Century Ireland: The Search for a Christian Social Order* (Dublin, 2000), 68.

126 Bolger, *Co-operative Movement*, 114.
127 Henry Kennedy, 'Agricultural Prosperity and Urban Employment', *Studies* 32 (1943), 63.
128 Bolger, *Co-operative Movement*, 217.
129 Diarmaid Ferriter, '"A Peculiar People in Their Own Land": Catholic Social Theory and the Plight of Rural Ireland 1930–55' (unpublished PhD thesis, UCD, 1996), 40.
130 Kennedy to L. Egan, 10 March 1944. NAI, ICOS/1088/591/4.
131 *Southern Star*, 3 October 1942.
132 Michael McNamara to Kennedy, 26 October 1943. NAI, ICOS/1088/348/36.
133 McNamara to Lemass, 25 May 1943. NAI, ICOS/1088/348/37.
134 Report of West Cork Conference of IAOS, 19 May 1943. NAI, ICOS/1088/348/37.
135 McNamara to Lemass, 17 November 1942. NAI, ICOS/1088/348/37.
136 McNamara to E.J. Coyne S.J., 13 April 1943. NAI, ICOS/1088/348/37.
137 *Anglo-Celt*, 8 April 1939.
138 L. Egan to Kennedy, 30 November 1944. NAI, ICOS/1088/591/4.
139 Kennedy to Egan, 11 December 1944. NAI, ICOS/1088/591/4.
140 T.J. McElligott to Editor, *Irish Times*, 11 December 1944.
141 H.A. Ferry to Riddell, 17 January 1943. NAI, ICOS/1088/227/7.
142 Riddell to T. O'Mahony, 8 January 1941. NAI, ICOS/1088/5/16.
143 O'Mahony to Kennedy, 6 October 1941. NAI, ICOS/1088/5/16.
144 Kennedy to O'Mahony, 16 October 1941. NAI, ICOS/1088/5/16.
145 F.J. Hegarty to Riddell, 19 June 1943. NAI, ICOS/1088/5/16.
146 P. Whelan, Report of Visit to Achonry Co-operative Agriculture and Dairy Society, 7–10 February 1944. NAI, ICOS/1088/5/16.
147 Whelan, Report of Visit. NAI, ICOS/1088/5/16.
148 MIOA, Donal O'Donovan, b. c. 1920, Cullane, co. Cork. Interviewed 6 March 2000, p. 1. See also MIOA, Mairéad Dwyer, b. 1929, Gooldscross, co. Tipperary. Interviewed 7 April 2000, p. 3.
149 See, for instance, memo on Ballinhassig Co-operative Creamery, county Cork. NAI, ICOS/1088/38/3.
150 MIAO, Donal O'Donovan, b. c. 1920, Cullane, co. Cork. Interviewed 6 March 2000, p. 3.
151 Thompson, 'The Moral Economy', 178.
152 See MIOA, Anne Blake, b. 1921, BirdHill, co. Tipperary. Interviewed 10 April 2000, p. 5.
153 R. Langford to Kennedy, 5 July 1948. NAI, ICOS/1088/152/3.
154 Kennedy memo, 3 July 1948. NAI, ICOS/1088/152/3.
155 Cors O'Shea to Kennedy, 21 July 1948. NAI, ICOS/1088/152/3.
156 E. Roche to J. Creed, 15 February 1949. NAI, ICOS/1088/152/3.

5

Smuggling

Have been staying on the border. It is perfectly easy to cross it with no interference ... was cycling to and fro the whole time and jumping hedges from Eire into Six counties fields.

John Betjeman, 20 April 1941

The contested frontier

Nowhere was popular defiance of the state's Emergency economic measures more evident than in Ireland's border region. The 1920 Government of Ireland Act created the new territory of Northern Ireland, establishing separate jurisdictions. Ireland's border region was formed: an extensive land frontier which spans nine of the country's thirty-two counties. During the Emergency, the Irish Republican Army (IRA) continued to target Customs posts along the border.[1] These violent actions were strongly condemned by the Fianna Fáil government, yet the 1937 Constitution of Ireland claimed sovereignty over Northern Ireland, and de Valera frequently condemned the Stormont administration as a 'government governing an unwilling population'.[2]

Political dispute was accompanied by economic defiance. In the 1930s, prices in the Free State and Northern Ireland diverged considerably, and an extensive cattle smuggling trade developed.[3] Writing in 1935, Northern Ireland Minister for Agriculture Basil Brooke commented that the 'monotonous regularity of seizures' indicated 'the smugglers are succeeding'. Whereas there were just under 7,000 cattle seized in 1931, Brooke noted that this figure had increased to 33,000 by the start of the Anglo-Irish tariff conflict in 1932. This figure rose to 50,000 in 1933 and just under 80,000 in 1934.[4]

Throughout the 1932–1938 Economic War between independent Ireland and the United Kingdom, the attitude of Stormont ministers to all-Ireland economic relations was marked by the lack of a conciliatory attitude. Their outlook was hardened by their sideline status during the Anglo-Irish coal–cattle pacts between 1935 and 1937.[5] Northern Ireland assumed greater prominence in the Anglo-Irish Trade Agreement talks of April 1938. After these talks, John Leydon and William Scott, Secretary of the Stormont Ministry of Commerce, came close to agreeing a substantial degree of cross-border collaboration on smuggling in the event of war. Chief among these considerations was the issue of food pricing and petrol rationing.[6]

Economic relations between the two territories were to be seriously undermined a few months later, though. Stormont reacted negatively to de Valera's outline of a federal solution to partition in a *London Evening Standard* interview of October 1938.[7] Relations soured and the stubborn attitude of the northern administration towards cross-border collaboration was confirmed to Leydon in April 1939, when he was engaged in negotiations with the British Board of Trade in London. Leydon learned that Scott, his opposite number in Stormont, was also in London and saw it as an opportunity to establish some common ground in the management of the coming crisis, but was rebuffed.[8]

In the absence of a pre-war agreement between Belfast and Dublin, the border remained a hotly contested economic and political frontier between 1939 and 1945. Cross-border price differentials continued as in the previous decade, but it was the disparity in supply, rather than price, which now drove cross-border smuggling. Separate rationing schemes were introduced on either side of the border, leading to demand for items more readily available in one territory than the other. Butter, bacon, eggs, sausages, ham, beef and jellies were lapped up by hungry northerners, and items of clothing such as stockings and blankets were also imported north illegally.[9] In the opposite direction flowed soap, wireless batteries, candles, white bread, paraffin oil, sugar, cycle tyres, contraceptives and, most commonly, tea and flour. These trends were part of the 'new' smuggling of the Emergency era, which was based predominately around consumer items and encapsulates the sometimes contradictory interplay of political, economic and religious factors in popular illegal activity of the era.

On Parr? Political relations, administration and the movement of labour

The uneasy relationship between Ireland's two administrations was reflected in the suspicious manner in which border officials viewed each other during the Emergency. Customs officials and Royal Ulster Constabulary (RUC) police officers generally viewed their counterparts south of the border as inefficient.[10] Gardaí and Irish Customs officials, they thought, were reluctant to apprehend smugglers because they worked for a state opposed to the very existence of the border. This perception was reinforced by British propaganda. After the 'American Note' controversy of 1944, when Dublin refused United States representative David Gray's request that it expel Axis legations, a British Movietone News film claimed that Irish disregard had resulted in 'German and Japanese agents roaming at large in Ireland'.[11] On the other side, the Gardaí were irked by reports that the RUC were not observing the land boundary. A Garda report of 1944 alleged incursions of RUC men into independent Ireland, pointing to the bonuses which the RUC offered its men in return for catching smugglers.[12]

Although northern border officials viewed their southern counterparts as complacent, there were significant internal disputes within their own ranks. In the early years of the Economic War RUC policemen had 'no more power than the ordinary citizen' in apprehending cross-border smugglers.[13] In 1936, this changed when Stormont decided that RUC officers would have the same powers as Customs officers. The RUC claimed that this reduced smuggling because in contrast to the former 'ludicrous position', 'every policeman was then recognised as a preventative officer'.[14] This empowerment had, however, excited the 'jealousy' of Customs officers. After the Anglo-Irish Trade Agreement of 1938, Customs unsuccessfully sought the revocation of these powers from their police colleagues.[15]

Northern Customs retained a dislike for their RUC colleagues during the Emergency. By virtue of experience, Customs men claimed to be able to spot the slightest indicators of smuggling, the telltale particulars that would be overlooked by their police colleagues. In a 1940 court case, a Northern Ireland Customs man pointed out to an astonished judge the discreet hallmark of cigarette smuggling. In the words 'W.D. & H.O. Wills' printed on every cigarette, the symbol '&' had no tail above the downward stroke on the Northern Ireland cigarette, whereas a tail appeared on cigarettes originating south of the border.[16] The RUC, for its part, was confident that its manpower would overcome Customs' regional staffing shortages that had, on occasion, resulted in whole trains entering Northern Ireland without having been inspected.[17] Customs was, according to the RUC, overstretched and hamstrung by a target culture in which Customs men would 'collect the requisite five millions and after that the smuggling that was taking place didn't matter very much'.[18]

Tensions between northern Customs officers and the RUC persisted throughout the Emergency but were mitigated by a greater common disdain: for their counterparts south of the border. The switch in Dublin's economic management of the Emergency, discussed previously, was crucial in reinforcing this negative impression. The Irish state lurched from a somewhat complacent initial approach to the supply crisis towards strident interventionism as the British supply squeeze tightened. Mirroring the state's priorities, between the years 1939 and 1941, Irish Customs officials used discretion when small quantities were being smuggled by individuals.[19] But by the crisis year 1941, the Department of Supplies noted, cross-border smuggling was becoming 'serious'. Dublin now resolved to take a firmer stance to eradicate it.[20] Northern consumers were now seen exerting pressure on the straitened supply situation south of the border. As the chief superintendant of the Drogheda Gardaí complained, 'middle-aged women [from Belfast] all armed with capacious shopping bags' had developed 'from being a joke into being a huge drain on the food reserves of this town.'[21]

Concerns that neutral Ireland was being drained of its food prompted Seán Lemass to introduce the Emergency Powers (Sunday Trading) Order in 1941. This prevented traders in border counties from selling butter, bacon, eggs, sugar, jams, jellies, marmalades or clothes on a Sunday.[22] Additionally, Supplies' Inspection Branch employed plain clothes officers to detect the sale of ration books to visitors from Belfast at Amiens Street Station in Dublin.[23] The department's Historical Survey claims that these restrictions, combined with stricter Customs enforcement and the introduction of full rationing in 1942, 'effectively curtailed illegal export'.[24] Considering the continuing disparity in the price and supply of goods between the two territories, this is a highly dubious assertion.

To northern officials, this switch from light to heavy regulation was a selfish one, and the lack of cooperation between border officials remained entrenched, as a 1941 incident on the Monaghan–Fermanagh border illustrates. The *Anglo-Celt* newspaper relayed the story of a young male smuggler apprehended by the RUC with two loaves of white bread, attempting to smuggle them south. Managing to escape the policemen's clutches, he cycled at a furious pace towards the border with RUC officers hot in pursuit. The northern policemen eventually succeeded in pulling him from his bicycle. However, at this point, the youth had just crossed the border and, in a twist certain to have warmed the hearts of republicans, a local potato digger came to the boy's aid and warned the RUC men off with a spade. To the further frustration of his former captors, when the Gardaí arrived from Clones, they refused to arrest the smuggler.[25] That this incident occurred late in 1941 demonstrates that although the Irish crackdown on smuggling may have reduced the flow of goods north, Irish authorities' practical disregard for petty smuggling persisted. It is a matter of conjecture as to whether this was the sort of incident John Leydon had in mind when, in defending his department's failure to ensure the fair distribution of white flour that was coming over the border and being sold via the black market, he praised 'risk-takers'.[26] From a northern perspective, the smuggler was a criminal compromising equitable distribution in the wartime moral economy, not merely a roguish miscreant. Naturally though, their southern counterparts were more concerned with stopping the export of goods north than their import south.

The northern system was administered by the Divisional Office of the UK Ministry of Food. Like the Department of Supplies, its principal responsibility was to secure equitable distribution. Northern Ireland's equivalent of Lemass was Chief Divisional Food Officer for Northern Ireland, G.H.E. Parr. Like their equivalents south of the border, Parr's inspectors relied on gossip and tip-offs. The Ministry received rather finicky complaints from self-appointed guardians of public economic morals. These included letters from the female proprietor of a temperance lodge accusing traders of deliberately keeping butter until it deteriorated so that they could sell it to soap factories[27] and a man from County Down so concerned with butchers' definitions of 'thick' and 'thin' streaky bacon that he had purchased a foot rule from Woolworth's to measure the slices.[28] Parr possessed the same extensive powers as Lemass when it came to the distribution of resources and was also responsible for a dimension of moral economy not witnessed in independent Ireland: the preference given to disabled ex-servicemen in the granting of licences for grocery shops.[29]

Compared to efforts in independent Ireland, the campaign against the black market in Northern Ireland was part of the greater bureaucratic nexus of the British war economy. The UK Ministry of Food's 'Food Economy' and 'Dig For Victory' initiatives rested on voluntary organisations. The Ministry provided groups such as city missions, churches and women's institutes with 'talkie' films and an abundant literature advocating frugality and denouncing the black market.[30] While officials admitted that people, particularly in 'crowded quarters', had 'neither the time nor the inclination' to avail of such information,[31] Parr could draw on more anti-black market educational material than Lemass, through the vast reams of propaganda churned out by the British Ministry of Information.

Like their counterparts in Supplies, however, the market restrictions operated by Ministry of Food officials in Northern Ireland brought them into conflict with business interests. In one case, a Derry baker protested to Prime Minister John Andrews that correspondence between him and Parr had descended into 'the vile use of histrionics'.[32] Like Lemass, Parr regularly quarrelled with the North of Ireland Grocers' Association.[33] Most significantly, Parr had to contend against a pervasive sectarianism. There was much controversy over Parr's appointments of Catholic food officers. To take one example, the mid-Armagh Unionist Association wrote to Basil Brooke (who took over from John Andrews as Prime Minister in May 1943) complaining of the 'disloyal tendencies' of their local food officer. This man, they claimed, had not only remained tight-lipped during a rendition of 'God Save the King' at a Red Cross fundraiser but was the son of a German mother and an Irish nationalist father.[34] Parr, a conscientious civil servant in the mould of Leydon, stood by his appointments, and so did Brooke.

In defending the growth of red tape, Ministry of Food officials and Stormont ministers frequently justified measures by pointing out that they were only following Whitehall's diktats: a tactic which shared certain similarities with the Irish government's justification of domestic regulation by blaming the depredations on imperialist warmongers. Arguably, social conditions in Northern Ireland were more challenging than those encountered by Ministry of Food officials in Britain. In the opening months of the Emergency, tensions between the unionist majority and large nationalist minority were heightened when the new British Prime Minister Winston Churchill announced that the introduction of conscription in Northern Ireland had been discussed at cabinet. Unemployment, moreover, was well above the British average. Aggravated by the dependence of the linen industry on raw materials from Europe and the social snobbery of James Craig and John Andrews, unemployment rose, exacerbating political and religious divisions. Fear of market disruption caused by an influx of Catholic workers from south of the border was a significant factor in Westminster's decision not to introduce conscription to Northern Ireland and Stormont's introduction of Residence Permits in 1943.[35] With these concerns in mind, Stormont also made all skilled workers register at employment exchanges.[36]

Yet despite the worry that Catholics would capitalise on wartime conditions to take all the available jobs, in the early years of the Emergency, the Northern Ireland

Ministry of Labour actively recruited unskilled labourers from independent Ireland. Between February and December 1941, 7,000 citizens of independent Ireland legally entered Northern Ireland for work. In addition to those legally working in Northern Ireland, private firms regularly recruited cheap labour from south of the border without going through official channels.[37] Although manpower committees were established to stabilise agricultural and industrial labour,[38] the Northern Ireland Ministry of Labour never exercised anything like its full powers to coerce and control the workforce.[39] Unlike the state coercion of labour promoted by Lemass, which is discussed later, or the even greater powers to direct working people that the British government possessed under the 1940 Statutory Rule for the Conscription of Workers, social and political sensitivities ensured that the Northern Ireland Ministry of Labour trod tentatively.[40]

It is evident, then, that there was much labour movement between the two territories during the early 1940s, despite belated moves from Dublin to place embargoes on this form of emigration.[41] This regular movement of workers reinforced the 'black' aspect to economic exchanges between the two sets of populations. Migrant workers, whether legally or illegally toiling on building sites in Belfast and other Northern towns, did not experience the same restriction of movement that workers in Britain and neutral Ireland did. Rather, these workers experienced the uncoordinated regulation of consumer supply in the two territories and the price and wage disparities that went with it. Naturally, where they could, they enthusiastically exploited these conditions by smuggling.

Corsets and cross-dressers: the 'new' smuggling

The Irish black market was 'most prevalent in the areas contiguous to the Northern Ireland frontier', as a Department of Supplies memorandum asserted.[42] Cattle smuggling, that staple of the Economic War, continued during the Emergency. Cattle were no longer dutiable, but imports were heavily restricted by the British authorities.[43] Illustrative of the almost comic dynamic to cattle smuggling is a letter to Northern Ireland Prime Minister James Craig from a Derry farmer, who wrote to complain that two plain clothes RUC constables had called to his farmhouse to demand he draw up a detailed list of the colouring and shading of each of his seventy cows.[44] Meanwhile, the Dáil heard complaints of cattle 'racketeering on the border',[45] and Stormont lamented the continuation of the black trade.[46] During the Emergency, agricultural officials from both jurisdictions ruminated on the net loss to revenue that smuggling of cattle and pigs represented.[47] Border farmers, too, pointed to the glutting of markets and the negative effect on price of the continued smuggling of livestock.[48]

Significantly, though, livestock smuggling was accompanied, in the words of the RUC Inspector General Charles Wickham, by a 'new form of smuggling'.[49] In the popular imagination and in alarmist media pieces, bootleggers and smugglers of the time were sinister characters, plying their trade from dark, cavernous hideouts in mountains.[50] Even the *Sunday Independent* children's cartoon 'Curlie Wee and Gussie Goose' had its anthropomorphic heroes infiltrating a smuggler's cave.[51] In fact, smuggling was a more quotidian matter altogether. In contrast to the smuggling of beasts during the Economic War, the 'new smuggling' meant small quantities of food and other consumer items. This new smuggling activity was parodied in a *Dublin Opinion* cartoon of 1941 depicting a man sitting astride the border as he ate his meal (consisting of beef and butter on one side and tea and white bread on the other).[52]

This new smuggling of consumer goods did not develop immediately after the outbreak of war. Customs surveyors in Fermanagh and Armagh recorded 'no material change in the cross boundary traffic compared with the pre-war period' in September 1939.[53] From 1940 on, however, there was a sharp increase in correspondence between border officials and their Belfast central offices as the 'new' smuggling took hold. In October 1940, Lemass, worried that imports of flour were dwindling, fixed wheat extraction at 75%, slowly ushering in the completely black loaf by February 1942.[54] White flour (still available in Northern Ireland) therefore became a commodity subject to great demand. Flour smuggling was described by Inspector General Wickham as 'more difficult to deal with than cattle smuggling.'[55] As the Northern Ireland Divisional Food Office noted, there had been a significant increase in flour smuggling after the introduction of the completely black loaf south of the border. Bags of the coveted white flour brought in from Northern Ireland were selling at three times Lemass's fixed price. 'Everybody appears to know of the overcharging in regard to flour except the Minister's inspectors', commented Irish Labour Party leader William Norton, 'somebody should whisper something to them on the matter.'[56]

Bakers, bread delivery men and millers from Northern Ireland smuggled flour and bread south to meet the demand for white bread that soared from 1941 onwards as bread in neutral Ireland became gradually darker. A Northern Ireland government analysis of millers' deliveries in 1942 showed an increase of 45% over the pre-war average, whereas the corresponding increase in Great Britain was only 19%.[57] At a 1941 trade conference, an official from the Ministry of Food claimed that the involvement of bread delivery men in smuggling represented 'the blackest of the black markets': not only were offenders depriving the poor of their staple, they were undermining their own trade. It was agreed at the conference that traders would compare bread delivery accounts 'before and after Eire went off white bread' and expel the 'bad eggs' from their midst. Under pressure from the Ministry, the Master Bakers' Association agreed that those traders whose records showed an increase in profits from illegally exporting south would be blacklisted.[58]

The authorities on both sides of the border were also keenly aware that the railway was an active smuggling corridor. As discussed earlier, Lemass introduced petrol rationing in October 1939. By April 1942, petrol shortages were so severe that Lemass announced the end of all non-essential road transport. The railways, although hamstrung by inferior coal, therefore provided the only viable transport arteries for the nation.[59] Cross-border services were operated by the Great Northern Railway (GNR) and the Sligo, Leitrim and Northern Counties Railway (SLNCR).

To Sunday excursionists and more serious smugglers alike, the cross-border train became a sort of deus ex machina amidst the banality of shortages. An excited John Betjeman composed his reflection on the porousness of the border while 'in a flash-jazz cocktail bar on the train'.[60] Train staff, too, misbehaved. GNR files record the 'smuggling of merchandise (butter etc.) into Northern Ireland by enginemen' and 'smuggling of foodstuffs by road motor staff'.[61] In 1944, the engine crew of a GNR Dublin–Belfast train were fined and imprisoned for smuggling activity.[62] Employees of the SLNCR also engaged in illegal activity.[63] Like bread servers, railway men enabled the black trade in the course of their daily work patterns. The reminiscences of railway employees, such as Joe McGrew from Omagh, County Fermanagh, illustrate this. McGrew joined the GNR in 1944, by which stage, according to Supplies' Historical Survey, smuggling had been 'effectively curtailed'.[64] However, McGrew had reason to fear Customs inspection. In 1945, his fear of apprehension for smuggling butter led him to empty a station's fire bucket of its sand, replace its contents with his smuggled butter, turn it upside down and sit on it smoking while Customs men walked by.[65] McGrew suggests that smuggling was so extensive that it was common among railway employees as well as the public.

The GNR's cheap excursion rates resulted in a great number of people from Northern Ireland's towns and cities visiting border towns to purchase goods which, for them, were in short supply.[66] GNR's Belfast–Dundalk route proved popular with these Sunday excursionists. Predominately middle-aged, working class and female, snobbery soon arose at the sight of these women eating in train dining cars.[67] Although such women were the most conspicuous consumers on the route – a 'joke', as the Dundalk Garda described them – the Belfast–Dundalk route was popular not just with Belfast women but with women resident in outlying counties. One South Armagh resident testifies: 'my grandmother, Big Annie, would shift butter and eggs from Dundalk every Monday. Her twelve children would await her arrival with something exotic from the 26 counties – a tomato, or even an orange'.[68] Although the firmer stance of Supplies from 1941 had an effect in reducing the volume of smuggled goods detected, it is unlikely that the trade was ever 'effectively curtailed' on the Belfast–Dundalk line.

In comparison to the Belfast train, little attention has been given to the smuggling that thrived on a similar Emergency excursion route operating on the opposite side of the country: the GNR route from Omagh to Bundoran, County Donegal, on which Joe McGrew worked. Due to the opportunity it presented to overcome the restrictions imposed by rationing in Northern Ireland, the people of Tyrone nick-named it 'The Sugar Train'.[69] Like the Belfast–Dundalk train, the Sugar Train was popular with housewives, but children were also heavily involved. Oliver Gibson of County Tyrone remembers 'a young lad would be supplied with a list of items - sugar, orange peel, raisins, sultanas. You got a pound note, you were to make the purchases. Above all, you weren't to lose it to the Customs man. So you learned the guile of being able to look innocent, to keep the parcel out of the Customs' man's eye.'[70] Brian O'Neill, another child smuggler during the Emergency, recalls the 'nervous tension that went right through the train' when the words 'Anything to Declare?' were heard, the determination 'not to lose the bob or the tanner you'd been lent by your neighbours' and how adults would open the carriage windows and lift children out so that they could conceal smuggled items on the roof.'[71] The tension was heightened by the rumour, which usually began at Pettigo Junction, the border town straddling counties Donegal and Fermanagh, that Customs men had boarded the train.[72] For those smugglers travelling in the 'Quiet Carriage' (reserved for women), the 'Lady Searcher' was to be reckoned with: a female Customs officer who could search women more thoroughly than her male colleagues.[73]

Because it involved the certainty of Customs inspection at the border, smuggling on the train required ingenuity. Imaginative ways of concealing smuggled goods included under seats where bolts had come loose, in the gas cylinder box in the buffet car, in train battery boxes, in the locker of the tea car, in the inner sheeting boards under seats and in the steps of horse boxes.[74] 'The receptacle at the rear of rail cars' was identified as a favourite smuggling compartment by the Northern Ireland Customs surveyor of Enniskillen, who wrote to the manager of the SLNRC in 1943 to insist that railway staff secure the box by lock.[75]

Many individuals engaged in the black market because they saw it as a matter of necessity rather than greed. Cross-border trade rested on the geographical impracticalities of the border. Ministry of Food officials noted that 'unlike Great Britain, Northern Ireland has a large exportable surplus of a number of foods, particularly livestock products, and it is therefore clearly more difficult to convince the local public than it is to convince a public which is entirely dependent for its food supplies on imports'.[76] Whitehall expressed concern to Stormont that border controls were operating unfairly. Referring to the seizure of a Donegal farmer's cattle by the RUC in June 1939, a British official pointed out that the farmer's route to market crossed the border four times over the course of three miles. Farmers who had their cattle seized in such circumstances often had a greater moral economic claim than the authorities, claimed the official in London.[77] Traders from border counties complained of apprehension by the RUC even when travelling, for instance, between one town in Cavan and another, because the road crossed the border.[78] There were obvious difficulties in imposing fines for smuggling on people resident on the other side of the border in any case. Due to this administrative difference, border settlements such as Derry became smuggling hotspots.[79]

The stronger moral claim of local people intersecting the border is further evidenced by the recollections of Lettie Hill. Lettie was nineteen when the Emergency began, living with her parents on the family farm in County Cavan. Northern Ireland was only one mile away, but before the Emergency, she had never crossed the border. When the domestic supply of oil declined drastically from 1941, it fell to Lettie to undertake journeys by bicycle into Fermanagh to purchase candles and paraffin oil from country shops and smuggling sheds because her brothers and father were working on the farm. Lettie continued to smuggle even after apprehension by the RUC: 'sure all the girls did it'.[80] At times, officials on both sides dealt with smugglers in an 'under the counter' manner; other times, they were fastidious. A schoolgirl from County Monaghan stopped at the border with a basket of eggs was reported as being upset not at the seizure of the eggs but the RUC's insistence on confiscating her little basket as well.[81]

As Lettie Hill's recollection illustrates, the bicycle was the most common means of transport for small-scale smugglers who lived within cycling distance of the border. There is a popular myth about Emergency smuggling which tells of a man who regularly travelled to Northern Ireland by bicycle and was methodically searched by a particularly diligent Northern Ireland Customs official who could never find anything on him. With the relaxing of restrictions post-war, the Customs man asked him what he had been smuggling. 'Bicycles!', replied the man.[82] Unfortunately, this story is unlikely to have any historical foundation. Alert to the export of bicycles, the Northern Ireland authorities frequently confiscated and impounded them in a Belfast warehouse.[83] A release fee of ten shillings applied on top of the fines incurred for any goods smuggled, which were considered 'forfeit to the crown' and confiscated.[84] If they did not have the money to pay the bicycle release fee, the smuggler could be left stranded miles away from home. Most people smuggling bicycles or bicycle parts were offered the option of paying a fine or facing legal proceedings. Some, who refused to pay fines or repeatedly offended, were sentenced a short period of imprisonment.[85]

Compared to professional smuggling outfits, the booty of the typical Northern 'excursionist' or farm girl was trifling.[86] Lettie Hill, for one, would only smuggle what she could carry in her bicycle basket or her pockets. Indeed, in 1942, a male smuggler dressed in a skirt and shawl was recognised as a cross-dresser because of the ease with which he was carrying an eight-stone sack of flour on his shoulder.[87] Female attire and accoutrements afforded greater opportunities for concealment. In at least one instance, a female smuggler was intercepted by Customs officers when they removed the baby from her pram to find two loaves of white bread.[88]

Likewise, the women of Omagh would return from Bundoran with as much lace as they could fit on the inside of their umbrellas (prompting genial fellow passengers to remark 'you must have been expectin' bad weather missus') or as much flour as they could stash in their clothing ('When's your baby due, missus?').[89] As one smuggler of the era recalled, 'many a skinny girl went down on the morning train to return on the evening train heavily pregnant'.[90] It was not just women who feigned bulk either. In 1943, a Louth man caught in possession of smuggled goods at Crossmaglen enlisted the help of a solicitor, who wrote to Customs officials in Newry claiming his client had been caught with an amount of tea that did not exceed that which visitors to neutral Ireland were allowed to take for holiday purposes. The Customs surveyor replied sarcastically that 'among the rations carried for his holiday by, if I may so describe him, your *robust* client, were six packets of boot protectors, two lamp globes, one pound of springs, one pound of paint, one pound of candles and three bars of soap'.[91]

The goods smuggled by most women, whether those returning North or South, were for use in the domestic sphere. In this regard, female involvement in smuggling conformed to the common type of labour of Irish women from struggling backgrounds documented by Caitriona Clear: unpaid and centred around the home.[92] Smuggling activity afforded one significant and overlooked difference to Clear's representation of female economic activity during the era, however: it afforded women and girls the opportunity to get out of the house. Indeed, there are records of housewives travelling to Northern Ireland from as far away as south Mayo to smuggle candles south.[93] Women also tended to smuggle in groups of three or four, whereas seizures of goods from men, when not part of smuggling gangs, were more likely to be from lone individuals. Occasionally, women were caught with amounts so copious they suggested commercial intent rather than domestic use. In 1944, a housewife from Sligo was found with twelve candles, a pound of tea, mustard, eight bars of soap, ovaltine, oatmeal, ten pairs of silk stockings and a pound of margarine.[94] In another case, the *Anglo-Celt* reported on a 'bulky beggar woman' found, on inspection by the lady searcher, to be carrying dozens of stockings and underpants.[95] In 1941, one Josephine Gibbons, obviously something of a smuggling phenomenon, was illegally exporting enough food to Northern Ireland to have a Garda file devoted exclusively to her activities.[96]

As the Emergency progressed, authorities became more adept at spotting the techniques of the new smuggling. However, the wartime movement of large numbers of servicemen and women helped sustain the illicit trade. The large presence of Allied troops in Northern Ireland from 1942 mitigated the increased anti-smuggling surveillance on both sides of the border. This is evidenced by the encroachment of service people into records of border seizures. Women were conspicuous by their involvement in this dimension of the black market as well. Women of the Auxiliary Training Service were apprehended for smuggling, including the export of tea to sell for a profit south of the border.[97] Men and women from the large Royal Air Force garrisons accounted for a sizeable proportion of smuggling offences. In 1943, two female RAF personnel were caught attempting to cross the border with fifteen hair clips, eight lipsticks, four hair combs, perfumes and silk stockings.[98] The availability of luxury clothes and cosmetics from independent Ireland was demonstrated later that year when two male RAF officers were caught at Belleek, Fermanagh, with a large quantity of ladies' corsets and stockings.[99]

The arrival of American troops from January 1942 also proved something of a boon to the smuggling trade. The number of American service personnel stationed in Northern Ireland peaked at 120,000 in December 1943, the equivalent to one tenth of the statelet's pre-war population,[100] and Northern Ireland hosted an aggregate of 300,000 American troops over four years.[101] An IRA manifesto of September 1942 predicted that 'British tactics' would result in conflict between American troops and

'Irish guerrilla forces.'[102] This never materialised and, availing of the post-exchange stores (shops for American military personnel), American soldiers introduced chewing gum and Camel cigarettes to the streets of Northern Ireland. Occasional street brawls, both internecine and with local men, provided the only real conflict. With rationing restricting the supply of foodstuffs in Northern Ireland, American goods became coveted and many black market exchanges took place between locals and troops. Like their British counterparts, US army personnel would visit neutral Ireland to purchase liquor. The victim of the largest individual seizure recorded was a private William McCrea who was caught at Brookeborough, County Fermanagh, in 1944 with ten bottles of whiskey hidden unconvincingly about his person.[103]

Dumps, donkeys and dinghies: different modes of smuggling

For many, cross-border smuggling was based around the train journey. For those living closer to the border, small purpose-built shops and huts were opened by shrewd traders to better facilitate the black trade. These sheds acted as dumps for goods to be smuggled or sold to people on the opposite side. Continuous surveillance by Customs men only resulted in the sheds temporarily ceasing business. Despite renewed efforts by Irish border authorities to clamp down on smuggling activity from 1941 onwards, the closeness of the sheds to the border made detection difficult because it proved almost impossible to secure convictions unless suspects were caught in the physical act of taking goods across. Even when the proprietors of the sheds and their customers were witnessed doing business by Gardaí or Customs officers, this proximity spared the participants from prosecution: 'In one case the shop was so close to the border that even with Customs stationed on the road, customers were able to escape with goods through a field at the back of the border.'[104]

This unhappy situation for Customs officers was ostensibly remedied by Lemass through Emergency Powers (no. 267) Order (1943). This legislation forbade the owners of any such premises south of the border to sell certain items and empowered Customs to close the businesses. It also prevented the opening of any new retail premises within three miles of the border without the permission of the Minister for Supplies. Again, the effectiveness of the legislation is questionable: only five such premises were closed and each one eventually reopened; the owner of a shop operating from a labourer's cottage was prosecuted, but the case failed on technical grounds.[105]

Professional smuggling outfits grew up and were sustained because of the profits to be made, based on the demand for goods that were scarce on one side but plentiful on the other. The smuggling of large quantities of alcohol is evidenced in contemporary newspaper accounts. In October 1942, a dump of 100 bottles of brandy and gin was discovered in a Clones graveyard,[106] and in 1944, a number of men were imprisoned for smuggling spirits (of the liquid variety) across the border in coffins.[107] Wine was not a popular drink in Ireland at the time, but nevertheless, Customs records reveal that the illegal importation of wine north increased considerably during the

Emergency;[108] the smuggling of champagne was also detected with some frequency.[109] These trends reflected the growing demand for alcohol among a population enlarged by service people. Those who smuggled in great quantities took greater risks. If caught with a substantial amount of any goods, the fines imposed by District Courts south of the border and petty session courts north of the border were hefty. Imprisonment was a much more likely outcome for bigger smuggling offences. For instance, a man caught with seven bottles of brandy and five bottles of whiskey in 1944 was handed four months' imprisonment by northern authorities.[110]

There was at least one significant engagement between gangs of flour smugglers and the authorities where the latter came off worse. In March 1940, over 100 young men, accompanied by several dozen donkeys and ponies, over which were slung bags of smuggled flour, quietly passed over the border from Fermanagh into Cavan. Early in the morning, and two miles into the southern state, they unwittingly marched straight into a Customs patrol. A moonlight battle ensued between smugglers, armed with sticks and stones, and baton-wielding Gardaí. Donkeys and ponies, terrified, added to the confusion as they charged through the crowd of fighting men. Several members of the Gardaí were injured.[111] The guards were forced to retreat and called in the military from Sligo, who dispatched live rounds. The men escaped but left two tons of abandoned flour and several donkeys behind them.[112] The incident made the Italian newspaper *La Tribuna Illustrata* which, bizarrely, covered the story as an anti-British propaganda piece highlighting the injustice of partition. The Italian article, sent to the *Leitrim Observer* by an Irish priest based in the Vatican, even mentioned where the smugglers were apprehended: Dowra. This led the solicitor defending some of the men at a later trial to remark proudly that Dowra was noted, but never before in Rome.[113]

The sheer number of men involved in the incident illustrates the extent and organisation of smuggling rackets operative during the Emergency. This was indeed a 'battle royal', as a local newspaper termed it, between smugglers, Gardaí and Customs officials.[114] This type of smuggler was undoubtedly more of the 'Bill Sykes type' than 'the pompous and respectable looking citizen', as Lemass put it. For instance, in a 1940 incident, a Customs man was hospitalised after being repeatedly kicked in the face and stomach by a smuggler.[115] The 'Spiv' character – young, male, brash and suave – was a fixture of cross-border black market exchanges. An example of 'Spiv' activity was the 1942 trial in Belfast of two young men accused of selling 2,500 smuggled silk stockings manufactured in Dublin to gullible commercial travellers.[116] Unlike individual smugglers, smuggling rackets – particularly those operating from Northern Ireland, where petrol was more readily available – sometimes availed of cars and lorries.[117] Boats were used as well. Due to hull space, smuggling by boat lent itself to gang activity. In Down, so-called Smart Boys would row across to County Louth to trade tea for butter. The appearance of Customs men on the opposite bank resulted in many a load of butter being jettisoned, floating out to sea from Carlingford Lough.[118] The black market trade at Carlingford Lough was noted in a

Garda report of 1941, which provides evidence that 'a system of barter' had developed on both sides.[119] Observing the shores of Lough Erne in County Fermanagh at night, RUC men were able to detect smugglers through the disturbance of swans by their boats and dinghies.[120]

Smuggling by waterway afforded secretive access denied when crossing the heavily policed land border. In 1942, a court official from Fermanagh revealed the huge expenses he had incurred when issuing a petty sessions summons to a man who had been caught smuggling butter and blankets in a boat. The smuggler had sailed to Fermanagh from the isle of Inishturk, off the Mayo coast, up the river Erne. This Odyssean journey illustrates the gravity of shortages off Ireland's west coast. The court official travelled south to issue the summons, but after he had revealed his identity as an official from the northern statelet, no local men would row him to the island, and he had to eventually pay a 'colossal' sum to get to Inishturk.[121] Lough Erne itself, dotted with 365 islands, provided a fertile geography for smuggling activity.

Another frequently overlooked but significant means of smuggling during the Emergency was through parcel post. The development of this postal black trade demonstrates, once more, the frustration of officials in other departments of state at Supplies' omnipotence and the practical limitations of the war against smuggling. Responding to a request by the UK Trade Commissioner, Irish postal censorship provided sample data for a week in the summer of 1940. In those seven days, it was revealed that 1,000 pounds of tea and 1,700 pounds of sugar had been exported by Irish people to relatives in Northern Ireland and Britain.[122] Often, fictitious particulars were listed on the Customs declarations forms attached to parcels. There was also much concern in Dublin at the practice of Belfast men coming to Dublin, buying up quantities of needles, flints, haircurlers and other such goods and exporting them north through parcel post. One man was reputed to have posted 125 parcels in one day.[123] Ostensibly, this form of smuggling could have been averted through instructing postal workers to exercise greater diligence. However, the 'haphazard' and frequently changing list of articles banned for export by Supplies proved understandably difficult for postal workers to comprehend. Although a Customs official was likely to know that the section of Supplies' list of articles banning 'cutlery, hardware, implements and instruments' included wristwatches, a postal worker was unlikely to possess the same level of understanding. In a well-publicised 1945 case, a gang which had smuggled £50,000 worth of wristwatches was almost acquitted on the grounds that the acceptance of the parcels by postal staff meant that they had never needed an export licence.[124] Earlier in the Emergency, Supplies' strong-arm tactics to eradicate the parcel post trade were met with a cool attitude from the Irish post office. In August 1943, inspectors from Supplies were refused entry into post offices to open parcels bound for Northern Ireland because workers had been informed by management that no interference with the post was permissible except via individual warrants from the Minister for Justice.[125]

Elite forms of smuggling also affected wartime Ireland. The British secret service identified Lisbon as the epicentre of the Europe-wide black market in fake bank notes, some of which made their way to Irish banks. The fraud, facilitated by German agents, was aided by the concealment of currency in diplomatic bags, which were exempted from customs inspection. Noting that a number of counterfeit Bank of England notes had turned up in Ireland, the British sounded a note of political anxiety: 'it is usually impossible to trace the recipients of £5 notes in Ireland and it is never very satisfactory to find suspect notes turning up in that country'.[126] While currency may have been brought into Ireland by merchant sailors on the Lisbon route, these notes are likely have been introduced by German spy Gunther Schuetz, one of a number of Nazi agents at large in Ireland hoping to exploit anti-partitionist sentiment.[127]

Reflections on the moral economy of smuggling

Although it is impossible to quantify, the new smuggling was certainly intensive. A Garda report of September 1941 details 183 petty seizures at Omeath, County Louth, in one month alone.[128] As a 1941 *Irish Times* piece correctly identified, this black market thrived on the political dividend which the contested nature of the border afforded. 'The authorities on both sides of the border seem to be shutting their eyes to this pleasant little game of money-making', the columnist mused; 'unless the civic conscience of the people can be mobilised it will continue'.[129] However, civic conscience was one thing, Ireland's prevalent political and economic culture another altogether. While 'Sunday excursionists' did not go as far as to make 'shopping bags the weapons in a new economic war',[130] they certainly used the politically contested nature of the border to legitimate their activity.

During the Emergency, popular anti-partitionism was stoked by several influential publications. Of these, 'Orange Terror', which appeared in the *Capuchin Annual* in 1940 and 1943, was the most widely read. Republished in pamphlet form, its cover depicted a monstrous Protestant crushing Catholics in a vice labelled 'pogrom'. In its account of the harassment of the Catholic population, it struck a moral economic note specific to wartime conditions, claiming that Catholic 'small business folk, coal vendors, shopkeepers' had been displaced by 'war-vultures with money to speculate'. Unemployed Catholics were, the pamphlet claimed, 'offered the alternative of going to England to danger areas to work, or being put off the dole'.[131]

For Catholics in Northern Ireland, smuggling could provide economic opportunities which were otherwise unavailable. As a County Down Catholic from a middle-class, large farming family stated 'as a Catholic everything was closed to ya'.[132] Smuggling provided access to cheap food and resources or – if undertaken frequently – a form of work. Likewise, appealing to popular republicanism, the flour smugglers of Dowra could have reasonably complained that their apprehension and prosecution buttressed the very border which their government and constitution opposed.

One of the favourite themes of the *Irish Press* was anti-partitionism, underlined by its resoundingly negative coverage of proceedings at Stormont. In the European context, engagement on the black market was often construed as an act of resistance to the occupier.[133] If pressed to legitimise their activity, smugglers from nationalist communities in Northern Ireland may have justified their behaviour in similar terms.

Adding to this tension, relations between Catholics' spiritual leaders and the Northern Irish state were certainly rocky during the Emergency. Tensions were inflamed in 1941 when the Lenten pastoral of Cardinal Joseph MacRory, Archbishop of Armagh and Primate of All Ireland, was withheld by censorship officials in Northern Ireland. 'It is an intimate, important and exclusive document, which a civil government has no right to uphold', fumed MacRory.[134] MacRory's main theme was not the condemnation of partition and discrimination against Catholics in Northern Ireland. It is likely that the censor was irked by his more general articulation of Ireland's moral neutrality. He claimed that God had inflicted the war to punish 'a wicked world', that it would continue until God's justice was satisfied and that materialist statesmen had encroached upon 'the God-given rights of the Church, the family and the individual'.[135] As such, it seems unwise that MacRory was censored for expressing his worldview, rather than criticised for encouraging crime through his explicit anti-partitionism. The anti-partitionist sentiment of many other Catholic bishops in Ulster certainly did little to deter smugglers who justified their activity by pointing to a moral and political cause. At his enthronement as Bishop of Clogher in 1943, Eugene O'Callaghan claimed that 'the evil of partition' militated 'against the possibility of good citizenship'.[136] Similarly, at his enthronement as Bishop of Derry in 1939, Neil Farren referred to 'the mutilation of our country'.[137] In his Lenten pastoral of 1942, he delivered a message which noted the 'occasions and temptations of mischief' that had arisen due to the different rationing restrictions but blamed them on 'the unnatural border'.[138]

Smuggling was not seen by many of its participants as a selfish act undermining a moral economy. Instead, according to an *Irish Independent* editorial, it was a crime commonly regarded with a genial tolerance.[139] All manner of people engaged in the black trade in small goods around the border: publicans, teachers, waitresses, labourers, housewives, soldiers and policemen. Restaurants and pubs in Belfast openly sold southern ration books. Similarly, in Donegal resorts female inspectors from Supplies posing as visitors from Northern Ireland were able to purchase a massive amount of goods without using coupons.[140] In the popular nationalist mentality, anti-partition sentiment acted as a potent political motive for illegal cross-border market activity. This anti-partitionist attitude was conveyed by a Derry priest who wrote to de Valera in 1944 to complain of his apprehension by Gardaí for using his car in non-essential circumstances. In complaining against a fine issued by Supplies for doing so, he claimed 'Mr Leydon is enforcing partition'.[141]

Moreover, the impracticalities of the land frontier were commonly resented by those residents in the border counties whose daily patterns of life it threatened.

Smuggling, an established activity in these areas, thrived during the Emergency. However, it is evident that for residents in both territories and for members of both political traditions, adherence to the common weal, even in time of emergency, frequently vied not only with the base want created by shortages but also with more selfish manifestations of historically and economically rooted Irish 'individualist values'.[142] Engagement with the black market, then, does much to dispel the popular representation of independent Ireland during the Emergency as a Catholic, rural and conservative nation suffering from an absence of deviance and a surfeit of spirituality.

All the same, to represent theft and smuggling as an enactment of moral economic principles rooted in political tradition rather than the rumblings of hungry stomachs or avarice would be simplistic. Involvement in the black market, even at the lowest level, satisfied greed and compromised equitable distribution. Not all smuggling operated on a moral economic understanding between the Irish state and its citizens (or northern adherents) that plunder of the neighbouring demesne was quietly sanctioned. Religious leaders in both territories complained of the damage to the common good caused by smuggling, denouncing its particularly corrupting influence on the many children involved.[143] As a County Roscommon clergyman insisted in 1944, the black market, with its 'grisly train of injustice and perjury', had led to the 'exploitation of the needs of the poorest in the land'.[144] Smugglers may have disagreed with the somewhat contradictory anti-border/anti-smuggling stance of church and state, but their activities were also frequently borne of a greed that was popularly disliked. Indeed, in 1942 a large number of locals on the Fermanagh–Monaghan border attacked smugglers loading white loaves, tea and bicycle tyres into a lorry, incensed at professional gangs increasing the price of the loaf from five pence to nine pence in that area.[145]

But for all that, officials from the two administrations subsequently took diverging post-war attitudes toward state regulation. In doing so, the smuggling experience of the war years was highly influential. As mentioned above, when it came to flour smuggling, Leydon wavered from an unequivocally firm anti-black market stance.[146] With the end of the Emergency in sight, Lemass, in his 1944 speech to retailers, similarly claimed to favour trade self-regulation and a return to normal trading conditions.[147] In contrast to the return to post-war harmony between business and state south of the border, officials in Belfast stridently opposed post-war calls from the bread trade that it continue to be self-regulated. Rubbishing the continuation of trade interests blacklisting their own 'bad eggs', senior civil servants in Northern Ireland claimed that this would lead to 'a series of abuses' because the bread trader would 'favour his better-to-do customers, the member of his own church, his own lodge'. Instead, they favoured the introduction of bread rationing so that 'poor people get their proper share'.[148] These differing visions exemplify the post-war distaste for state interventionism and the willingness to embrace it, respectively.

Conclusion

Wartime smuggling was certainly exacerbated by both the border and anti-partition-ism, but was not unique to divided Ireland. Thousands of Spaniards were attracted to the higher wages of the German war economy and were able to supplement their income by smuggling coffee and cognac into Nazi-controlled Europe to sell on the black market there.[149] In Switzerland and Sweden, reliant on certain fuel and food imports from occupied Europe, illegal goods also found a ready market. Thanks to film and literature, some of this black market activity is now almost proverbial; in particular, Michael Curtiz's *Casablanca* (1942) ensured that the black markets of wartime Lisbon (infused with political dimensions, as in Ireland) became famous.

Smuggling had been a feature of life in the Irish border region since the border was imposed and it intensified during the Economic War. Such activity did not end with the resolution of this conflict in 1938. Rather, it changed significantly in nature during the Emergency due to the restrictions imposed by rationing. Differing mar-ket regulation in both territories was the main reason why a 'new form of smuggling', as the RUC Inspector General described it, developed.[150] Many northerners desired more meat and butter than their ration permitted, and many southerners desired more white flour and tea. Hence, a reciprocal trade developed in commodities restricted in one territory but more readily available in the other.

It is unclear whether the smuggling of the Emergency was greater in volume than that of the Economic War years. Naturally, police reports from both sides of the bor-der emphasised the success of the authorities through listing seizures and prosecu-tions in both periods. Cattle smuggling continued during the Emergency, particularly in counties where it was something of a tradition, like Monaghan. However, the easy concealment of goods made the new smuggling easier and more accessible. Signifi-cantly, smuggling was incorporated into daily economic patterns by the considerable movement of labour between the two territories. Despite the class-based disdain for 'Sunday excursionists', smuggling transcended the neat classification of participants by class, occupation and status. Professional operations aside, smuggling was carried out by children, servicemen and workers and – most notably – women.

Smuggling was discouraged by authorities on either side of the border as a dero-gation of the wartime moral economy of rationing and equitable distribution. But while there is every evidence that greed and racketeering was popularly resented, it is also apparent that in almost every regard, the issue was infused by politics. Politi-cal discord underlay the absence of unilateral trading agreements between Northern Ireland and independent Ireland during the Emergency. This lack of cross-border collaboration secured the persistence of the material motive for smuggling as well as its political legitimation. After the British trade squeeze of 1941, the Irish govern-ment began to take cross-border smuggling more seriously. The short supply of cer-tain commodities, however, ensured that smuggling was quietly tolerated. Therefore, the anti-smuggling message of church and state did not assume the clamour of the anti-black market message. After all, the latter, focused domestically, was politically less contentious. The somewhat contradictory pronouncements of Catholic Ireland's spiritual leaders on the border and smuggling provide a good example of the nationalist anti-partitionist hegemony of the age,[151] and the church's broader attitude to the economy in Emergency Ireland is discussed subsequently.

As for much of the twentieth century, uneven market regulation and price disparity characterised cross-border trade during the Emergency; consequently smuggling – and the many forms of smuggler – thrived.

Notes

1 See Michael Kennedy, *Division and Consensus: The Politics of Cross-Border Relations in Ireland, 1925–1969* (Dublin, 2000), 95.
2 *Dáil Debates*, vol. 74, col. 2, 8 February 1939.
3 See David S. Johnson, 'Cattle Smuggling on the Irish Border, 1932–38', *Irish Economic and Social History*, 6 (1979), 41–63.
4 Basil Brooke, Memorandum on the Smuggling of Cattle from the Irish Free State into Northern Ireland. Public Record Office of Northern Ireland (PRONI), Cabinet Files (CAB)/4/348/18.
5 David S. Johnson, 'Northern Ireland as a Problem in the Economic War 1932–1938', *Irish Historical Studies*, 22, 86 (September 1980), 150.
6 Kennedy, *Division and Consensus*, 70–73.
7 Kennedy, *Division and Consensus*, 73–78.
8 Supplies, 'Record of Activities'. NAI, IND/EHR/3/15, p. 7.
9 See PRONI, Customs Files (CUS)/1/7/1/1–3, CUS/1/7/2/7–9 and CUS/3/7/1/1–2/12 for comprehensive registers of seizures from Belfast, Enniskillen, Crossmaglen and Newry, respectively.
10 Brian Barton, *Northern Ireland in the Second World War* (Belfast, 1995), 10.
11 'Eire Border Check Up', broadcast 27 March 1943. PRONI, Northern Ireland Digital Film Archive (NIDFA).
12 Garda report, 7 December 1944. NAI, FA/P305/1.
13 G.S. Robertson to D.E. Vandepeer, 20 September 1938. PRONI, CAB/9/R/57/5.
14 Robertson to R. Gransden, 8 February 1937. PRONI, CAB/9/R/57/5.
15 Robertson to D.E. Vandepeer, 20 September 1938. PRONI, CAB/9/R/57/5.
16 *Anglo-Celt*, 30 November 1940.
17 *Report of Customs and Excise Surveyor*, Enniskillen, 10 July 1943. PRONI, CUS/1/7/2/8.
18 Robertson to Vandepeer, 20 September 1938. PRONI, CAB/9/R/57/5.
19 Supplies, 'Historical Survey'. NAI, IND/EHR/3/C4, part XI, p. 505.
20 'Historical Survey'. NAI, IND/EHR/3/C4, part XI, p. 505.
21 'Purchase of quantities of foodstuffs by people traveling on Belfast Excursion Trains', NAI, JUS/8/868.
22 'Historical Survey'. NAI, IND/EHR/3/C4, part XI, p. 506.
23 'Inspection Branch'. NAI, IND/EHR/3/4, p. 5.

24 'Historical Survey'. NAI, IND/EHR/3/C4, part XI, p. 506.
25 *Anglo-Celt*, 25 October 1941.
26 John Leydon to J. Connolly, 24 May 1941. MA, OCC/2/57.
27 M. Lee to Craigavon, 23 November 1939. PRONI, CAB/9/CD/4/4.
28 R. Courtney to Craigavon, 17 May 1940. PRONI, CAB/9/CD/4/4.
29 'Food Control Licensing of Retail Food Businesses'. PRONI, CAB/9/CD/4/5.
30 *Report on Ministry of Food's 'Food Economy' Campaign in Northern Ireland*, 27 November
    1940. PRONI, AG/16/19/3.
31 Meeting of the National Food Campaign Consultative Council, 22 May 1940. PRONI,
    AG/16/19/3.
32 F. Stewart to Andrews, 6 July 1942. PRONI, CAB/9/CD/4/4.
33 Parr to W.D. Scott, 13 February 1940. PRONI, CAB/9/CD/4/2.
34 Mid-Armagh Unionist Association to Brooke, 1 May 1944. PRONI, CAB/9/CD/4/3.
35 Phil Ollerenshaw, 'War, Industrial Mobilisation and Society in Northern Ireland,
    1939–45', *Contemporary European History*, 16, 2 (2007), 169–197.
36 Minutes of the cabinet sub-committee on Infiltration of Workers from Eire, 5 February
    1942. PRONI, CAB/4A/21.
37 Sub-committee on Infiltration of Workers, PRONI, CAB/4A/21.
38 For the minutes of the first manpower committee (1941), see PRONI, CAB/4A/18;
    for the minutes of the second (1943), see PRONI, CAB/4/545.
39 Minutes of the cabinet manpower committee, 16 June 1943. PRONI,
    CAB/4A/24/1/1.
40 Minutes of the cabinet sub-committee on Labour, PRONI, CAB/4A/24/1/1.
41 Cabinet minutes, 5 May 1942. NAI, DT/S13029 A.
42 Supplies, 'Inspection Branch'. NAI, IND/EHR/3/4, p. 5.
43 C.M. Martin-Jones to R. Gransden, 20 January 1940. PRONI, CAB/9/R/57/5.
44 F. Gilliland to Craigavon, 13 October 1941. PRONI, CAB/9/CD/4/4.
45 William Davin, *Dáil Debates*, vol. 81, col. 15, 2 October 1940.
46 Minutes of cabinet meeting, 18 March 1941. PRONI, CAB/4/466.
47 *Sunday Independent*, 25 September 1940.
48 *Anglo-Celt*, 3 February 1940.
49 C.G. Wickham to W.A.B. Iliff, 18 October 1941. PRONI, CAB/9/CD/4/4.
50 Censor's Report for September 1944. UCDA, Aiken papers, P104/3499.
51 *Sunday Independent*, 18 June 1943.
52 *Dublin Opinion*, December 1941.
53 *Report of Customs and Excise Surveyor*, Enniskillen, 16 and 27 September 1939. PRONI,
    CUS/1/7/2/8.
54 Wills, *Neutral Island*, 241.
55 Wickham to Iliff, PRONI, CAB/9/CD/4/4.
56 *Dáil Debates*, vol. 83, col. 352, 14 May 1941.
57 Divisional Food Office to R. Gransden, 19 June 1943. PRONI, CAB/9/CD/4/4.
58 Northern Ireland Master Bakers' Association and Divisional Food Office Conference,
    29 September 1941. PRONI, CAB/9/CD/4/4.
59 See Rigney, *Trains*.
60 John Betjeman to John and Myfanwy Piper, 20 April 1941, in Green, John Betjeman, 286.

61 GNR Mechanical Engineers' Office Letter Index 1940, Louth County Archives (LCA), Mallon collection, PP206/002, p. 353.

62 *Irish Independent,* 3 October 1944.

63 Customs and Excise Surveyor, Enniskillen, to Manager, SLNCR, 23 September 1943. PRONI, CUS/1/7/2/9.

64 'Historical Survey'. NAI, IND/EHR/3/C4, part XI, p. 506.

65 Joe McGrew, b. 1929, Omagh, co. Tyrone. Interviewed 4 August 2008.

66 'Historical Survey'. NAI, IND/EHR/3/C4, part XI, p. 505.

67 Wills, *Neutral Island,* 154.

68 Ann McGeeney, cited in Paddy Logue ed. *The Border: Personal Reflections from Ireland North and South,* (Dublin, 1999), 105.

69 Joe McGrew, b.1929, Omagh, co. Tyrone. Interviewed 4 August 2008.

70 www.bbc.co.uk/ww2peopleswar/stories/88/a5865988.shtml. Accessed 4 December 2008.

71 Brian O'Neill, b. 1937, Omagh, co. Tyrone. Interviewed 4 August 2008.

72 Joe McGrew, b. 1929, Omagh, co. Tyrone. Interviewed 4 August 2008.

73 Sheila O'Neill, b. 1928, Omagh, co. Tyrone, letter received 29 September 2008.

74 Letter Index, 42/488, p. 55; 40/1053, p. 59; 40/1222, p. 58; 40/1053, p. 58; 42/1298, p. 346.

75 Customs Surveyor, Enniskillen, to Manager, SLNRC, 23 September 1943. PRONI, CUS/1/7/2/9.

76 'Food Economy Campaign in Northern Ireland'. PRONI, AG/16/19/3.

77 C.M. Martin-Jones to R. Gransden, 20 January 1940. PRONI, CAB/9/R/57/5.

78 *Report of Customs and Excise Surveyor,* Enniskillen, 25 September 1939. PRONI, CUS/1/7/2/8.

79 Blake, *Northern Ireland,* 98.

80 Lettie Hill, b. 1920, Ballyconnell, co. Cavan. Interviewed 17 July 2008.

81 Record of Seizures, 26 February 1945. PRONI, CUS/1/7/1/3.

82 Pat Masterson, b. 1922, co. Leitrim. Interviewed 17 July 2008.

83 Record of Seizures, PRONI, CUS/3/7/2/4.

84 Customs and Excise Surveyor, Enniskillen to Bridget Gallagher, 4 January 1944. PRONI, CUS/1/7/2/9.

85 Report of Seizures, PRONI, CUS 3/7/2/5.

86 *Anglo-Celt,* 25 October 1940.

87 *Anglo-Celt,* 11 April 1942.

88 *Anglo-Celt,* 29 November 1941.

89 Brian O'Neill, b. 1937, Omagh, co. Tyrone. Interviewed 4 August 2008.

90 Barton, *Northern Ireland,* 10.

91 John Sinder to Messrs. Collins and Collins, PRONI, CUS/3/7/2/6.

92 Clear, *Women of the House,* 202–215.

93 Record of Seizures, 15 October 1943. PRONI, CUS/1/7/1/1.

94 Record of Seizures, 5 August 1944. PRONI, CUS/1/7/1/2.

95 *Anglo-Celt,* 29 November 1941.

96 339 (13 June 1941), Dublin Garda Index to Special Files, 1929–1945.

97 Record of Seizures, 14 September 1944. PRONI, CUS/1/7/1/2.

98   Record of Seizures, 6 March 1943. PRONI, CUS/1/7/1/3.
99   Record of Seizures, 6 November 1943. PRONI, CUS/1/7/1/1.
100 Leanne. McCormick, "One Yank and They're Off": Interaction between U.S. Troops and Northern Irish Women, 1942–1945', *Journal of History of Sexuality*, 15, 2(2006), 228.
101 Blake, *Northern Ireland*, 289.
102 *Belfast Newsletter*, 2 September 1942. NAI, JUS/8/940.
103 Record of Seizures, PRONI, CUS/1/7/1/1.
104 'Historical Survey'. NAI, IND/EHR/3/C4, part XI, p. 507.
105 'Historical Survey'. NAI, IND/EHR/3/C4, part XI, p. 508.
106 *Anglo-Celt*, 10 October 1942.
107 *Anglo-Celt*, 24 June 1944.
108 See Record of Seizures, 21 April 1944. PRONI, CUS/1/7/1/2.
109 See *Report of Customs and Excise Surveyor*, Enniskillen, 13 October 1943. PRONI, CUS/1/7/2/9.
110 Record of Seizures, 6 January 1944. PRONI, CUS/1/7/1/1.
111 *Anglo-Celt*, 18 May 1940.
112 *Leitrim Observer*, 30 March 1940.
113 *Leitrim Observer*, 18 May 1940.
114 *Anglo-Celt*, 18 May 1940.
115 *Anglo-Celt*, 24 February 1940.
116 Brief for Counsel – the King versus Alexander McBratney and Bernard Henry Collins, 8 April 1942. PRONI, D2587/3/7.
117 Record of Seizures, 11 December 1944. PRONI, CUS/1/7/1/2.
118 Tony Canavan, *Frontier Town: An Illustrated History of Newry* (Belfast, 1989), 210.
119 Garda report, 8 August 1941. NAI, FA/P305/1.
120 *Anglo-Celt*, 4 January 1941.
121 George G. Magrath to G.G. Down. PRONI, CUS/3/7/2/5.
122 'Historical Survey'. NAI, IND/EHR/3/C4, part XI, p. 510.
123 'Historical Survey'. NAI, IND/EHR/3/C4, part XI, p. 511.
124 'Historical Survey'. NAI, IND/EHR/3/C4, part XI, p. 512.
125 'Historical Survey'. NAI, IND/EHR/3/C4, part XI, p. 513.
126 'Report on the Operation of B.I.B. in connection with Financial and Currency During the War 1939–1945', NAUK, MI5 records, KV4/465.
127 Stephan, *Spies in Ireland*, 187.
128 Garda Report, 11 September, 1941. NAI, FA/P305/1.
129 *Irish Times*, 8 September 1941.
130 Wills, *Neutral Island*, 153.
131 Ultach, 'Orange Terror: The Partition of Ireland' (Dublin, 1943).
132 MIOA, Jack Magill, b. 1927, Saul, co. Down. Interviewed 16 April 2000, p. 8.
133 Milward, *War, Economy and Society*, 282.
134 *Irish Independent*, 20 May 1941.
135 *Leitrim Observer*, 4 March 1941.
136 Eugene O'Callaghan, cited in Daithí Ó Corráin, *Rendering to God and Caesar: The Irish Churches and the Two States in Ireland, 1949–73* (Manchester, 2008), 44.
137 Neil Farren, cited in Ó Corráin, *Rendering*, 44.

138 *Irish Press*, 16 February 1942.

139 *Irish Independent*, 27 July 1943.

140 'Inspection Branch'. NAI, IND/EHR/3/4, p. 5.

141 Father Felix O'Neill to de Valera, 8 August, 1944. NAI, DT, RA/103/44.

142 Cormac Ó Gráda, 'Primogeniture and Ultimogeniture in Rural Ireland', *Journal of Interdisciplinary History*, 10, 3 (Winter 1980), 495.

143 Barton, *Northern Ireland*, 10.

144 Father D. Doorly, Lenten Pastoral on the black market, cited in *Leitrim Observer*, 26 February 1944.

145 *Anglo-Celt*, 28 February 1942.

146 Leydon to Connolly, 24 May 1941. MA, OCC/2/57.

147 Lemass to the National Convention of Retail, Grocery, Dairy and Allied Trades' Associations, 29 November 1944. NAI, Tweedy Papers, 98/17/5/5/43.

148 G. Scott Robertson to Frank Tribe, 25 June 1946. PRONI, CAB/9/CD/4/5.

149 Bowen, *Spain*, 120.

150 C.G. Wickham to W.A.B. Iliff, 18 October 1941. PRONI, CAB/9/CD/4/4.

151 See Stephen Kelly, *Fianna Fáil, Partition and Northern Ireland, 1926–1971* (Dublin, 2013).

6

Church and state

The key to Ireland is the Church, its pontiffs, the Nuncio, MacRory and McQuaid and
I think we should bother less about relations, good or bad, with the Government and
more with relations with the Catholic Church.

John Betjeman, 21 March 1943

Subsidiary function

The exercise of collective responsibility to overcome material shortages infused political, economic and social debate during the Emergency. It also came to affect many
aspects of everyday life: Irish people were not used to queuing, yet during the Emergency, food queues became a 'fact of life'.[1] These new 'facts of life' were ordered by the
state. At the same time, Catholic social thought proffered an alternative form of social
and economic organisation. In this schema, by contrast, the state's role was reduced
to a 'subsidiary function'.[2] Catholic social doctrine was based on the papal encyclicals
Rerum Novarum (1891) and *Quadragesimo Anno* (1931). The latter elaborated papal
doctrine on twentieth-century social and economic questions, declaring that in its
pursuit of the 'common good', the state should extend 'special care and foresight' to
the 'great mass of the needy'.[3] On the other hand, the state should not encroach on the
just freedom of individuals and families. It reaffirmed the rights of private property
and declared that the state was 'not permitted to discharge its duty arbitrarily'.[4]

Party political affiliations to Catholic social thought became confused in the tur-
bulent political circumstances of the 1930s.[5] De Valera's 1937 Constitution was per-
vasively Catholic in comparison to the Free State Constitution of 1922. Nonetheless,
a substantial number of clergy and theologians remained unreconciled to Fianna
Fáil, and around the middle of the decade, several senior ecclesiastics endorsed the
United Ireland Party, an amalgamation of the Blueshirts, Cumann na nGaedheal
and the Centre Party.[6] During the Emergency, social Catholicism, or vocationalism,
persisted as an influential form of public opinion, and conformity with the church's
moral and social principles remained a priority for Irish Catholics.[7]

The government responded to the growing prominence of vocationalism by
establishing the Commission on Vocational Organisation in January 1939. The

commission's 1943 report warned of the danger, on the one hand, of 'competitive anarchy' and, on the other, of 'state regimentation'.[8] The latter consideration united a commission delayed in its appointment and hamstrung by its size and diversity of interests. To quote its chairman, Bishop Michael Browne of Galway, 'the one point on which all the members are agreed is that they abhor totalitarianism or state-domination in any form ... whether communist, socialist or fascist'.[9] During the Emergency, the state accumulated power and initiated schemes which, in encroaching upon individual freedom and property rights, tickled this particular nerve. This chapter details the complex interactions between church and state at this time in the spheres of the regulated marketplace, civil and canon law, and money and credit.

'A sin that cries to heaven for vengeance': church, state and marketplace

Using the *Irish Press*, Radio Éireann, and its power of censorship over the rest of the media, the Fianna Fáil governments of the Emergency carefully cultivated an image of the Irish people as exceptional in shunning the base lure of materialism. Yet they did not shy from attacking the spiritual failings of the Irish populace either. As mentioned previously, in 1943, Minister for Justice Gerald Boland expressed concern that 'our morality is not as deep-seated as it ought to be'.[10]

Typically, pronouncements from the Catholic hierarchy and the clergy chimed with this anti-materialist message. A Lenten pastoral of 1941, for example, celebrated the 'comparative poverty' of Ireland as having saved her from war.[11] Evidently though, the wide-ranging market regulation and moral economic rhetoric introduced by Seán Lemass failed to combat consumer demand in a period of short supply. In particular, the flouting of Lemass's sporadic Control of Prices Orders was widespread. The seriousness of the situation was highlighted by a letter to the editor of the *Irish Independent* in mid-1943. It claimed that 'every shop in the country is a black market', with flour and other goods openly being sold at prices well in excess of fixed prices.[12]

The significance of such breaches to the state's fixed prices was discussed in a series of responses in the 'Notes and Queries' section of the monthly publication *The Irish Ecclesiastical Record*. In these, Maynooth theologian John McCarthy supported the state's role. In December 1941, McCarthy discussed the case of the metaphorical 'Caius', who had smuggled tea over the border to sell in Dublin at ten shillings per pound. 'The maximum retail price of tea in Éire has been fixed by an order of the Minister of Supplies at three shillings per pound', wrote McCarthy. In selling tea at 'the much higher price', 'Caius' was guilty of 'a very serious violation of commutative justice'.[13] He added that even theologians who considered tax and pricing legislation as purely penal 'admit that whoever violates these laws is bound, if the violation is discovered, to accept the penalty imposed'.[14] Therefore, according to McCarthy, 'Caius' had committed an offence under both canon and civil law, offending God as much as Caesar.

But while McCarthy's response represented an endorsement of the state's version of moral economy, it contained loopholes. He noted that people were bound through both conscience and commutative justice to observe the legally fixed price 'unless it is *manifestly* unjust' and 'Caius' was at fault for selling tea at 'the *much* higher price'.[15] The article prompted a flood of letters to the *Ecclesiastical Record*, unusual for a clerical scholarly publication which lacked a wide general readership. The content of letters on the subject was noted in the journal. This suggests that flouting of controlled prices was prevalent and justified by reference to a higher authority than the Minister for Supplies.

One letter claimed that 'the general opinion among the people is that ten or twelve shillings per pound for tea is not unfair' and that there was no excessive profiteering in Caius's case.[16] Another was from a man who had 'stored in plenty of tea according to the past orders of the Government' and questioned whether he was acting unjustly by selling it to his neighbour (who could not get enough tea) at ten shillings per pound.[17] This letter reflected the confusion caused by Lemass's public announcements on supply shortages. These pronouncements varied per commodity and per availability, resulting in the transmission of a paradoxical mixture of advice ranging in its recommendations from hard-nosed self-help to the discouragement of hoarding.

McCarthy responded by denouncing those who 'from the comfortable shelter of anonymity felt free to make varied and vaporous accusations'. He stated that 'legal justice binds in conscience but also under pain of mortal sin if the matter at hand is grave' which, given the supply crisis, he deemed it to be. The state's moral economic right in fixing legal prices was such that 'the Government need not, does not, and sometimes should not take into account the factors of supply and demand'. Black market activity was 'a sin that cries to heaven for vengeance'.[18] McCarthy explicitly defended Lemass from the charge that market regulation was applied 'haphazardly' and declared profiteering 'unjust, whether by private citizen, retailer, wholesaler or manufacturer'.[19]

McCarthy's support for the kind of moral economy offered by the state during the Emergency was mirrored by the endorsement of the hierarchy. In his Lenten pastoral of 1942, for example, Bishop James McNamee of Ardagh and Clonmacnoise attacked the 'materialistic conflict in Europe'. He went on to remind people that a lack of 'co-operation with the civil authority' by involvement in the black market would result in 'a shortage of food more terrible than the failure of the potato crop in the Black Forty Seven'.[20] This anti-black market theme was reiterated in a succession of annual Lenten pastorals throughout the Emergency. In 1943, the *Irish Independent* summed up the message of pastorals read around the country:

> All our problems, even those which at first sight seem to deal with purely material affairs, have a moral and spiritual aspect as well. The backwash of the world upheaval has brought to this country a new spirit of worldliness and a craving for luxury. Many people are benefiting by the necessities of the needy to carry on shameful black market transactions, undeterred alike by the laws of the State and the laws of God. Embezzlement,

robberies, cheating and stealing are becoming painfully common, and often are committed by people whose social standing should designate them as the leaders to whom others ought to be able to turn for guidance. We should lend our united strength to eliminate them, root and branch, from the land.[21]

Other pieces in the *Irish Ecclesiastical Record* repeated McCarthy's stance. E.J. Hegarty, a theologian who in a post-war Dáil debate, claimed that state care 'from the cradle to the grave' would threaten the institution of marriage,[22] aligned closely with the state's version of moral economy during the Emergency. In a 1944 article, he asserted the right of the state to fix prices and regulate the market.[23] Church and state were singing from the same hymn sheet; or so it seemed.

'There's nothing like a nice cup of tea': differing approaches to moral economy

Although the state could count on the general support of the church, there were limits to the coalescence of these two bodies. Although shortages continued towards the end of the Emergency, trade prospects had clearly improved by 1943/1944 as an Allied victory in the war became more likely. At the same time, a small but noticeable shift took place in the public addresses of the hierarchy. Bishops became less introspective. The emphasis on fairness in the domestic marketplace began to share space with broader talk of the coming peace, the character of the future world order and the evils of communism. Although sins taking place at home were still mentioned, by 1944, the bishops expressed concern about 'plans for the post-war world', chiefly the 'danger of deifying the state'.[24] This was in contrast to the pastorals of 1941, 1942 and 1943, which mentioned the war but focused principally on the black market and the food and fuel drive.[25] The principal theme of the Lenten pastorals issued by Irish bishops in 1945 was that the destruction wrought by war had prepared the way for universal 'pagan ideas and practices'.[26]

This general transition was reflected in theological debate. Even McCarthy responded in more conciliatory terms to an acerbic letter to him on the issue of fixed price. 'You have no right to manufacture moral obligations', the letter declared, asserting the popular claim that the state's legal price was merely penal and comparing the self-righteousness of Ireland's theologians to the Pharisees sitting on the chair of Moses. In contrast with his angry earlier denunciations of 'varied and vaporous accusations', McCarthy replied 'it is not within our province or competence to force our view on anybody' and that, in his advocacy of the state's version of moral economy, he had 'merely stated the traditional theological teaching at the point of issue'.[27]

While the laws of the state and the laws of God were often conflated by speakers from political platform and pulpit alike, the essential distinction between spiritual and temporal authority was to lead Catholic intellectuals to point to the theological loopholes in the state's version of moral economy. Noticeably, this questioning spirit took hold in the latter years of the Emergency, as the supply situation began to look somewhat healthier. The theologian E.J. Hegarty, for example, although supportive of the state's measures, endorsed them with more caveats than McCarthy. Hegarty stressed that Catholics were not bound to obey state law if it was excessive. It was not sinful for sellers to 'charge something more' than the controlled price for goods 'provided that the excess is within reasonable limits'. Charging twenty shillings for a pound of tea was wrong, therefore, but charging a shilling or two over the controlled price was justified. After all, he reasoned, 'there's nothing like a nice cup of tea'.[28]

Similarly, another contributor to the *Ecclesiastical Record* cited the Spanish government's control of grain prices in the late sixteenth century. These were unfair, he claimed, as they took no account of changed conditions and variable harvests year-on-year.[29] Again, the 'just price' was established as different to the state price. These theological musings had their popular complement as well. Citing the opinion of 'many theologians', a letter to the *Irish Independent* implied that Lemass's fixed prices were merely an example of penal law. The letter went on to argue that the only sin those charging higher prices than set in the order were committing was one 'against obedience to the State'.[30] These differences between church and state, based on the essentially spiritual vision of the former and the material objective driving the latter, were small but significant. For many people, engagement with the black market and the compromise of equitable distribution that this entailed may have begun with the desire for a 'nice cup of tea'.

If the Emergency's long denouement prompted a less vigorous promotion of the state's type of moral economy by Catholic intellectuals like McCarthy than had been the case amidst the supply crisis of 1941, there were always those of a more radical bent who had questioned the state's role from the very beginning. In two 1941 pieces, *The Standard*, a popular press manifestation of social Catholicism, struck a note against capitalist excess which was typically ambiguous in its attitude towards Lemass's measures to regulate prices and profits. The newspaper declared little sympathy with small retailers who had been prosecuted by the Department of Supplies: 'the retailer must take his share of the hard times which are the lot of us all'.[31] However, it also criticised the banking system and detailed the 'profits in disguise' hidden by big business, contending 'the state which doesn't limit profits and supervise prices is sowing the seed for profiteering, for social unrest, for bloody revolution'.[32]

A piece also written in 1941 by Cornelius Lucey, an outspoken and often anti-establishment cleric, implied criticism of Supplies by declaring business profits 'scandalously excessive' and condemning 'profiteering'.[33] Supplies relied on censorship officials to inform its officials of advertisements that promoted the black trade, but when it came to misleading advertising, the department proved reluctant to censor. Many consumers would have sympathised with the frustration of Lucey, writing earlier in the year, at 'the three different brands of soap advertised in the newspaper before me, all claiming to be the best'.[34] Officials at Supplies, though, were unwilling to extend censorship of advertisements to cover purely ethical issues at corporate level. Instead, the department concentrated on the more quotidian realm of small black market advertisements. Clearly, the state's version of moral economy had limits influenced by more material concerns than Lucey.

Catholic Action provides another example of the social radicalism of church initiatives outstripping those of the state in this period. Reflecting the slowdown in house building and slum clearance, new Dublin Archbishop John Charles McQuaid did little to endear himself to members of the Dublin Corporation when they came to offer him an address of welcome in 1940, berating them for not building more homes for the poor.[35] In April 1941, McQuaid oversaw the creation of the Catholic Social Service Conference (CSSC), a federation of thirty existing Catholic charities comprising nine subcommittees.[36] During the Emergency, the Dublin poor were heavily reliant on the CSSC, which provided thousands of free meals to hungry schoolchildren and by March 1942 had an impressive seventy-seven free clothing guilds alone.[37]

In broad terms, the philosophy of Catholic Action subscribed to that of the vocational lobby, which was critical of the invasive state. Vocationalists were not, though, absolutely opposed to state intervention, as has been seen. Generally, they supported it in so far as it served the common good in a time of crisis. McQuaid, like other bishops, publicly endorsed the state's efforts in this regard. In 1940, he said that Catholics were to accept, in a spirit of obedience, the censorship and food rationing measures which the 'Supreme Civil Authority' found it necessary to ordain and were not to resort to black market activity.[38] The following year, he led by example by agreeing to a request from John Leydon that the number of candles used on altars and shrines in his archdiocese be reduced to overcome shortages in supply.[39]

Essentially, though, the CSSC exhibited a paternalism typical of the corporatist desire to emulate the medieval order and more redolent of a classic pre-capitalist moral economy than state initiatives to this end. As the CSSC grew during the Emergency, the paternalist networks established by McQuaid grew too. Creameries donated milk, butchers gave bones and oxtails, farmers gave sacks of potatoes, Dublin distilleries provided free storage for the CSSC's turf for the poor, and the army stockpiled it.[40] Ultimately, and unlike the state, McQuaid embraced the practical application of an Emergency moral economy on his own, sectarian terms. Alongside a genuine compassion for the poor, there is little doubt that McQuaid entered the field of social services in order to counteract the activities of other, non-sectarian organisations. Unsurprisingly, then, McQuaid was virulently opposed to well-meaning non-state social initiatives if they were not Catholic. He disliked the Irish Housewives Association because of its largely Protestant membership. Similarly, when asked to endorse the Mount Street Club, a secular urban cooperative for unemployed men, he refused, claiming that 'whatever its good work, of set purpose it excludes consideration of the Catholic faith'.[41]

Petrol, priests and protest

Most priests steadfastly promoted the state's vision of moral economy. At the outbreak of war, the *Irish Press* publicised the hierarchy's support for the state. 'Bishops Remind People of Duty in Crisis' ran the headline, accompanied by the bishops' joint appeal to the public to 'place the common good above every private interest' and to 'support loyally the measures which the authorities may deem necessary'. The piece was accompanied by a rather threatening notice to priests notifying them that 'all bishops except three' were present at the meeting from which the remarks were quoted.[42]

Not all priests were obedient, though. At a rally of his 'Rural Reform League' in Gorey in 1942, radical Wexford priest J.F. Sweetman juxtaposed the conditions of life for the small farmer and the agricultural labourer with those of government ministers, judges and higher civil servants, telling the crowd 'the system and order of things' which perpetuated the injustice was 'wrong and immoral'. He urged them to 'unite and work' for their 'social elevation'.[43] In his *public* dissent, Sweetman was exceptional for a clergyman. The attitude of some within the church towards state interventionism during the Emergency diverged markedly from their public stance, but was generally expressed privately. A case in point is Lemass's ban on all 'non-essential motoring', announced in 1942. Under this order, priests were still allowed to use their cars but were restricted to 'urgent and necessary' clerical duties such as visits to people who were gravely ill or dying. Reflecting the fuel crisis and Supplies' concern that priests were availing of their cars for more workaday pursuits, the department issued a 'Warning to Clergymen' in January 1943. Footed by the signature of John Leydon, it reminded clergymen that the use of their cars was confined to 'immediate spiritual consolation' and, as such, subject to strict regulation:

> It has come to the notice of the Minister for Supplies that Clergymen have been using their motor vehicles for the purposes of attending retreats and conferences, and for clerical duties outside their parishes. In view of the numerous reports of misuse of vehicles by clergymen received by this department it has become necessary to warn all clergymen that misuse of their vehicles will involve the immediate withdrawal, for the duration of the emergency, of the permits and petrol allowances issued in respect of these vehicles.[44]

Archbishop McQuaid had evidently not foreseen the warning and was perturbed by its abruptness. He wrote to Leydon in scolding tones, complaining that the warning had been addressed to him 'without even a covering note' and that he required an immediate explanation.[45] McQuaid sent Leydon another letter the following day, curtly enquiring 'for the second time' whether Leydon had received his initial communication.[46] Leydon, the scrupulous civil servant, was not going to be bullied. Remarkably, he did not receive a reply from Leydon until sixteen days after his first letter.[47]

McQuaid's indignation was eventually indulged by Lemass, with whom he enjoyed warmer relations. Whereas others experienced great difficulty in securing permits for their vehicles, Lemass immediately issued McQuaid with a new permit when the Archbishop decided that he wanted a new car.[48] Throughout the Emergency, Lemass also regularly granted the Archbishop an ample supplementary allowance of petrol.[49] Later in the Emergency, McQuaid wrote to Lemass to express his gratitude for these extra petrol coupons.[50] In contrast to the warm exchanges between Lemass and McQuaid, Leydon granted the supplementary allowance grudgingly. His attitude was understandable. By November 1941, McQuaid was receiving a bloated allowance of fifty-one gallons per month. As discussed earlier, at the start of that year, the ration for the general public had reached a low of one gallon per month. 'I assume there is some exceptional reason', Leydon enquired when writing to McQuaid to authorise his massive monthly allowance in late 1941.[51] McQuaid composed a reply listing his reasons for needing so much petrol, but, angered by what he perceived as Leydon's impertinence, the letter was furiously crossed out and never sent.[52]

McQuaid's irritation at petrol restrictions was matched by that of some less prominent clergymen. The letters of seventy-five-year-old Derry priest Father Felix O'Neill to de Valera exhibit the outrage of a priest who had been reprimanded by the Gardaí for driving his car in non-essential circumstances. In August 1944, O'Neill wrote to Leydon requesting that he be allowed to drive his car south of the border. He was denied a permit by Leydon, who reminded Father O'Neill that a priest's 'urgent and necessary' clerical duties only extended to the boundaries of his own parish.[53] O'Neill resorted to a series of paroxysmic letters to de Valera in protest. He complained that he had had to travel on foot to anoint a boy killed by lightning, assailing the government's 'tyrannical disregard' for 'priestly dignity'. 'Don't touch the Lord's Anointed!' he warned de Valera, reminding him 'You owe your position to people like me!' before asking 'Are the days of the priest hunters going to be renewed in Ireland?' His plight was, he claimed, a symptom of the 'insular and narrow-minded bureaucracy' running the country.[54]

O'Neill's response to the ban on non-essential motoring is echoed in numerous other letters to de Valera from priests requesting he grant them greater use of their cars. Another indignant letter to de Valera came from a Father Michael McCarthy of Kilmallock, County Limerick. In its drive to eradicate non-essential motoring, the government had also cut race meetings by half and banned the use of motor transport to get to and from races. Father McCarthy obviously thought priests were exempted from this law, for between 1939 and 1942 he had repeatedly used his car to convey horse owners, trainers and jockeys to race meetings at Ballyheane. In his letter to the Taoiseach, he described his apprehension by local Gardaí as 'petty', the product of a 'vendetta' and 'ruthless victimisation'.[55]

In another such letter, a Father Considine of Ardrahan, County Galway, claimed that he had been unfairly apprehended by local Gardaí for the 'non-essential' use of his car in the moral policing of local hurling matches. How else, he asked, was he supposed to combat the 'sheer blackguardism' that occurred on such occasions?[56] 'I sit in my car during the progress of the match', he explained, 'I never leave the car as on my person I carry the Holy Oils and Most Blessed Sacrament. I cannot let these mingle with the onlookers.'[57] As an example of the 'urgent and necessary' clerical duties the use of his car enabled him to perform, he cited a recent hurling match where 'I had the misfortune to cross back through the yard of a local public house and was unlucky enough to come upon a travelling woman of tinker class, helplessly drunk, and publicly acting immorally with four young men'.[58]

These letters demonstrate that distaste for state intervention during the Emergency was not only articulated by common men but also by 'people of standing', as John Leydon termed them.[59] Most parish priests steadfastly supported the national drive for greater food and fuel production and the sacrifices this entailed. But while priests publicly advocated compliance with measures such as rationing and compulsory tillage, some made noisy protests in private at their perceived loss of privilege as a result of Emergency restrictions. Instead of speaking out against the sometimes coercive role of the state during the Emergency, a significant minority simply used their status to privately flout government restrictions. It is perhaps unsurprising therefore that, confronted with priestly hypocrisy, a significant proportion of their parishioners continued to privately engage with the black market as well.

Attitudes towards money in Emergency Ireland

Ireland's monetary reformists represented an influential vein of opinion in Emergency Ireland. The monetary reform lobby was a disparate group but generally subscribed to the social and economic vision outlined in the papal encyclicals. After undergoing a split, the Commission of Inquiry into Banking, Currency and Credit (1934–38) produced a radical third Minority Report. It advocated monetary reform, citing *Quadragesimo Anno* and blaming the decline of rural Ireland on the absence of a national monetary policy.[60] It recommended that the Irish pound be allowed to find its own level dependent on the price level in Ireland and not on maintaining parity with sterling and that an Economic Development Commission be given power to control actions by companies which lowered the standard of living or failed to provide for the unemployed. Significantly, its authors – headed by the leading intellectual advocating Irish monetary reform, Alfred O'Rahilly – declared that its conclusions paid 'unique' attention to 'the teaching of the popes'.[61]

Pius XI's views on monetary reform were summarised by O'Rahilly, who quoted the encyclical *Quadragesimo Anno* in his best-selling 1941 book *Money*: 'those who hold and control money also govern credit and determine its allotment, for that reason supplying the life-blood to the entire economic body and grasping in their hands the very soul of production, so that no-one can breathe against their will'.[62] O'Rahilly proposed a State Reserve Bank with a strict measure of social control over commercial banking and the creation of full employment. He also opposed the establishment of an Irish central bank in February 1943, arguing that it would make the state subservient to the banks. Instead, he proposed a central bank controlled by the state and geared to national social interests and held the view that 'Men must be the masters of money, and not the reverse.'[63]

Although by the Emergency O'Rahilly had distanced himself from politicians and political affiliation, the Irish Monetary Reform Association (founded in 1939) established a political platform for monetary reform arguments. The monetary reformists favoured shifting control of the economy from London to Dublin by exerting Irish control over credit, currency, interest and capital. Seán Lemass had proposed a similar reformist approach to banking in 1932, but this plan was vetoed at an early stage by the Department of Finance.[64] By the Emergency, Fianna Fáil's unwillingness to fundamentally alter the state apparatus was confirmed. By this point, O'Rahilly's ideas were far enough removed from the liberal centre that the Monetary Reform Association was viewed with suspicion by Gardaí in Dublin.[65] The Monetary Reform Association nonetheless won three seats in the 1942 local elections, and a year later, Oliver J. Flanagan, a Fianna Fáil dissident, won a Dáil seat on a monetary reform ticket.[66] During the Emergency, monetary reform held considerable appeal within the political establishment as well. Within Fianna Fáil, Hugo Flinn was a prominent opponent of the practice of depositing sterling assets in the Bank of England. During the war, these sterling assets underwent an unprecedented growth.[67]

The monetary reform lobby deployed moral economic arguments which chimed with Emergency conditions. O'Rahilly attacked 'anti-social enterprise' and argued that the supply of money should be controlled 'in accordance with social needs'.[68] He also talked of the great stability in prices in Antiquity and the Middle Ages compared to modern capitalist price inflation. In arguing that the 'general price level is within our power of adjustment',[69] it is reasonable to assume that O'Rahilly privately looked favourably on Lemass's regulation of prices while opposing Fianna Fáil's continued refusal to remove Irish currency's tie with sterling.

O'Rahilly's writings consistently invoked 'the days when usury was regarded as subordinate to moral principles'.[70] Such opinions were not unique to the Emergency period. Turn-of-the-century intellectuals such as Horace Plunkett had argued that there was something hostile to moneymaking in the version of Christianity that dominated Ireland,[71] a notion underlying the paternalistic concern of Chief Secretary George Wyndham in 1903 that 'Jews in certain areas are getting the peasantry into debt'.[72] These imaginings of nation and alien prevailed in independent Ireland and are evident in popular Irish Catholic journals of the 1930s, which sometimes contained articles denouncing Judaism as underpinning both capitalism and socialism.[73] In outlawing moneylending on Christian holidays – Sundays, Christmas Day, Good Friday and St Patrick's Day – the Moneylenders Bill of 1933 provided some justification for the opinion, expressed by O'Rahilly and others, that such practices were antithetical to the Catholic moral economic order.[74] During the 1940s, Catholic journals continued to criticise materialism and condemned usury.[75] Such views closely resembled the rhetoric and ethos of popular Irish nationalism, particularly the hostility towards capitalism integral to the tradition of civic republicanism.

Neutral Ireland was not home to a sizeable Jewish minority. At the Wannsee Conference of 1942, the Nazis estimated that the number of Jews in Ireland was close to 4,000.[76] Comparatively, this meant that Ireland was home to less people of Jewish origin than neutral Switzerland, Spain and Sweden, but contained 1,000 more than neutral Portugal. In reality, due to a relatively parsimonious refugee policy, the number of Jews in Ireland lagged well behind neutral Portugal, where the actions of diplomat Aristides de Sousa Mendes ensured the influx of tens of thousands of Jews.[77] Nonetheless, O'Rahilly's moral hostility to Jewish economic practices was widely disseminated during the Emergency, a period when Ireland was experiencing an introspective moral surge. Between 1939 and 1945, the presence of 'aliens' became more conspicuous and was more frequently recorded by the authorities.[78] The Gardaí recorded the presence of 'aliens' on the basis of nationality rather than on the basis of religion or ethnicity.[79] But as shortages bit and moral economic notions underwent a discursive growth, some groups exploited these conditions in order to juxtapose the values of Christianity with the values of Judaism.

The 1939 manifesto of the 'Irish-Ireland Research Society' expressed hostility towards the perceived lack of morality of 'racial aliens, with their special moral code and values' and claimed that, by contrast, 'our society is ranged against world money'.[80] The manifesto clearly juxtaposed the Jewish 'moral code and values' with those pertaining to their version of an Irish moral economy. In June 1942, a far-right group calling themselves the Irish Christian Rights Association published a leaflet attacking the 'pernicious evils of money-lending'. This group's newspaper *Penapa* had previously been censored for reporting on moneylending trials involving Jews.[81] Hostility to usury was not confined to the lunatic fringe, either, with most Irish building societies condemning moneylending as exploitative. In 1942, with Emergency shortages at their worst, Fine Gael's James Dillon exhibited the common distaste for usury in the political mainstream when he urged Minister for Justice Gerald Boland to abolish the practice altogether.[82]

Open and public anti-semitism was notably espoused by the quasi-fascist *Ailtiri na hAiseirghe* and from the 'independent Christian' standpoint of Flanagan, who in his maiden Dáil speech in 1943 famously proposed that emergency orders be 'directed against the Jews, who crucified our Saviour nineteen hundred years ago and who are crucifying us every day of the week', and that 'Where the bees are there is the honey, and where the Jews are there is the money'.[83] Press coverage of a number of anti-semitic acts in Dublin during the Emergency was censored, but prominent incidents did take place, including the daubing of 'JEWS' in two-foot high letters on Jewish-owned premises on Grafton Street in 1944.[84] Gardaí in Dublin also monitored a group called *Clann na Saoirse*, which reports described as a 'Racial Resurgence Party'.[85] A.J. Leventhal, reflecting on what it meant to be an Irish Jew in *The Bell*, remarked of the underlying racism against his coreligionists that 'if you are Einstein you are a Swiss, but a Jew if you are a black marketer'.[86] During the trial of a Dublin Jew for black market offences in 1944, a letter from an anonymous Irish citizen to the *Irish*

World newspaper in New York came to the attention of the Censor's Office. It read 'When, oh when shall we get rid of this type who sneak in here and then begin their dirty business tactics? I hope the old judge gives this bird the works.'[87] The fact that it was highlighted proves that Irish censorship during the Emergency – frequently derided for its fastidiousness – also protected minority groups from slander.

The reputation of Ireland's Jews as synonymous with prohibited market practices can only have been augmented by newspaper reports for convictions carrying the names of the guilty. Among the men convicted for trafficking gold coins in the Dublin area in high-profile cases in 1945, Jewish surnames are conspicuous: Gittleson, Greeph, Wine, Mazure, Garber, Yaffe, Woolfson and Farbenbloom.[88] Similarly, the *Irish Times* reported that an Israel Cohen had been fined £100 and jailed for two months for selling cigarettes over the controlled price in 1942.[89] It would be trite to deny the involvement of Ireland's Jews in the Emergency black market, then, but while the Irish authorities undoubtedly shared some of the public prejudice towards Jews, suspicion of 'aliens' was not unusual for wartime, and, at an official level, they were treated no differently to other groups outside the Catholic Irish mainstream.[90] According to official figures, the number of Jews sentenced to imprisonment for criminal offences between 1940 and 1943 was twelve, representing just 0.01% of the total number of committals to prison for criminal offences in those years.[91]

These figures suggest that Ireland's Jews were not disproportionately involved in illegal black market activities as defined by the state. On the other hand, a relatively high proportion of Jews were involved in peddling, moneylending and pawnbroking – trades ostensibly antithetical to Catholic moral economy. Many of the Dublin poor continued to rely almost entirely on moneylenders, as documented in a miserable piece dictated by an anonymous slum woman in *The Bell* in 1941.[92] Moneylending remained for many a regrettable necessity, although a slum dweller during the Emergency recalled that Jewish moneylenders were in fact often fairer than Irish people involved in the dubious trade.[93] Significantly, in its paternalistic pursuit of a form of moral economy during the Emergency, the Irish state did not target moneylending. This suggests, once again, that the government's enforcement of 'fair' market practices fell short of targeting every activity identified as immoral by Catholic thinkers and writers.

The government's unwillingness to outlaw moneylending was attacked in the popular Catholic press. *The Standard*, which also covered calls from church figures for controls on Jewish interests in property and finance, criticised what it regarded as the government's failure in this regard.[94] The government's reluctance to extend controls on profits and prices to target moneylending indicates an attachment to liberal democracy and a rejection of the more radical Catholic definitions of moral economy. This was similarly reflected in Fianna Fáil's refusal to cement self-sufficiency by breaking with sterling. Once again, although underpinned by Christian notions of justice, the boundaries of the Irish state's moral economy fell short of those of some Catholic commentators.

Competing visions

The inconsistencies between church and state in this period reflect the broader clash of competing administrative visions that church and central government were locked in at the time. The vocationalist lobby was well known for its harsh criticisms of civil service bureaucracy and the expansion of state power.[95] The government, on the other hand, favoured strong central government. In its inaugural edition, contributors to *Christus Rex* (a journal edited by a group of theologians headed by Cornelius Lucey) attacked 'the authoritarian approach to many of our problems'[96] and stated 'we would prefer widely diffused ownership on a co-operative and vocational basis to state monopoly'.[97]

At cabinet level, a key division existed between Seán MacEntee, who generally opposed regulations impacting on individual liberty, and Lemass, who was often in favour of restriction in order that productive priorities were realised. This clash was demonstrated in debates over the emigration of agricultural labourers during the Emergency. MacEntee had argued against the intrusion of the state into areas of family life and the development of what many Catholic commentators termed the 'Servile State', a system borne of attempts to reform capitalism whereby state regulation removed the freedom of the individual and the family. But despite these differences, the delays in the Commission on Vocational Organisation's appointment, its large membership, and its considerable brief indicate that de Valera and his cabinet were united in their approach to Ireland's vocationalists.[98] The government would appease the lobby without compromising its grip on power in any way.

The commission completed its oral hearings by August 1941 and began writing up its findings shortly thereafter. The commission's brief did not cover short-term economic planning, but if its members had hoped their findings would impact upon the management of the Emergency, they were to be disappointed. By this point, the main aspects of Fianna Fáil's management of the Emergency were already in place: large-scale recruitment into the army and its ancillaries, compulsory tillage, turf and other labour schemes, the rationing of certain goods, mutual agreements with the British on emigration and industrial wage restriction. By this time, the government had also instituted an unprecedented degree of state control, exemplified in emigration embargoes and a system of full rationing.

The commission's report, published in November 1943, recommended the incorporation of all employers and workers into vocational groupings in six key sectors and the election of a National Vocational Assembly to manage the national economy.[99] Lemass, angered by the report's disregard for civil servants and bureaucracy, was able to dismiss it as 'a slovenly document'.[100]Although weak in offering alternatives and reactionary in places, the real significance of the *Report of the Commission on Vocational Organisation* is that it expressed widely shared opinions collected from across the country in the early 1940s.[101]

Frequently, these opinions were supportive of the government in time of war but overwhelmingly critical of Fianna Fáil's management of the country and the economy during the Emergency.

Lemass dismissed the commission's report in late 1943. By this point, and markedly so thereafter, Ireland's Catholic writers were already extending their gazes to the post-war world. Prior to this, when the outcome of the war appeared less certain, Catholic commentators generally disliked the character of Irish state intervention but viewed it as a regrettable necessity. After all, they reasoned, Ireland was experiencing a national emergency and, if used properly, state power could be ultimately derived from God.[102] An article published in the *Irish Monthly* in 1940 criticised totalitarianism as 'materialist' and 'a form of idolatry'. However, it justified the 'seemingly excessive state interference' witnessed in Portugal under António de Oliveira Salazar:

> The present régime in Portugal is in the nature of an experiment ... in the Corporative system. The latter is, after all, only in its swaddling clothes, and needs careful tending until it can be considered strong enough to fend for itself. It is as a foster mother that the state acts, a foster mother that encourages every sign of self-control and self-discipline manifested by its fosterling.[103]

Some Catholic writers certainly saw the growth of the Irish state during the Emergency as signifying the emergence of a 'foster mother' to an Irish corporative system and backed it for that reason. The historian John Whyte argued that Irish Catholicism was becoming 'increasingly right-wing'[104] in this period. This holds true in the social and cultural sphere post-war, but is less clear-cut in the heavily regulated economic realm operative during the Emergency, where profiteering was a key concern. In this respect, Irish Catholic social thought was indeed 'right-wing' in advocating market practices of mutuality redolent of a bygone medieval order. But Catholic theorists also condemned the excesses of liberal free trade, greed and profiteering: a position often associated with the 'left wing' of the political spectrum. Catholic periodicals of the era often contained articles pertaining to a spiritual vision of a moral economy which, although underlined by the objective of preparing Ireland for a Christian renaissance which would follow materialism's decline, deserve more than mockery.[105]

There was, then, a radical tinge to Irish Catholicism in this era. The 'individualism' of the 'capitalistic order' was wrong, one contemporary theological article asserted: 'a point on which 'Marxist and Catholic thinkers are in agreement'.[106] Another argued that 'the whole economic order must be moulded and shaped so that it may afford the conditions for a decent human livelihood'.[107] While commentators have paid much attention to the social and sexual concerns of the church over dance halls in this period,[108] the anti-capitalist sentiment of these concerns has been overlooked in favour of the racier denunciations of illicit sex. Bishop McNamee, for instance, devoted the majority of his 1942 Lenten pastoral to an attack on dance halls but chiefly to the 'private gain' and 'profiteering' that they represented rather than the sexual 'occasions of sin' that attendance at them may have prompted.[109]

The bishops were not devoid of material concerns and displayed awareness of the straitened material conditions that pertained during the Emergency by annually releasing people from their Lenten obligation to fast because of food shortages.[110] The church and the Catholic social movement were certainly outspoken in denouncing communism and the danger of excessive state control in this period. But in opposing selfish market behaviour and backing state regulation of the market, intellectual Catholicism was certainly not in thrall to business concerns either. An influential political and intellectual current in Emergency Ireland, social Catholicism promoted social justice and class harmony while criticising the organising concepts of both capitalism and communism and the practical applications of free market capitalism and state socialism.[111] It is significant that pastorals commonly identified people of 'social standing' as carrying out black market activity. This accusation was forcefully repeated in *Christus Rex* at the end of the Emergency.[112] It further reinforced Lemass's conviction that it was not the 'Bill Sykes type' who was the chief culprit when it came to black market activity, but the middle class wholesaler, the hoarder and the unscrupulous businessman.

Opposition to state control was a key aspect to the 'integralist' (as opposed to liberal democratic) ethos of Irish Catholicism identified by Whyte in the late 1940s.[113] Such post-war opinions were influenced by the upsurge in regulation during the Emergency. In the response of the clerical estate, however, time, place and the perception of how long shortages would last were crucial. Open rumblings of discontent from Catholic sources on the government's efforts to increase productivity were few. As in the case of the state's efforts to regulate the market and eliminate black market practices, these occurred most commonly in the later stages of the Emergency. With the end of the war in sight, contributors to Catholic publications reacted with hostility to the expansion of the British state through the Beveridge Plan, bemoaning 'state regulation and regimentation of economic life carried so far that individuals are freed from the task of working out their own economic salvation'[114] and rejecting the 'omnicompetent state' which the post-war world threatened.[115]

Conclusion

The church's advocacy of compliance with the 'civil authority' in overcoming scarcity was part of an introspective moral surge during the Emergency, witnessed in the importance of pastoral letters, Lenten regulations or, as retailers noted, in the heightened number of complaints about corsets in shop windows.[116] In general, the hierarchy, clergy and Catholic thinkers saw state encroachment as a regrettable aspect of the national emergency, but, crucially, they also saw it as

temporary. Although subscribing to the notion of moral neutrality, Ireland's bishops and intellectuals did not apply Catholic concepts of moral law in abstract.
Rather, they related them to the material shortages and increase in crime evident
in Ireland at the time. They saw it as their spiritual duty to imbue a moral economic ethic based on Christian principles to overcome what they saw as the
decline in public morality.[117]

But while differences between church and state during the Emergency should
not be overstated, neither should the coalescence of the two bodies. On occasion,
the privileged place of the church in Irish society clashed with the moral economic
role of the state. While promoting a cooperative ethic, a number of priests selfishly
resented the implied loss in status that the equitable application of rationing delivered. Likewise, the extension of moral economy to a more total Catholic 'integralist'
society, one ranged against monetary capitalism, centralisation and excessive state
control and based on widely diffused ownership and guild structures, was dismissed
by Fianna Fáil, unwilling to act as a 'foster mother' to Irish corporatism. Tensions
also existed between church and state over the widely held belief that state price
control was merely penal and not morally binding. The importance of these keenly
debated differences was subtle yet significant. It lay in the potential for the development of a spiritual counter-hegemony to state intervention and the propaganda that
legitimised it.

Ultimately, however, Ireland did not suffer the widespread disruption to social
order that combatant nations did through the sheer devastation wrought by bombs
and the collective experience of struggle. Hence, differences over the just price of a
'nice cup of tea' and the vanity of the clergy and the hierarchy aside, the close relationship between church and state in Ireland emerged fractured but substantially
intact after 1945. There is a certain resonance with authoritarian nationalist Europe –
not least with the rustic Catholic ethic of *Travail, Famille, Patrie* in Vichy France,
where the crucifix replaced Marianne on schoolroom walls. In Ireland, though,
much greater differences existed in the views of each camp on the exercise of state
power and the essence of the social order. The socialist republican Peadar O'Donnell,
addressing the rural poor, differentiated between the 'Catholic fascism of Cardinal
MacRory' and the 'Catholic Democracy of de Valera'.[118] Nonetheless, during the
Emergency, church and state reached a definite accommodation, at times uncomfortable, sometimes challenged from below, but never surmounted by latent tensions and never the subject of a major breach.

Notes

1 Phil O'Keefe, b. 1928, Dublin. Interviewed 18 March 2009.
2 Pius XI, *Quadragesimo Anno* (Rome, 1931), point 80.
3 *Quadragesimo Anno*, point 25.
4 *Quadragesimo Anno*, point 49.

5 J.J. Lee, 'Aspects of Corporatist Thought in Ireland', in Art Cosgrove and Donal McCartney eds, *Studies in Irish History* (Dublin, 1979), 324.

6 Patrick Murray, *Oracles of God: The Roman Catholic Church and Irish Politics, 1922–37* (Dublin, 2000), 295.

7 Murray, *Oracles of God*, 406–420.

8 *Report of the Commission on Vocational Organisation* (Dublin, 1943), 142.

9 *Irish Press*, 14 October 1939.

10 Gerald Boland, *Dáil Debates*, vol. 89, col. 1834, 8 April 1943.

11 Bishop of Kilmore's Lenten Pastoral, *Irish Press*, 24 February 1941.

12 *Irish Independent*, 30 June 1942.

13 In Catholic social theory, commutative justice demands respect for the equal human dignity of all persons in economic transactions.

14 J. McCarthy, 'Smuggling and Profiteering', *Irish Ecclesiastical Record*, 58 (July–December 1941), 554–557.

15 McCarthy, 'Smuggling and Profiteering', 554–557. The italics are my own.

16 J. McCarthy, 'The Legal Price', *Irish Ecclesiastical Record*, 60 (July–December 1942), 438.

17 J. McCarthy, 'The Just Price of Stored Tea', *Irish Ecclesiastical Record*, 60 (July–December 1941), 298.

18 J. McCarthy, 'The Legal Price', 442.

19 McCarthy, 'The Just Price of Stored Tea', 298–300.

20 *Leitrim Observer*, 12 April 1942.

21 *Irish Independent*, 8 March 1943.

22 *Dáil Debates*, vol. 125, col. 225, 5 April 1951.

23 See E.J. Hegarty, 'The Black Market', *Irish Ecclesiastical Record*, 64 (July–December 1944), 38–43; M. Mansfield, 'Theologians and the Legal Price', *Irish Ecclesiastical Record*, 63 (January–June 1944), 301–311.

24 See the *Irish Independent*'s summary of the pastorals on 21 February 1944.

25 See the *Irish Independent*'s summaries of the pastorals on 3 March 1941, 6 April 1942 and 8 March 1943.

26 See the *Irish Independent*'s summary of the pastorals on 12 February 1945.

27 J. McCarthy, 'Is the Legal Price a purely Penal Regulation?' *Irish Ecclesiastical Record*, 62 (July–December 1943), 269–270.

28 Hegarty, 'The Black Market', 42.

29 Mansfield, 'Theologians and the Legal Price', 310.

30 *Irish Independent*, 25 March 1943.

31 *The Standard*, 8 August 1941.

32 *The Standard*, 21 November 1941.

33 Cornelius Lucey, 'The Just Profit Rate', *Irish Ecclesiastical Record*, 58 (July–December 1941), 400.

34 Cornelius Lucey, 'The Ethics of Advertising', *Irish Ecclesiastical Record*, 57 (January–June 1941), 7.

35 Whyte, *Church and State*, 77.

36 John Cooney, *John Charles McQuaid: Ruler of Catholic Ireland* (Dublin, 1999), 136.

37 Dublin Diocesan Archives (DDA), McQuaid papers, AB8/B/XIX/1a.

38 Cooney, *McQuaid*, 133.
39 Leydon to McQuaid, 23 June 1949. DDA, McQuaid papers, AB8/B, Industry and Commerce.
40 Cooney, *McQuaid*, 146.
41 'The Mount Street Club'. DDA, McQuaid papers, AB8/A/XVIII/37.
42 *Irish Press*, 11 October 1939.
43 Garda Report on Rural Reform League, Gorey, county Wexford, 12 September 1942. NAI, JUS/8/903.
44 Leydon, 'Emergency Powers (Mechanically Propelled Vehicles) Order' (1942). DDA, McQuaid papers, AB8/B, Supplies.
45 McQuaid to Leydon, 30 September, 1943. DDA, McQuaid papers, AB8/B, Supplies.
46 McQuaid to Leydon, 1 December 1943. DDA, McQuaid papers, AB8/B, Supplies.
47 Leydon to McQuaid, 16 December 1943. DDA, McQuaid papers, AB8/B, Supplies.
48 Lemass to McQuaid, 14 September 1942. DDA, McQuaid papers, AB8/B, Supplies.
49 O'Doherty to McQuaid, 14 July 1944. DDA, McQuaid papers, AB8/B, Supplies.
50 McQuaid to Lemass, 15 July 1944. DDA, McQuaid papers, AB8/B, Supplies.
51 Leydon to McQuaid, 13 November 1941. DDA, McQuaid papers, AB8/B, Supplies.
52 McQuaid to Leydon, 15 November 1941 (not sent). DDA, McQuaid papers, AB8/B, Supplies.
53 John Leydon to O'Neill, 4 August 1944. NAI, DT/RA 103/44.
54 Father Felix O'Neill to de Valera, 8 August 1944. NAI, DT/RA 103/44.
55 De Valera to John Leydon, 18 July 1945. NAI, DT/RA 103/44.
56 Father J.F. Considine to de Valera, 10 October 1945. NAI, DT/RA 103/44.
57 Considine to Gerald Boland, 19 July 1945. NAI, DT/RA 103/44.
58 Considine to Boland, 18 August 1945. NAI, DT/RA 103/44.
59 Leydon to de Valera, 1 September 1943. NAI, DT/RA 103/44.
60 E.J. Coyne, 'The Papal Encyclicals and the Banking Commission', *Irish Monthly*, 77 (1939), 82.
61 Coyne, 'The Papal Encyclicals', 76.
62 Pius XI, *Quadragesimo Anno* (Rome, 1931) cited in Alfred O'Rahilly, *Money* (Cork, 1941), 250.
63 O'Rahilly, *Money*, 254.
64 Dunphy, *The Making of Fianna Fáil Power*, 147.
65 73 (7 February 1941), Dublin Garda Index to Special Files, 1929–1945.
66 Gaughan, *Alfred O'Rahilly*, 352.
67 John Busteed, 'Our Sterling Assets', *The Bell*, 11, 4 (January 1946), 857–860.
68 O'Rahilly, *Money*, 431; 45.
69 O'Rahilly, *Money*, 46.
70 O'Rahilly, *Money*, 339.
71 Garvin, *Preventing*, 51.
72 Stanley Price, *Somewhere to Hang My Hat: An Irish-Jewish Journey* (Dublin, 2002), 57.
73 Dermot Keogh, *Jews in Twentieth Century Ireland: Refugees, Anti-Semitism and the Holocaust* (Cork, 1998), 92–99.
74 See *Dáil Debates*, vol. 48, col. 1500–1502, 28 June 1933.
75 See, for example, E.J. Coyne, 'What Is Credit?', *Irish Monthly*, 71 (1943), 281–292.

76 Keogh, *Jews*, 101.
77 Lochery, *Lisbon*, 41.
78 220–289 (1939), Dublin Garda Index to Special Files, 1929–1945.
79 A notable exception to this rule was the Jehovah's Witnesses, described as a 'religious sect'. 1026 (1 November 1940), Dublin Garda Index to Special Files, 1929–1945.
80 *Irish Times*, 23 February 1939.
81 O'Drisceoil, *Censorship in Ireland*, 187.
82 *Dáil Debates*, vol. 82, col. 467, 15 April 1942.
83 *Dáil Debates*, vol. 91, col. 569, 9 July 1943.
84 O'Drisceoil, *Censorship in Ireland*, 112.
85 70 (24 April 1944), Dublin Garda Index to Special Files, 1929–1945.
86 A.J. Leventhal, 'What It Means to Be a Jew', *The Bell*, 10, 3 (June 1945), 211.
87 Censor's Report for December 1944. UCDA, Aiken papers, P104/3502.
88 *Irish Times*, 14 November 1945 and 30 April 1946.
89 *Irish Times*, 12 August 1942.
90 O'Halpin, *Defending Ireland*, 224.
91 Gerald Boland, '*Dáil Debates*, vol. 93, col. 1667, 26 April 1944.
92 'Slum Pennies', *The Bell*, January 1941, 75.
93 Johnston, *Banks of Pimlico*, 122.
94 *The Standard*, 21 November 1941.
95 O'Leary, *Vocationalism*, 89–103.
96 Thomas A. McLaughlin, *Christus Rex*, 1 (1947), 11.
97 Cornelius Lucey, 'The Ethics of Nationalisation', *Christus Rex*, 1 (1947), 19.
98 See Lee's 'Aspects of Corporatist Thought'.
99 *Report of Commission on Vocational Organisation*, 330–350.
100 J.J. Lee, 'Aspects of Corporatist Thought in Ireland: The Commission on Vocational Organisation, 1939–1943', in A. Cosgrove and D. McCartney, eds, *Essays in Irish History in Honour of R.D. Edwards* (Dublin 1979).
101 Whyte, *Church and State*, 107.
102 'Extracts of Social Wisdom: Catholic Theory of the State', *Irish Monthly*, 69 (1941), 88.
103 John J.M. Ryan, 'Is Portugal Totalitarian?', *Irish Monthly*, 68 (1940), 1–9. Ryan, 'Is Portugal Totalitarian?', 1–9.
104 Whyte, *Church and State*, 160.
105 Susannah Riordan, "The Unpopular Front': The Catholic Revival and Irish Catholic Identity, 1932–48' (unpublished M.A. thesis, UCD, 1990), 157.
106 Wilfred Parsons, 'The Function of Government in Industry', *Irish Monthly*, 72, 1944, 148–161.
107 Lucey, 'Spending of the Living Wage', 143.
108 Wills, *Neutral Island*, 31.
109 *Leitrim Observer*, 12 April 1942.
110 See, for instance, *Anglo-Celt*, 17 February 1945.
111 See O'Leary, *Vocationalism*.
112 'Vigilans', 'As I See It', *Christus Rex*, 1 (1947), 37.
113 Whyte, *Church and State*, 163.

114 Father Paschal, 'The Responsibility of Economists', *Irish Ecclesiastical Record*, 59 (January–June 1942), 432.

115 Peter McKevitt, 'The Beveridge Plan Reviewed', *Irish Ecclesiastical Record*, 61 (January–June 1943), 149.

116 Nesbitt, *At Arnott's*, 115.

117 *Dáil Debates*, vol. 89, col. 1834, 8 April 1943.

118 Peadar O'Donnell, *The Bothy Fire and All That* (Dublin, 1937), 10.

7

Coercion in the countryside

All surrounding houses either nunneries or burnt-out ruins, and bog in all directions
John Betjeman, 6 July 1942

The geopolitics of food supply

During the Second World War, at least 20 million people died of starvation and its related diseases: a number exceeding the 19.5 million military deaths.[1] Wielded as an economic weapon, food supply could be horrifically effective. During this period, food supply became a truly international issue. Generally speaking, nations which granted concessions to the Allied powers received support for their domestic agricultural policies in return. A number of Middle Eastern countries, for instance, received British and American supplies of food crops, fertilisers and agricultural machinery after granting shipping space to the Allies.[2] Ireland, by virtue of her neutrality, was removed from such aid.

Without Allied help, the Irish food supply situation became critical. Ireland's was an overwhelmingly agricultural economy and the sector expanded during the Emergency. By 1942, net *industrial* output was nearly a quarter below its pre-war level.[3] The agricultural sector's overall share of national income, on the other hand, rose from 28% in 1938 to 37% by 1945.[4] Yet agricultural productivity remained relatively poor. By the end of 1941, Ireland was importing 1,000 tons of grain a week, but consumption was 1,000 tons a day and domestic production was not making up the deficit.[5]

In an effort to improve productivity, state intervention in the agricultural sphere increased. The overriding aim of such action was to provide the population with enough bread to prevent starvation. The central wartime initiative to this end, Fianna Fáil's compulsory tillage scheme, represents an important initiative in the social and economic history of Ireland.[6] The scheme forced Ireland's farmers to prioritise the tilling of their land, cultivating wheat and other cereal crops, rather than using it for dairy or other uses. Prices and productivity levels were also controlled closely by central government to ensure enough food was produced and that it would be equitably distributed. In the Allied nations, similarly, governments switched from instructing farmers to grow less (to prevent food surpluses) to compelling them to cultivate every inch of their land (to prevent starvation).[7]

In 1941, with Ireland choking under Churchill's supply squeeze, Irish Minister for the Coordination of Defensive Measures Frank Aiken travelled to the United States in an attempt to secure much-needed food, fuel and weaponry for the country. While held up in Lisbon prior to his trip, he met Portuguese leader António de Oliveira Salazar. Salazar told Aiken that Portuguese efforts to obtain 'war material' from the United States had come to naught. Portugal, like Ireland, was being punished by Britain and America for her neutrality. Whereas the farmers of Allied Britain, the United States and Canada shared modern tractors, fertilisers and pesticides – emerging from the war with nutrient-rich soil – neutrals like Ireland were forced to over-farm land using archaic methods. As in Ireland, Spanish and Portuguese agriculture remained largely unmechanised and imports of fertilisers fell dramatically. Rather than new tractors, these countries reverted to donkey and plough. As Salazar reflected ruefully to Aiken, 'It is the neutrals who are paying for this war'.[8]

The genesis and implementation of compulsory tillage

A key tenet of Irish nationalist ideology associated land with the essence of the nation.[9] Established under the 1881 Land Act, the Irish Land Commission oversaw the transfer of agricultural holdings from landlords to tenants. Its work in acquiring and redistributing untenanted land continued after independence, but the historiography of this body largely departs after the 1923 Land Act. That act not only completed land purchase begun under the British acts but gave the Land Commission powers to compulsorily acquire and redistribute land.[10] Although it possessed the power of land confiscation, the Land Commission represented a form of interventionism that was popular among landless labourers and smallholders, who stood to gain most from it. Its work was halted by the government during the Emergency as the production of food became the priority.

During the First World War, all occupiers of ten acres or more had to till one tenth of their land.[11] In Ireland, the measure was initially opposed by the majority of large grazier farmers due to the greater outlay compulsory tillage demanded. On the other hand, it appealed to smallholders and agrarian labourers, who anticipated that it would deliver extra land and extra work. In practice, it became another issue in the welter of nationalist political agitation and agrarian dissidence of the time, with Sinn Féin highlighting the fact that some landowners were using it as an excuse to let land to tenants at exorbitant prices and demanding the full-scale division of land.[12]

After Fianna Fáil assumed power in 1932, the government instituted a number of economic policies derived from early Sinn Féin policy. Much of the party's support was based on their anti-grazier attitude to land distribution; the party professed to represent small farmers and labourers and signalled its departure from Cumann na nGaedheal by giving preference to the landless in the allocation of land through the

Land Commission.[13] The government's emphasis on tillage had its roots in Sinn Féin's socio-economic hostility to large-scale grazing, itself a product of nineteenth-century nationalism. During the ensuing Economic War, trade restrictions also meant stock was not earning what it once did. Consequently, for both ideological and material reasons, it had been government policy vigorously to encourage wheat-growing in the years preceding the Emergency.[14]

Significantly, though, the first scheme of compulsory tillage in independent Ireland was much grander in scale than its predecessor and much more intensive than the tillage drive of the previous decade. Compulsory tillage formed the centre-piece of the Irish government's emergency controls on agriculture. The government announced that farmers with holdings below ten acres would be exempted, while the rest were required to till one eighth of their arable land.[15] Those who failed to meet the requirements would be liable for a fine of up to £100 or six months' imprisonment. Rough mountain land, bog, sand dunes, forestry land and land subject to flooding were exempted,[16] but unlike measures imposed during the First World War, widows who held land were not exempted from having to till it.[17] Inspectors had the power to enter onto holdings, repeatedly if necessary, and to provide the evidence that could result in prison, fines, dispossession or all three.[18]

Most significantly, before the harvest of 1940, Minister for Agriculture James Ryan announced that he had instructed his officers 'to enter on to and take possession of holdings' in the case of any farmer who failed to comply with the quota.[19] This empowered the department's inspectors to act as bailiffs in dispossessing farmers who were considered unproductive and to seize their land for the state. After confiscation, the department would let the land to tenants considered more reliable. Up to this point, the Irish state had interfered with private land by subdividing large estates rather than smaller holdings.[20] Compulsory tillage, by contrast, raised the prospect of a widespread derogation of property rights in the opposite direction.

Propaganda: famine and the Irish farmer

In 1938, officials from the Department of Agriculture drew up plans for the wartime role of the state in the agricultural sector. They noted that the average yield for tillage crops had declined in the late 1930s because the intensity of the government's tillage drive propaganda had been relaxed from 1935.[21] During the Emergency, the department therefore placed a premium on propaganda because they saw it as essential to securing higher yields. They also noted that in 1915 and 1916, the imperial authorities had relied on a food production campaign that combined public meetings and propaganda, but farmers had continued to devote most of their efforts to livestock.[22] By contrast, when compulsory tillage was introduced under the draconian terms of the Defence of the Realm Act in 1917, the area under tillage had increased by one million acres. These figures convinced Agriculture officials that 'intensive tillage developments cannot be obtained without compulsion'.[23]

During the Emergency, then, the state adopted a twin-pronged approach to enforcing compulsory tillage, combining the legal requirement to till with a comprehensive propaganda campaign. The scheme followed that instituted in Northern Ireland in September 1939 by the Craigavon administration, itself following Westminster's lead. At the time, the *Irish Times* commented 'farmers are notorious anarchists, and it remains to be seen how those of Northern Ireland will respond to the new discipline'.[24] Shortly after, compulsory tillage was implemented south of the border, and these were to prove prescient words indeed.

In an effort to manage shortages and increase productivity in the Irish countryside, state propaganda invoked a historical spectre almost one hundred years old. The government used the impending centenary of the Great Famine to add legitimacy to the methods employed in its campaign to produce more food and undermine the Emergency black market.[25] The 'Grow More Wheat!' campaign became ubiquitous: the slogan was repeated on the wireless, in political speeches from town square platforms and even on the franking of postage stamps.[26] The government regularly published notices in newspapers encouraging farmers to till. Some provided emotional stimulus, depicting children in a field of wheat above the words 'they depend on you'.[27] 'We have no army in the fighting line to feed', said Minister for Agriculture James Ryan shortly after the outbreak of war in 1939, 'but we have the old, the infirm, the children, the masses'. It was the farmers' duty, he continued, 'to supply their fellow men'.[28] In February 1942, Cardinal MacRory declared 'the farmers, and they alone, stand between us and famine'.[29] Official government announcements soon adopted the motif.[30] Such exclamations were augmented by images of harvest toil in newspapers, magazines and periodicals.

There was more to the state's efforts than the manipulation of historical memory, however. After the fall of France in June 1940, grave concerns arose about the possibility that Ireland would run out of food and other essential supplies. Famines occurred in Leningrad (1941/1942) and Bengal (1942/1943). More worrying for the Irish government, Western Europe saw famine in Greece (1941/1942), the Netherlands (1944/1945) and Poland (1944). In February 1944, reports of the 1943 Chinese famine landed on de Valera's desk. They vividly depicted the erosion of a progressive, hard-working social system by hunger. First, people sold clothing and bedding to make money to buy food. Next, houses were torn down to sell timber. A desperate population then resorted to digging up crops half-grown and eating roots and leaves. Finally, banditry reigned and over one million perished.[31] According to the report, there were two main reasons for this descent into death and barbarism: firstly, not enough rice had been grown and, secondly, the province was overreliant on imports.[32] The substitution of the word 'rice' with 'wheat' provided a chilling parallel with Ireland's supply crisis at the time.

Although most accounts of starvation in Europe were censored and never reached the Irish public,[33] some reports did make it past the censors. In 1945, for instance, a report on the 'menace of starvation' was published which claimed that 'half of

Europe, to mention nothing of Asia, is facing famine such as the world has not known since the Black Death.'[34] Wireless and press propaganda depicted farmers as the shock troops in the war against such apocalyptic possibilities. Ryan repeatedly stressed the 'very important position' of farmers and their responsibility to 'prevent any want or famine in this country'.[35] Compulsory tillage had been introduced as a matter of necessity, de Valera stated in 1939, 'to meet the conditions created by the European war'.[36] Appealing to farmers in 1941, Lemass reiterated this message, urging farmers to increase production as a matter of urgency, revealing that 'outside sources of supply are virtually cut off', reserves 'insufficient' and insisting 'people need bread'.[37]

Albeit specific to Emergency scarcity, this was a continuation of the post-independence nationalist idealisation of the small farmer and the ruralist ethic, embodied in the ploughman – back hunched, tilling the soil with his horses beneath a beaming sun – depicted on the Irish pound note from 1929.[38] The government's theme was echoed by church figures, a continuation of the Irish hierarchy's own invocation of ruralism in the decades after the Great Famine and in the early twentieth century. This concept was not depicted as a complex social or theological issue, but an all-embracing embodiment of the very spirit of Irishness.[39] In his Lenten pastoral of 1942, the Bishop of Clonfert thanked the farmers for ensuring 'starvation will not stalk our land again'.[40] State propaganda in the press repeated this essentialist, stoical and anti-materialist message. For instance, an article which purported to be written by a farmer declared 'I'm all for tillage; no, not because it is supposed to pay. It won't ... But it's farming, husbandry, *our job* ... very likely the crop will be too flattened and we will have an expensive harvest for small return. Yet till we must!'[41]

'Till or go to jail': enforcement

When the compulsory tillage scheme was announced in October 1939, it excited protest from a number of farmers' organisations. Ryan refused to meet their representatives.[42] In an address to the Dáil in late September 1939, de Valera expressed his hope that compulsion in agriculture would not be necessary, citing his preference for the voluntary organisation of agricultural production involving parish committees.[43] Less than two weeks later, though, compulsory tillage was introduced. The McGillycuddy of the Reeks, a Kerry landowner, argued in a 1939 Seanad debate on the introduction of the scheme that compulsory tillage took little account either of the variations in land or the ability of different farmers to pay for seed, labour or tillage crops and implements. Compulsory tillage was, The McGillycuddy contended, a form of compulsion, an instruction to the farmer: 'you must forthwith go and till as much land as I require you to do'.[44]

This phrase encapsulated Ryan's hard-headed approach, which set the tone for the government's implementation of the scheme from the outset. As Ireland's supply situation worsened from early 1941, the government's stance in the press switched noticeably as well. Official notices soon changed from legitimation of compulsory tillage with reference to external wartime disruption to an increasingly inward and punitive focus on disobliging farmers. The Department of Agriculture published statistics of farmers dispossessed of their land or fined under the order.[45] Such notices appeared more frequently during harvest time and were complemented by calls from the bishops for greater food production.[46] In March 1942, de Valera surpassed the mild duress of the 'Grow More Wheat!' message with the blunt instruction 'Till or Go to Jail'.[47] The following year, in keeping with this warning and in contrast to his conciliatory tone of four years previously, de Valera attacked what he called the 'black sheep' among the farming community who were failing in their tillage obligations.[48]

By the later years of the Emergency, tillage orders were revised by the Department of Agriculture to take greater account of the heterogeneity of Irish farming land: in 1944, the country was divided into three districts to ensure that quotas reflected the quality of land.[49] This revision was, however, unlikely to have abated farmers' scorn for the scheme because it came after the annual intensification of tillage stipulations in the preceding years. Initially, farmers were required to till one eighth of their land if they possessed ten acres or more.[50] The following year, Ryan upped the requirement to till one eighth of arable land to one sixth.[51] In 1941, Ryan announced that the requirement to till one sixth had now become one fifth.[52] Later in the year, he increased this mandatory quota to a quarter.[53] In 1944, the ten-acre ceiling was reduced to five acres and the quota increased to three eighths.[54] In 1942, to boot, the government passed a bill increasing the maximum penalty for failing to comply with tillage orders from £100 to £500.[55]

Evidencing the intensification of Agriculture's twin-pronged campaign, the amount of money the department requested for press advertising also rose with the punitive aspect of the order. The department had estimated that the yearly cost of the propaganda campaign in the press would be £7,000.[56] In fact, the department overspent and had to justify to Finance a figure of £8,350 for the year.[57] This figure increased to an annual sum of £10,000 for the remaining four years of the Emergency.[58] By 1944, Agriculture had even persuaded the Department of Education to issue a pamphlet to all schools 'to be used in reading and discussion' entitled 'Why Compulsory Tillage?'[59] An elderly Dublin man remembers attending a summer school in County Waterford as a child: the term Curadóireact Éigeantach (Compulsory Tillage) is his 'best piece of Irish to this day'.[60] As well as an effort to convince farmers, through their sons and daughters, that compulsory tillage was a national necessity, this move reflected the fact that many children were employed on the farm in an effort to meet quotas. After the government introduced compulsory tillage, there was a noticeable decline in school attendances in rural areas.[61]

By the spring of 1940, six holdings had been taken over by the state and sixty-eight farmers brought to court for failing to till enough land.[62] Between January and April 1941, the department announced that it had taken possession of 385 acres

from seventeen farms.[63] Although a small number, these figures relate to just the first
few months of the scheme's operation. They also reflect the time and costs incurred
by the state in confiscating and running a farm, a point raised by politicians opposed
to the measures.[64] Effective inspection was also hindered by fuel shortages and the
foot-and-mouth outbreak of 1941. In 1947, the *Irish Independent* reported that
300,000 farms came under compulsory tillage regulations, yet the average yearly
number of convictions (from 1940 to 1946) was only 236: 'in other words, not even
one farmer in a thousand failed in his duty'.[65] However, it is evident that by including
the data for 1946, the figures were distorted. This had the effect of exaggerating the
extent of cooperation with tillage orders. As stated in Dáil records, there were a mere
ten prosecutions listed for 1946 because prosecutions were still proceeding and the
intensification of the campaign had abated.[66] A more accurate yearly mean for convictions (from 1941 to 1945) is 305. In this period, the Irish state dispossessed
farmers of some 7,365 acres of farm land.[67] This figure represents a relatively high
proportion of evictions. In Northern Ireland, where farmers received ploughing and
fertiliser subsidies from the UK exchequer and more decisions were 'left to the good
sense of farmers', voluntary compliance was more forthcoming: in the ten years of
the scheme's operation, only four farmers were dispossessed of their land.[68]

'Cursing and threatening to sink his teeth into his belly': resistance

When compulsory tillage was announced, the *Irish Independent* reacted with typical
bluster, attacking the power to confiscate holdings in the strongest terms. Minister
Ryan was accused of a 'repugnant', 'high handed threat' which would allow the state
to act as 'judge, jury, sheriff and bailiff'.[69] The issue of land repossession was a particularly sensitive one in Ireland. If historical memory of the Great Famine was powerful during the Emergency, that of the land agitation of the late nineteenth century
exerted a similarly compelling presence in the collective mindset. Given this history,
the scope of the powers enjoyed by the Department of Agriculture's tillage inspectors proved contentious. Compulsory tillage, it was claimed, was 'state instruction at
the point of the bayonet'.[70]

    In implementing the scheme, the state faced various forms of resistance. Some
farmers used litigious strategies of resistance to oppose tillage orders. As with prosecutions for rationing offences, judges proved lenient towards the defendants on a
number of occasions. In several court cases in 1940, judges found that the state had
prosecuted prematurely. In November 1940, for instance, the judge at Longford Circuit Court reversed the decision of the Clonmel District Court and the convictions
of five farmers for non-compliance with the order. The farmers had been initially
convicted of not tilling their quotas in acreage 'in 1940'. The judge reasoned that
they could not be prosecuted as the year had not yet expired: two months of the year
remained.[71] The legal precedent for defences of this sort was set by a high-profile
case that went before the High Court in January 1941. A Blanchardstown farmer

had cultivated only one acre – a vegetable garden – of his 33.5 acre holding. The defence argued that the issuing of the summons by the Department of Agriculture in October 1940 was premature. The court agreed, pointing to the loophole in the 1940 Compulsory Tillage Order which ensured that prosecutions could be success-fully contested if the year had not expired when the summons was issued. Mr Justice Hanna criticised the order as 'drafted either by a farmer who knew no law or by a lawyer who knew nothing about farming'.[72]

The verdict represented the upholding of legal loopholes in the face of state pres-sure. The case took place amidst the weighty moral economic justification used by the government to validate tillage orders and denunciation of those farmers who did not carry out their 'patriotic duty'.[73] Due to the supply crisis, statements on the necessity to till as much land as possible appeared on nearly every front page of the *Irish Press* throughout early 1941. Covering the case, the *Press* unsurprisingly paid most attention to the words of Mr Justice Black, who contended 'a man who does not carry out his obligation to till is a public enemy and should be dealt with as such'.[74] The state solicitor's reminder that 'the production of food supplies is essen-tial to the very life of the community' was also widely cited.[75] The case did not pro-vide a lasting precedent for the evasion of compulsory tillage quotas because new orders were issued every year and those which followed the 1940 order were drafted to allow no leeway. Donegan's acquittal nonetheless provided an important example of the courts ruling in favour of the farmer and against the state. Mirroring the annoyance of civil servants from Supplies when a prosecution was not secured, de Valera stormily claimed that judges who acquitted farmers on such grounds 'did not realise the seriousness of the situation'.[76]

The case stands in contrast to examples where harsh sentences were imposed with the sort of unflinching rigour that, in the department's view, the supply crisis warranted. In a 1942 hearing, a judge launched a lengthy attack on a defendant, criti-cising him for his 'disobedience to the law and indolence'.[77] In another case in the same year, Agriculture successfully fined the owner of land which, unbeknownst to him, had not been tilled by his tenant farmer.[78] The burden that tillage quotas proved to the majority of farmers is demonstrated in satirical representations of exhausted farmers attempting to plough in the middle of the night in their pyjamas.[79] Leeway was not forthcoming in several instances to elderly farmers who pleaded that they could not fulfil the quota because they were too old and there was a lack of labour available in the local area.[80] In 1942, a number of successful defences at circuit court level against the order encouraged the government to move swiftly. Two Emergency Powers Orders were swiftly passed which removed the possibility of action against the Minister and enabled the referral of appeals by circuit court judges to a higher court (at which there would be less chance of success).[81]

State instruction faced other obstacles though. The rule of law was relatively weak during the Emergency, particularly in the nation's peripheries. According to John McGahern, himself the son of a Garda, 'In the Ireland of that time the law was still looked upon as alien, to be feared and avoided, and kept as far away as possible'.[82] The lowly status of the rule of law in Emergency Ireland may help to explain the actions of Leitrim small farmer Stephen Dalton when he was visited by a tillage inspector from the Department of Agriculture in late 1941. Seeing the inspector approach, Dalton ran towards him, chasing him off his land 'cursing and threatening to sink his teeth into his belly'.[83]

It may be that Dalton was, in the words of the judge who had charged another Leitrim farmer earlier that year for not complying with a tillage order, 'a stupid bovine creature'.[84] His reasoning may, on the other hand, have rested upon a common antipathy to stiff-necked and fussy outside authority similar in sentiment to Winston Churchill's criticism of his own officials for their 'petty, meticulous arrogant officialism'. In Emergency Ireland, there was a popular vocationalist mood, articulated in 1939's *Irish Monthly*: 'if our system of government makes it more attractive to produce more and better civil servants and poorer farmers, then the next generation will hardly pray for us'.[85] The implication was that Agriculture's Inspectorate did not understand that much of Ireland's land, particularly in the west, was unsuitable for wheat-growing.[86] In an article in 1940's *Capuchin Annual*, Robert Barton, chairman of the Turf Development Board, wrote of regional differentiation in Irish agriculture, describing the farming community at large as 'extraordinarily heterogeneous' in methods and means and noting 'Louth and Wexford farmers may not be any more industrious than those of the western counties, but soil and climate certainly afford them conditions more favourable for tillage than, say, Kerry'.[87] In implementing compulsory tillage, however, Barton's Fianna Fáil associates were accused of possessing a crudely homogeneous outlook that did not display adequate consideration for such differences. In Northern Ireland, by contrast, concessions were given to Fermanagh and South Antrim, where the soil was less suited to intensive cultivation.[88]

Those affected by compulsory tillage during the Emergency were disproportionately members of the lower socio-economic band of Irish farmers. Despite the expansion of the urban population during the Emergency, Ireland remained a nation of smallholders working unmechanised farms. According to the 1936 census, half of Ireland's working population was employed in agriculture, and the prevailing size of farms was small: over 50% of farms were thirty acres or under.[89] A 1941 source claimed that as much as 60% of Irish farms were thirty acres or (much) less.[90] Whatever the correct figure, such conditions promoted emigration as an option. As a Clare farmer attested, 'it was too hard to make a living out of thirty acres, so I went to England'.[91] In a Dáil debate of 1944, the Monetary Reform Party's Oliver J. Flanagan claimed that the compulsory tillage scheme had not affected the 'ordinary farmer', but had succeeded in targeting the 'rancher', 'one of the greatest enemies that we have in this country'.[92] On the contrary, evidence of court proceedings overwhelmingly demonstrates that 'ordinary' farmers – generally those whose farms were unmechanised and under thirty acres – were punished under the legislation.

Protesting against petrol rationing, a County Galway farmer bemoaned the 'deplorable position of the people especially the small farmers owing to the Government's compulsory tillage order'.[93] Others, fuelled by the widespread perception that compulsory tillage was fostered on them by a brutish and heedless Dublin bureaucracy, practised disobedience. Elsewhere in the west, a farmer was fined for not tilling the required acreage despite claiming at his trial that he thought Leitrim was exempt.[94] Some farmers went even further in attempting to circumvent the order. According to veteran broadcaster Mícheál Ó Muircheartaigh, a County Kerry farmer decided to act as if he was mad in order to avoid being allotted a tillage quota. Before the inspector visited, the farmer brought his horse into the house. While talking to the inspector, he repeatedly dropped his hand into the horse's feed – a bucket of mangels – and started to eat them, to the inspector's astonishment. As the inspector was about to leave, he produced a lump of coal, placed it on the table and smashed it to dust with a hammer, eating the dust as he did so and inviting the inspector to join him.[95]

Some farmers remained defiant. In February 1942, three Roscommon farmers were charged with not complying with tillage orders. It is uncertain whether these men (all of whom were in their sixties) were unable to till the required acreage because they were too old and all the local labour had been taken up on turf schemes, as they claimed, or whether they were merely idle. Either way, all three challenged the fines imposed by the judge, one telling him 'Do what you like with me. I am doing all I can and can do no more' and another 'I have never had an inspector tell me what to do in my life'.[96] Such disobedience demonstrated the disruption that tillage orders brought to the elderly countryman's pattern of life, a yearly round that followed the innate rhythms of the seasons and was, in some instances, unchanged in generations. In passionate *Dáil Debates* early in the Emergency, representatives from farming communities pleaded the farmers' case. They urged the government to take account of the varied nature of farming by exempting dairying land[97] because when many mixed and dairy farmers turned their attention to cultivating arable land, it resulted in a drastic fall in dairy production.[98] However, as James Ryan repeatedly insisted, Ireland simply did not have enough land under tillage to produce the sugar, wheat and animal feeding stuffs required by the shortfall in supplies: milk simply had to come second to wheat.[99]

In traditional grazing counties, the transition to tillage was generally resented. Some ploughed the required acreage and merely planted what they had always planted, leaving the rest fallow; others sowed oats among the wheat or claimed ownership of fewer acres than they really had. Shortly after Ryan announced the scheme, a farmer in Meath hired a private aeroplane to fly over local churches and GAA pitches on a Sunday morning, dropping thousands of leaflets opposing compulsory tillage.[100] Resistance to the scheme appears to have been just as robust in the grazing counties, where the transition to tillage was more difficult. In 1940, 35% of those inspected in Meath (415 farmers) failed to comply fully with the order; in Westmeath, 41% (219 farmers) were found guilty of non-compliance.[101]

With the end of the Emergency in sight, a number of county committees of agriculture openly wavered from the government's consummate drive for productivity
and passed resolutions calling for an end to compulsory tillage.[102] Such widespread
unpopularity was an important factor in the first Inter-party government's abolition
of the scheme in July 1948. There was a notable rise in dispossessions as the Emergency progressed. This was a symptom of the desperate need to grow more food but
also, as in the case of the Department of Supplies, demonstrated the growing capacity and confidence of the Department of Agriculture's Inspectorate. The *Irish Independent*'s figure of 236 convictions obscures the number of cases where court action
was threatened but not realised and the number of cases in which district justices or
judges dismissed charges. Of the latter, the dismissal of summons in 1940 against an
immobile eighty-year-old farmer of 'hopelessly feeble mind'[103] is illustrative not
only of the unwillingness of the judiciary to summarily punish offenders but also the
determination of the Inspectorate to secure convictions against deviants.

Newspaper reports of prosecutions illustrate that those farmers who did not comply with the state's instruction were often obstinate characters but also frequently old
and infirm. Summoned for non-compliance with a tillage order in 1940, an aged and
hard-of-hearing Meath farmer was guffawed at in court when he confessed to the
judge: 'Damnit, I can't hear a word at all.'[104] The presence of the farmer in the dock –
commonly unfamiliar with even basic court proceedings – provides an alternative
symbolism to the ploughman on the pound note. In a separate case, a farmer explained
that he was too old and too ill to till the required acreage and refused to pay the fine
imposed by the court.[105] In another case, a seventy-year-old County Tipperary farmer
was fined £20 for falling just an acre short of his quota.[106] It was not just old men who
felt the negative consequences of the scheme either. Perhaps the ultimate snub to the
iconic Ploughman was the revelation that a young farmer, who happened to be the
all-Ireland ploughing champion, had been forced from the land by compulsory tillage regulations and had instead taken to selling gravel in Dublin.[107]

'From the twentieth to the seventeenth century': in comparative perspective

For all the disruption, the quota demanded of the Irish farmer was lighter than that
demanded by the British war economy from Northern Ireland. There, from the earliest stages of the war, farmers were required to till one third of their land.[108] Farmers
south of the border were only obliged to till this proportion of their land from 1944.
In Northern Ireland, the tillage quota reached the upper heights of 45% (1943),[109]
whereas the most farmers south of the border were required to till was 37.5% (1944).
In England, everything produced by farmers was dictated by local war agricultural
committees, whereas in both Irish territories, the government dictated a minimum
tillage requirement but, after this was met, left the activity of the farmer to his or her
own discretion.[110] Neither did Ryan's Inspectorate expand to the same proportions
as Lemass's. Ryan stipulated that tillage inspectors 'must be men experienced in

judging land'[111] and the department's inspectors appear to have had less of the offi-cious swagger of their cousins in Supplies. Although some inspectors were seconded from the Land Commission, inspectors were usually already recognised local offi-cials of the department. By 1943, the department employed fifty inspectors and sixty-three tillage supervisors: a much smaller number than Supplies.[112] There was no large-scale recruitment of a new Inspectorate as with Supplies and no cannibalis-tic attempts to subsume civil servants and swell its functions. Instead, Agriculture preferred to curtail some of its activities so that compulsory tillage would be effec-tively administered. The department was unwilling to take on new staff and did so rarely and somewhat begrudgingly.[113]

Yet farmers south of the border faced a harder task than those in Northern Ire-land in a crucial regard: the abysmal lack of supplies. Farmers' disdain for outside interference was exacerbated by the lack of modern aids to production available to them. Although many farmers toiled hard to meet tillage quotas, the absence of fer-tiliser and lime made cultivation much harder and in some cases almost impossible. In 1939, Ryan had announced a subsidy for farmers to purchase lime, fertiliser and machinery,[114] but due to the rapid deterioration in the trade situation with Britain, supplies of these goods soon disappeared. Many would have concurred with James Dillon's contention that 'tillage without manure is not farming. It is mining – e.g. taking the fertility out of the soil without putting anything back.'[115] As a result of mineral depletion caused by compulsory tillage, there were disproportionate num-bers of deformities recorded in farm animals in the years following the scheme.[116]

Defending the scheme in early 1940, Ryan's Department of Agriculture claimed that compulsory tillage would be an easier proposition for the farmer than in 1917 because there were more farm horses and tractors available.[117] Farmers could have reasonably countered that not only was the burden of tillage offset in 1917 by better agricultural prices but that a lack of essential supplies (such as petrol, com-ponent parts and the machines themselves) had rendered compulsory tillage a back-breaking task during the Emergency. During the First World War, the depart-ment consulted more widely with county committees of agriculture, substantially increased wage rates for agricultural labourers, guaranteed higher prices for agri-cultural produce, dispossessed less land comparatively and greatly increased the number of tractors in the country.[118]

The lack of access to farm machinery was a major difference in the experience of compulsory tillage in the two states of Ireland. In the short course of the Emergency, old farming practices in Northern Ireland were substantially overhauled as Basil Brooke's Ministry of Agriculture took over the control and distribution of agricul-tural machinery. The productive gains which this transition to mechanisation brought were conveyed plainly by a County Down farmer: 'people said that a tractor couldn't plough like horses ... sure the tractor was ploughing three times as much' although, he added, 'when the horse is working he's not eating, but when a tractor's working it's eating an awful lot'.[119] Unfortunately for Ryan, bringing widespread mechanisation to Ireland's farmers was not an option. As mentioned, Lemass and Leydon were wrong-footed by Britain reneging on trade guarantees for agricultural machinery.[120] Lemass's department also continued to sanction the export of machinery to Britain in the first fourteen months of the Emergency, only securing the exchange of agricultural machinery for beer in the closing stages of the war.[121] Even this barter arrangement only resulted in Ireland receiving 100 tractors and twenty threshing sets.[122] By 1944, the number of tractors in Northern Ireland had risen from 550 (1939) to 7,000 (1944).[123] These machines worked on a sophisticated hydraulic three-point linkage system which allowed the plough to be connected directly to the tractor rather than on a trailer; the increased efficiency allowed for three to five furrow ploughing, cutting ploughing time from days to hours.[124] By contrast, as the official history of Northern Ireland during the war years smugly notes, 'to go south was to be transported in a matter of minutes from the twentieth to the seventeenth century'.[125] Whereas the modern machine was increasingly apparent on the farms of the six counties, the horse was still very much in evidence in the twenty-six counties. Due to its government's adherence to the British war effort, farmers in Northern Ireland also had greater access to fertilisers and phosphates as well, and when the tillage ceiling was reached in 1943, Brooke was able to relax restrictions and extend the use of fertilisers.[126] A combination of poor planning and British intransigence ensured Ryan could not revert to chemical solutions to ease the tillage burden.[127]

Interestingly, in 1917, Ireland's golf courses did not escape compulsory tillage, but during the six years of the Emergency, the country's links were spared the plough and spade.[128] In the northern statelet, by contrast, not even the lawns of Queen's University or Stormont survived compulsory tillage. Contemporary newsreel footage shows Minister for Agriculture Brooke overseeing the ploughing of Stormont estate with newly imported tractors in 1940.[129] Even Brooke's own country estate was subject to tillage regulations. In her first entry since 1924, Lady Brookeborough recorded in her diary '1941 – much ploughing last year ... arable acreage 90 acres ... have now one Ferguson, one Ford/Ferguson and only two horses'.[130]

In independent Ireland, Agriculture considered that 'state lands should be tilled at least to the extent stipulated in the order to act as an example to private owners'[131] but found itself frustrated by the unwillingness of other departments to permit tillage on its lands. The Department of Defence sought the exemption of all military lands from the order,[132] Industry and Commerce resisted its application to the fields of Dublin Airport,[133] and the Office of Public Works (OPW) declared many lands on large state properties and national monuments 'unsuitable'.[134] Thwarted officials from Agriculture even sought the removal of common rights of pasture on the Curragh of Kildare so that large areas could be put to tillage.[135] The use of the greatly expanded Irish army could have eased the burden that compulsory tillage placed on the farmer. Proposals to do so were vetoed, however. Ryan was fearful of the social disruption that would be caused by deploying soldiers from urban backgrounds onto rural farms, and Oscar Traynor, the Minister for Defence, argued that the army was already heavily involved in the turf drive and that its priority was national defence.[136]

Despite their seemingly insatiable quest for greater productivity in this sector, Seán Lemass and his developmentalist allies in the government and the civil service did not antagonise Catholic sensitivity to the family and the home to the extent of advocating a Women's Land Army – as seen in Britain – to aid the tillage drive.[137] During the First World War, by contrast, women in Ireland were able to attend special training courses to become agricultural workers.[138] In policymaking, Lemass was certainly less influenced by his Catholic faith than his colleagues in cabinet. There were clear limits, however, to the pragmatic progressiveness Tom Garvin sees the Minister for Supplies as embodying.[139] South of the border, the mass mobilisation of women into the workforce did not occur, whereas in Northern Ireland, it did, increasing women's economic liberty.[140] Although by the end of the Emergency Henry Kennedy's successor as president of the cooperative society the IAOS, the Jesuit E.J. Coyne, acknowledged the 'enormous potential productivity of our womenfolk' wasted during the Emergency, he envisaged women rearing poultry, practising horticulture and beekeeping rather than taking on farming duties such as tillage.[141] This was reflected in the propagandaic piece 'A Fresh Hand In The Harvest Field', which appeared in the *Irish Times* during the 1944 harvest season. 'Ireland's Land Army are going over the top to produce more wheat!' the author enthused. Unlike Britain's Land Army, though, women appeared in the narrative only to bring the men 'a big black kettle of tea and beef sandwiches'.[142] Despite the fact that between 1942 and 1945, one third of the Irish workforce in the British war economy was female,[143] the government did not encourage female labour in the Irish economy – either in the agricultural or industrial sphere.

Conclusion

When compulsory tillage was instituted under British rule in 1917, the *Irish Independent* noted the 'general feeling that a new body representatively constituted of the interests affected ought to have been established'.[144] When the scheme reappeared in 1939, there were again calls from farmers that compulsory tillage be instituted in a manner more sympathetic to local conditions and local opinions, as de Valera had suggested would be the case. The Monaghan Farmers' Trade Union, for example, resolved in December 1939 that 'any attempt to acquire holdings by compulsory tillage be decided by twelve local farmers with knowledge of the situation'.[145] Instead, the state carried out relatively little consultation. Compulsory tillage in the Irish case did not match the brute application of the scheme in neutral Spain, where farmers were subject to the more threatening surveillance of provincial Falange activists as well as state inspectors,[146] but it was instituted in a similarly punitive manner.

Relative to its impact, there is very little historical discourse surrounding compulsory tillage during the Emergency. The *1943 Report of the Commission on*

Vocational Organisation omitted mention of compulsory tillage from its criticism of the government's record in agriculture, a particularly puzzling oversight given that the commission consulted a number of farmers' representative bodies in the course of its enquiries. Emergency historiography, too, has largely ignored the scheme. While perhaps not the Stakhanovite effort desired by Lemass, as the following chapter explains, the country's farmers nonetheless raised the amount of land under corn crops from a five-year average of just under a million (between 1935 and 1939) to one and a half million acres (between 1940 and 1944).[147] Even with higher quotas and much greater mechanisation, the highest yearly acreage farmers in Northern Ireland reached was just over three quarters of a million acres.[148] As James Ryan, in a typical invocation of the Famine era, contended, 'you have to go back nearly one hundred years to beat that record'.[149] Meanwhile, the individual and collective resistance of a significant minority provides evidence that agrarian dissidence was alive and well during the Emergency. While resistance did not quite reach a pitch of 'notorious anarchy',[150] the evidence points to a greater degree of popular disobedience in the Irish countryside during the Emergency than previously documented.

Notes

1 Collingham, *Taste of War*, 1.
2 Milward, *War, Economy and Society*, 252.
3 Kennedy, *Modern Industrialisation*, 6.
4 Daly, *Agriculture*, 257.
5 Wills, *Neutral Island*, 241.
6 The best account is in Daly, *Agriculture*, 224–237.
7 Collingham, *Taste of War*, 81.
8 See Robert Brennan/Frederick Boland correspondence, March 1941. NAI, Washington Embassy file, Department of Foreign Affairs files (DFA)/10/P/35.
9 Terence Dooley, *'The Land for the People': The Land Question in Independent Ireland* (Dublin, 2004), 2.
10 Dooley, *'The Land for the People'*, 59.
11 Daly, *Agriculture*, 55–56.
12 Dooley, *'The Land for the People'*, 34.
13 Dooley, *'The Land for the People'*, 106.
14 Meenan, *Irish Economy*, 32.
15 *Irish Times*, 10 October 1939.
16 Emergency Powers (no. 12) Order 1939. NAI, FIN/S90/35/39.
17 James Ryan, *Dáil Debates*, vol. 81, col. 1297, 12 December 1940.
18 Ryan, Emergency Powers (no. 234) Order, 1942 - Motion to Annul, vol. 89, col. 1013, 4 March 1943.
19 *Irish Independent*, 25 March 1940.
20 Paul Bew and Henry Patterson, *Seán Lemass and the Making of Modern Ireland 1945–66* (Dublin, 1982), 21.

21 Interim Report of Departmental Committee on Increased Agricultural Production, 1938. NAI, FIN/S90/35/39.

22 Department of Agriculture, untitled memorandum, 4 September 1939. NAI, FIN/S90/35/39.

23 Agriculture, untitled memo, 4 September 1939. NAI, FIN S90/35/39.

24 *Irish Times*, 19 September 1939.

25 During the Emergency, the *Irish Press* frequently harked back to conditions 'a century ago' to promote tillage. See, for instance, F. Henegan, 'They Grew Wheat in Those Days', *Irish Press*, 8 February 1941.

26 Patrick Power, *History of Waterford City and County* (Dublin, 1990), 282.

27 *Irish Press*, 22 April 1942.

28 *Irish Press*, 11 October 1939.

29 *Irish Press*, 16 February 1942.

30 Wills, *Neutral Island*, 241, 257.

31 Department of the Taoiseach memorandum, 'Chinese Famine, 1943'. NAI, DT/T6/97/9/461.

32 NAI, DT/T6/97/9/461.

33 Censor's Report for February 1942. University College Dublin Archives (UCDA), Frank Aiken papers, P104/3486.

34 *Irish Independent*, 29 March 1945.

35 *Irish Press*, 16 January 1941.

36 *Irish Press*, 10 October 1939.

37 *Irish Times*, 18 January 1941.

38 The image is reproduced on the cover of Eugene Duggan's *The Ploughman on the Pound Note: Farmer Politics in County Galway during the Twentieth Century* (Athenry, 2004).

39 Ferriter, 'A Peculiar People', 33.

40 *Irish Press*, 16 February 1942.

41 *Irish Press*, 6 January 1941.

42 *Irish Times*, 13 October 1939.

43 *Irish Times*, 4 October 1939.

44 Seanad Éireann, vol. 23, col. 1303, 25 October 1939.

45 *Irish Times*, 1 April 1941.

46 *Irish Times*, 16 February 1942.

47 *Irish Times*, 2 March 1942.

48 *Irish Times*, 8 December 1943.

49 *Irish Independent*, 29 November 1946.

50 *Irish Times*, 10 October 1939.

51 *Irish Times*, 5 October 1940.

52 *Irish Times*, 9 January 1941.

53 *Irish Times*, 12 November 1941.

54 Ryan, *Dáil Debates*, vol. 92, col. 1106, 16 February 1944.

55 *Irish Times*, 2 July 1942.

56 L. Fitzgerald to T.S.C. Dagg, 2 November 1940. NAI, FIN/S3/1/40.

57 J.H. Hinchcliff to Hugo Flynn, 26 July 1941. NAI, FIN/S3/1/40.

58 D. Twomey to Flynn, 13 October 1941; 14 September 1942; 6 September 1943; 6 June 1944. NAI, FIN/S3/1/40.
59 *Irish Times*, 6 April 1944.
60 Tom Conlon, b. 1932, Dublin. Interviewed 6 November 2009.
61 *Southern Star*, 10 May 1941.
62 Ryan, *Dáil Debates*, vol. 81, col. 1816, 5 February 1941.
63 *Irish Times*, 1 April 1941.
64 General MacEoin, *Dáil Debates*, vol. 93, col. 417, 28 March 1944.
65 *Irish Independent*, 1 February 1947.
66 Ryan, *Dáil Debates*, vol. 104, col. 64, 22 January 1947.
67 *Dáil Debates*, vol. 104, col. 64, 22 January 1947.
68 Alan Greer, *Rural Politics in Northern Ireland: Policy Networks and Agricultural Development since Partition* (Aldershot, 1996), 23.
69 *Irish Independent*, 25 March 1940.
70 Patrick Baxter, Seanad Éireann, vol. 23, col. 1299, 25 October 1939.
71 *Irish Times*, 1 November 1940.
72 *Irish Press*, 16 January 1941.
73 *Irish Press*, 11 January 1941.
74 *Irish Press*, 16 January 1941.
75 *Irish Press*, 15 January 1941.
76 *Irish Times*, 2 July 1942.
77 *Connacht Tribune*, 6 June 1942.
78 *Irish Times*, 25 February 1942.
79 *Dublin Opinion*, February 1942.
80 See *Nenagh Guardian*, 28 February 1942 and 31 March 1945, for instance.
81 Daly, *Agriculture*, 236.
82 John McGahern, *Memoir* (London, 2005), 29.
83 *Leitrim Observer*, 12 December 1942.
84 *Leitrim Observer*, 28 February 1942.
85 T.J. McElligott, 'How the Farmers Can Organise', *Irish Monthly*, 67 (1939), 52.
86 Wills, *Neutral Island*, 241.
87 Robert Barton, 'The Agriculture of Leinster', *Capuchin Annual* (1940), 243.
88 Greer, *Rural Politics in Northern Ireland*, 24.
89 Seán MacEntee papers, '1936 Census'. UCDA, P67/262 (1).
90 Dominick MacCabe, Seanad Éireann, vol. 24, col. 2527, 4 December 1940.
91 MIOA, Vincent Hannery, b. 1926, Newmarket-on-Fergus, co. Clare. Interviewed 16 April 2001.
92 Oliver J. Flanagan, *Dáil Debates*, vol. 93, col. 487, 28 March 1944.
93 M. Haire to Henry Kennedy, 29 May 1941. NAI, ICOS/1088/222/4.
94 *Irish Times*, 7 July 1942.
95 Mícheál Ó Muircheartaigh, b. 1930, Dingle, co. Kerry. Interviewed 12 August 2009.
96 *Leitrim Observer*, 28 February 1942.
97 Patrick Belton, *Dáil Debates*, vol. 81, cols. 1256–1263, 12 December 1940.
98 George Bennett, *Dáil Debates*, vol. 91, col. 1566, 4 November 1943.
99 *Dáil Debates*, vol. 81, col. 1291, 12 December 1940.

100 *Irish Times*, 21 November 1939.

101 Daly, *Agriculture*, 235.

102 *Anglo Celt*, 19 May 1945.

103 *Meath Chronicle*, 28 September 1940.

104 *Meath Chronicle*, 28 September 1940.

105 *Connacht Sentinel*, 22 October 1940.

106 *Nenagh Guardian*, 23 January 1943.

107 *Irish Times*, 5 March 1943.

108 *Irish Times*, 12 September 1940.

109 Blake, *Northern Ireland*, 405.

110 *Irish Times*, 11 January 1940.

111 Ryan, Memorandum on Increased Food Production, 21 September 1939. NAI, FIN/ S90/35/39.

112 Daly, *Agriculture*, 235.

113 Department of Agriculture, untitled memorandum, 4 September 1939. NAI, FIN/ S90/35/39.

114 *Dáil Debates*, vol. 77, col. 642, 18 October 1939.

115 James Dillon to Editor, *Irish Times*, 1 April 1940.

116 Daly, *Agriculture*, 287.

117 *Irish Times*, 1 February 1940.

118 Daly, *Agriculture*, 55–62. James Ryan established a Consultative Council for Agricultural Production in 1939, but did not establish a committee devoted exclusively to the operation of the compulsory tillage scheme.

119 MIOA, Jack Magill, b. 1927, Saul, co. Down. Interviewed 16 April 2000, p. 6.

120 'Record of Activities'. NAI, IND/EHR/3/15, p. 7.

121 'Historical Survey'. NAI, IND/EHR/3/C4, part XI, p. 607.

122 Clement Attlee to Irish High Commissioner, 8 March 1942. NAI, FA/P58.

123 Blake, *Northern Ireland*, 410.

124 'Tractors', broadcast c. 1945. PRONI, NIDFA.

125 Blake, *Northern Ireland*, 410.

126 Blake, *Northern Ireland*, 405.

127 'Historical Survey'. NAI, IND/EHR/3/C2, part V, p. 223.

128 *Irish Times*, 18 November 1939.

129 Pathé Gazette, 'Dig for Victory!', broadcast 22 January 1940. PRONI, NIDFA.

130 Diary of Cynthia, Lady Brookeborough. PRONI, D3004/D/29.

131 J.H. Hinchcliff to Hugo Flynn, 29 April 1940. NAI, FIN/S90/35/39.

132 Defence memorandum on compulsory tillage, 8 April 1940. NAI, FIN/S90/35/39.

133 Industry and Commerce memorandum on compulsory tillage, 12 December 1939. NAI, FIN/S90/35/39.

134 P. Fagan to J.H. Hinchcliff, 17 April 1940. NAI, FIN/S90/35/39.

135 T.S.C. Dagg to secretary, Office of Public Works, 15 February 1939. NAI, FIN/S90/35/39.

136 Daly, *Agriculture*, 244.

137 See Penny Summerfield, *Women Workers during the Second World War* (London, 1982).

138 Daly, *Agriculture*, 56.

139 See Garvin, *Judging Lemass* and *Preventing*, throughout.

140 McCormick, "One Yank", 234.
141 E.J. Coyne, 'Agricultural Co-Operation', *Irish Monthly*, 73 (1945), 231.
142 *Irish Times*, 12 August 1944.
143 Ollerenshaw, 'War, Industrial Mobilisation', 192.
144 *Irish Independent*, 12 January 1917.
145 *Anglo-Celt*, 16 December 1939.
146 Bowen, *Spain*, 111.
147 *Statistical Abstract*, 1945.
148 Blake, *Northern Ireland*, 405.
149 *Irish Times*, 18 January 1945.
150 *Irish Times*, 19 September 1939.

8

The state and the small man

I am beginning to hate Ireland and the Irish

John Betjeman, 2 March 1941

Getting the bishops on-side: agricultural productivity

As an interference with private property rights and individual liberty, the Catholic Church might be expected to have opposed compulsory tillage. Yet there is no evidence of a major clash between the hierarchy and the government over compulsory tillage or other coercive state schemes. Why? In large part, the absence of a clash between church and state can be attributed to assurances secured from the bishops, both Protestant and Catholic, by ministers. In early 1941, Lemass wrote to John Charles McQuaid, Archbishop of Dublin:

> I am anxious to enlist your Grace's active assistance in the promotion of a campaign to safeguard our supplies of essential foodstuffs ... I would ask you, on behalf of the government, to use your influence with a view to getting farmers in your Archdiocese to produce the maximum possible crop ... I should be very glad if, in addition to using your own influence in this direction, you would ask the clergy, teachers, and other influential persons ... to help as much as they can so long as the emergency lasts.[1]

Lemass also wrote to McQuaid asking him to ensure the clergy encouraged the public to support the turf drive. He received assurances from him on both fronts. Lemass's approach was replicated in a letter addressed to all clergy the following year by a senior civil servant at the Department of Agriculture, Daniel Twomey. Falling back on the famine theme, Twomey warned of a return to 'the hardships endured during the forties of the last century' unless wheat production increased.[2] Twomey issued a similar letter to the clergy every year while shortages continued. McQuaid assured Lemass that he had his 'own way of quietly securing that the priests will assist you' in endorsing the government's campaign for agricultural productivity.[3] Echoing his assurance to Lemass, Twomey was informed by McQuaid that he had 'already taken steps in the matter' of getting priests to press the importance of food production.[4] De Valera also wrote to McQuaid to solicit his assistance 'in bringing the acute seriousness of the situation before the people'.[5] The apex of coalescence between church and state on this issue came in an extraordinary crossing of the boundary between church and state later in the Emergency when the Mayo county surveyor, Fianna Fáil's Seán Flanagan, himself issued a 'pastoral letter' to be read at all churches in the county calling for a ban on emigration so that turf would be saved.[6]

Compared with the other neutral Catholic states, the closeness of Fianna Fáil and the bishops on this issue was striking. In Franco's Spain, scientific advances in agronomy were stunted by the disruption of war and the decentralised conservatism of the new order.[7] Nonetheless, 'National Syndicalism', the Falangist agricultural reform project pursued during the war, initially assimilated even cooperative organisations – merging rural Catholic associations into a centralised structure – to the dismay of the Spanish hierarchy.[8] In Portugal, the apostolic nuncio told Irish diplomats in Lisbon that Salazar's regime relied on force in the economic sphere and had nothing in common with the ideals of the papal encyclicals.[9]

In Ireland, the cooperation of McQuaid and other bishops ensured that in its attempt to improve agricultural productivity, the state could rely on a constant stream of moral economic rhetoric from the church. The bishops' support for the tillage drive was tantamount to unanimous. It was enhanced by the fact that the use of horse and plough to increase productivity chimed with the consummate ruralism of clerical vocabulary in this period. The bishops' endorsement of the state's productivity drive was announced on the front pages of many newspapers, particularly in early 1941 when the supply crisis was relatively new and particularly grave. 'Speed The Plough! Bishops Support "More Wheat" Drive!' declared The Standard's headline;[10] 'Bishops: Farmers' Duty in Emergency', announced the Irish Press; 'every root of ground must play its part', declared the Bishop of Raphoe, William MacNeely.[11] 'This is not exactly a subject for the altar or the pulpit', admitted the Bishop of Cork, 'but the circumstances of the time are very exceptional' and require 'mutual help and co-operation'.[12] Both Catholic and Church of Ireland bishops expressed their strong support for compulsory tillage during a major Department of Agriculture meeting in Galway City in 1942.[13]

Some bishops, on the other hand, highlighted the hardship placed on farmers. MacRory urged farmers to 'respond wholeheartedly' to the state's tillage drive but stated that farmers could not 'do it all' and that better shipping and credit facilities and the use of the unemployed to dig turf were also needed.[14] Many bishops also declared their hopes that the state would provide fair prices for wheat to justify the farmers' hard work. The Bishop of Killaloe, Michael Fogarty, urged an 'economic price',[15] and MacRory urged the government to 'err on the side of generosity' in deciding wheat prices.[16] There were exceptions from the moral economic chorus, too. After the tillage ceiling had been reduced to a miserable five acres in 1944, the Bishop of Meath (later Cardinal Primate of all Ireland) John Francis D'Alton very deliberately and publicly declined Minister for Agriculture James Ryan's invitation to a 'Grow More Food' meeting in Mullingar. In a statement, he said that the 'burden may prove too heavy for some' if the government did not make more machinery and labour available.[17]

The popular Catholic newspaper *The Standard* was, predictably, more outspoken against the coercive measures employed by the state. Its arguments appealed to readers sympathetic to the organising concepts behind Christian parish-based rural renewal groups such as Muintir na Tíre, which advocated a subsidiary (rather than interventionist) role for the state based on intermediate groups between it and the citizen.[18] Discussing compulsory tillage in late 1941, an editorial declared that 'the farmer will provide a square meal if he gets a square deal'.[19] Earlier that year, the newspaper published a piece that remarkably escaped the censors. Following Lemass's proposal of a mobile turf corps in May 1941, it fell to Turf Controller Hugo Flinn to moot the idea that 'people may have to move from their homes to find work'. *The Standard* responded by branding Ireland 'A Nation Under The Lash'. Opposing the scheme, it drew attention to what it saw as a totalitarian concentration of power in the executive: 'The government have been given absolute power by the people. Then there's the Emergency Powers Acts. What more power does the government need?'[20] The following week, the newspaper called for 'justice' for the overworked and underpaid 'sons of the soil'.[21]

The intensification of tillage, however, also witnessed an intensification of rural essentialist discourse in *The Standard*, which was a staple of Catholic discourse in general. The newspaper supported the ethic of hardy self-sufficiency that the tillage drive represented. It is also significant that open expressions of discontent with compulsory tillage by Ireland's bishops were never publicly articulated in stronger terms than those of D'Alton. Despite the vocationalist dislike for the overbearing state, most priests and bishops fully endorsed the state's attempts to increase productivity. As mentioned previously, this support was based on the general willingness of Catholic bishops and writers to accept the view that the state 'derives its right, in certain grave necessities, to expropriate the private property of some of its citizens'. This right could be carried out 'in supremely critical emergencies without compensation'.[22] Although the extent to which the Emergency was 'supremely critical' in its later stages is questionable, the Irish hierarchy did not speak out against unpalatable aspects of the Irish war economy during the Emergency. Ultimately, harsh exactions in the production of wheat at home had to be weighed against English economic perfidy, an opinion encapsulated in the writings of Alfred O'Rahilly, the Cork economist and champion of social Catholicism, who wrote in 1941 that 'in case of war England would sell us wheat only at the price of Irish flesh and blood'.[23]

In its 1943 report, the Commission on Vocational Organisation criticised the centralisation of agricultural administration and stated its desire for 'the development of co-operation' to 'promote the economic, social and moral welfare of farmers'.[24] Writing about the commission, Don O'Leary argues that these recommendations were the most critical of the government.[25] The attack was hardly robust, though, and O'Leary overstates its significance, particularly given the lack of attention the Department of Agriculture paid to it. Earlier in its report, the commission praised cooperative dairying as an example of vocational organisation but admitted that 'the ideal of harmonious co-operation did not operate in practice'.[26] It is a pity therefore that the commission's recommendations for agriculture constituted little more than an idealisation of the parish guild structure and did not specifically condemn particular planks of the Emergency controls on agriculture.[27] In supporting the state's message, it is reasonable to assume that most priests envisaged the voluntary, cooperative cultivation of derelict land which was carried out during the Emergency by local guilds of the Irish Countrywomen's Association rather than state labour camps and land dispossessions: the grim reality of state efforts to improve agricultural productivity. But the report made no such complaints. In its reply, the Department of Agriculture was able to argue that farmers' often less-than-enthusiastic response to its Emergency measures demonstrated that they, and not the state, were against attempts to stimulate a cooperative spirit.[28]

Dictation and discourse

Alongside compulsory tillage, the state resorted to other forms of rural coercion during the Emergency. As with compulsory tillage, censorship was applied to smother collective agrarian dissent and criticism of the management of the foot-and-mouth crisis of 1941. The government claimed that publication would harm productivity and, thus, the wider community. Meanwhile, in an effort to increase fuel productivity, the state instituted camp labour and restricted the movement of agricultural labourers. These measures signalled an important departure in Fianna Fáil's broad approach to rural production. Significant market and social disruption resulted. In taking tough measures, Fianna Fáil insisted – and not without justification – that the national interest should come first. Yet even with the protection of censorship, this left the party open to political pressure. This centred on the effect of Emergency controls on the honest, hard-working small man. There were also strong divisions within the cabinet over the role of the state. Most significantly, in terms of power politics, Emergency measures in the countryside alienated a considerable proportion of Fianna Fáil's support base, as symbolised by the rise of the Farmers' Party, Clann na Talmhan, in this era.

James Ryan's Department of Agriculture oversaw the majority of Emergency controls on agriculture and Lemass's Department of Supplies dealt with the pricing of agricultural goods and complaints alleging overcharging.[29] As with many Emergency measures, the government's hand was forced by the British precedent of rationing and its strict price control mechanism.[30] These, together with the high insurance costs of transporting cattle during a time of marine warfare,[31] ensured that the export of livestock to Britain fetched very little profit. This situation presented a stark contrast to Irish farmers' ample returns during the First World War.[32] The government feared that farmers would attempt to overcome this loss of market and the increased cost of feed and fertiliser by overcharging for their produce. Consequently, to protect the consumer in a time of grave shortages, the government introduced price controls.

The government used its wide-ranging powers of censorship to enforce such controls, refusing to publish critical commentary on agricultural prices or productivity.

Such censorship soon came in for criticism. In 1939, a Westmeath TD claimed that 'in my county we cannot buy or sell milk'. He blamed the government's suppression of all information in the press in connection with a dairy strike. This had led to 'very serious inconvenience and confusion throughout the country'; farmers were isolated, he claimed, resulting in 'very strong indignation amongst the entire farming community'.[33] His protestations were met with a curt reply from the Minister for the Coordination of Defensive Measures, Frank Aiken, who told the deputy 'publication would have interfered with the provision of supplies essential to the life of the community'.[34] The following day, Aiken again faced questions on the use of censorship to safeguard agricultural productivity. He was accused of a 'disgraceful abuse of the Government's emergency powers' in censoring coverage of the Irish Farmers' Federation strike, a charge he met with the same reply as previously.[35]

These early exchanges set the tone for the rest of the Emergency, with Aiken pursuing an unwaveringly firm line against complaints that censorship was harming the economic viability of the sector. The government deemed any public discussion of agricultural prices a potential threat to productivity. The opposition claimed that the censorship of issues relating to the farming community was excessive. As mentioned in the previous chapter, the annual 'Grow More Wheat' campaign dominated the press during the Emergency. Each year, the government mounted a robust campaign to grow more wheat for the harvest. Any articles deemed to have deviated from the government's version of moral economy were ruthlessly cut. For example, in the midst of the government's frantic 'Grow More Wheat' campaign of February 1942, *The Farmers' Paper* was censored because it contained an article calling on the government for a 'fair and generous price' for wheat.[36] The article in question was particularly mild, conforming throughout to the obligatory moral economic rhetoric praising the farmer's 'sweat and toil'. Yet it was deemed to have run the risk of having a negative effect on the wheat-growing campaign due to this single reference to fair pricing.

During that same year's campaign, a press release by the Fine Gael Agricultural Committee, which merely stated that its members were going to government buildings to discuss the price of wheat, was censored.[37] In the ensuing bad-tempered exchanges in the Dáil, Richard Mulcahy accused Aiken of putting 'the hand of the censorship over everybody else's mouth' but his own. Aiken rounded on his opponent. Was Mulcahy, he asked, 'trying to argue that every galoot in the country should have the power to try and advocate starving people'?[38] Invoking the 'Step Together' spirit, Aiken claimed that 'when the life of this country is at stake, it is necessary for some disciplined, united effort' to protect 'the community generally'.[39] This was a classic deployment of the moral neutrality spirit, intertwined with the state's fundamental moral economic focus: the prevention of starvation.

Invariably, the opposition responded by offering an alternative and more popular version of moral economy, one in which farmers' honest work was exploited by big government's refusal to fix higher prices.

Censorship was also used to stifle criticism surrounding a disastrous episode for Ireland's farmers: the foot-and-mouth outbreak of 1941. In that year, there were a total of 556 outbreaks of the disease throughout the country, and 41,501 cows, sheep, goats and pigs were slaughtered.[40] The outbreak of the disease was devastating for Ireland's cattle farmers, necessitating the widespread destruction of livestock, particularly in counties Kilkenny, Carlow and Tipperary.[41] The first cases arose in January 1941, leading to a complete ban on meat exports. Agriculture officials placed disinfectant baths at the entrances to schools and creameries, but the disease spread rapidly.[42] James Ryan laid blame for the spread of the disease on those farmers who did not report outbreaks promptly.[43] These farmers were not compensated and instead faced prosecution and heavy fines.

Such punitive measures on irresponsible farmers were widely held to be just as the gravity of the outbreak became clearer. There was resentment, though, at Ryan's decision to ban cattle markets and fairs but allow race and coursing meetings to take place.[44] Ryan also faced criticism about the time lapse between the confirmation of the disease and the slaughter of the affected herds. In June 1941, he claimed that it was no longer than three days.[45] The following month, it was revealed that in some cases in County Kilkenny, the time lapse was five days because of the rapidity of the spread of infection.[46] Ryan denied that his department had failed to prevent the spread of the disease, citing its eradication in counties Donegal, Meath, Dublin, Wicklow, Offaly, Limerick, Kerry, North Tipperary and Laois by July 1941[47] and the presence of extra police on night patrols to prevent the transit of cattle in the still-affected areas of counties Tipperary and Kilkenny.[48] The elder citizens of the Local Defence Force (LDF) and the teenage members of the Construction Corps carried out much of the grim work of killing cattle and destroying carcasses, but foot and mouth persisted well into September 1941 in Kilkenny. The county's hurlers were even forced to withdraw from the all-Ireland championship that year due to the Department of Agriculture's travel restrictions.[49]

Clair Wills calls the foot-and-mouth outbreak 'a stroke of spectacularly bad luck'.[50] It certainly was, but it was also aggravated by ineptitude. Complacency in securing essential supplies was responsible for the lack of mechanical diggers in the country, which might have been used to bury carcasses quickly and effectively: an absence which hastened the spread of the disease.[51] This was, of course, not public knowledge at the time. The more biting criticisms of the government over the crisis were not published in newspapers either, due to censorship. The time lapse between detection and slaughter therefore did not become a cause célèbre, and despite his department and the authorities being evidently overstretched, Ryan was able to brand calls for the introduction of foreign experts to manage the outbreak 'unpatriotic'.[52]

Camp labour in the countryside

Censorship may have enhanced agricultural productivity by quelling dissent in rural communities, but economic measures were the fundament of state pressure in the sector. Seán Lemass's central position in the management of the Emergency economy ensured his disproportionate influence in this area. It is evident that Lemass held a disregard for the social factors underlying production. This is evidenced in his consistent placement of planning above social and even political considerations during the Emergency. In a memorandum composed in 1938, Lemass envisioned the Irish labour camp. It would be an essentially militaristic experience, he hoped. Participants would be 'subject to regulations as a soldier is subject to army regulations'. Harsh discipline would be imposed and recourse to ordinary courts denied.[53]

Lemass's desire to institute an experimental camp for coerced labourers was realised in 1939. It was opened at Clonsast near Portarlington in County Laois and proved an abject failure. Recruitment of unemployed men to Clonsast bog was dispersed between the Office of Public Works (OPW), the Turf Development Board, Employment Exchange officials and Gardaí.[54] Eighty per cent of recruits either failed to attend or dropped out within the first week.[55] Those who stayed complained of the poor pay and conditions and the monotony of turf digging.[56] In a clause obviously intended to add a favourable slant to the forcible enlistment of recruits, Lemass had advised that the 'voluntary enrolment of members would be assisted by withholding the dole from applicants'.[57] Clearly, however, most non-participants viewed the cessation of unemployment assistance payments as a less daunting prospect than employment and accommodation on a remote bog.

The Clonsast scheme bore all the hallmarks of Lemass's enthusiasm for grand schemes but also his willingness to erode liberties and regiment labour in the pursuit of economic targets. Another of Lemass's many schemes for camp labour in Ireland, brashly implemented with the illiberal testing ground mentality which the Emergency engendered in him, was the Construction Corps. Like its British equivalent, which was overseen by Minister for Labour Ernest Bevin, the scheme raised uncomfortable parallels with the fascist deployment of youth. Bevin assured the British cabinet that the scheme would 'resemble more closely President Roosevelt's Civilian Conservation Corps than any Fascist or Nazi youth organisation'.[58] Irish policymakers made similar assurances; after all, the first Irish advocate of such a scheme was Blueshirt leader Eoin O'Duffy back in 1934. The Construction Corps operated as an army battalion into which adolescent working class urban youth was coerced. Its members lived and worked in squalid conditions, under army discipline, frequently stationed to lonely bogs. Living conditions were compared to a 'concentration camp' by the father of one member who had complained of mistreatment.[59] If teenage boys refused to join, their dole payments were ceased. In 1943, it was alleged by Labour Party deputies that some 5,000 able-bodied young men had been refused unemployment assistance because they had refused to join the Construction Corps. 'Why should the state maintain a man who refuses to join the Construction Corps?' replied Lemass.[60]

During the Emergency, Lemass regularly adopted a similarly unbending attitude to the negative effects of compulsory tillage, turf camps and other forms of state compulsion. Reacting to the fuel crisis, the government placed emigration embargos on men with turf-cutting experience in October 1941 and in May 1942.[61] Garda records suggest that the state exercised such extraordinary controls on the movement of turf workers at an earlier stage. The Gardaí kept a file on workers employed by the Turf Development Board on their scheme at Glencree Bog, County Wicklow, and policemen were present at the camp.[62] Police surveillance of the personnel employed on state turf schemes during the Emergency underlines the seriousness of the nation's fuel situation but also the authoritarian aspect to these ventures. Under the first emigration embargo, leaving Ireland was prohibited to men under twenty-two years of age to whom work was available, with allowances made for areas with a strong tradition of seasonal migration.[63] Under the second, men with agricultural experience who were resident in tillage districts were prevented from emigrating.[64]

Lemass's cabinet rival Seán MacEntee favoured the extension of emigration embargoes, particularly in the 'congested districts' – areas of western counties where the land was poor and unemployment high.[65] Lemass, assuming his familiar place in the opposite corner to MacEntee, was against the extension of embargoes and instead proposed labour camps staffed by a 'reserve pool of labour' to be drawn from these rural areas.[66] The reserve pool would feature 'a class of worker' that would partake of employment instead of remaining at home idle, the victim of 'inequitable' embargoes.[67] Lemass's proposals are contextualised by the problem of rural unemployment due to the seasonality of agricultural employment. Illustrative of the hardship of rural unemployment is a letter he received in early 1940 from an unemployed agricultural labourer from County Wicklow, pleading 'this is a Christian state. Please don't let us starve and die' and warning that unless something was done, 'a very ugly situation' would develop 'in the near future'.[68] The letter's author was a recipient of 'rotation' relief, a scheme whereby a man could usually expect work for three days in every week. After each period of employment, the worker faced a compulsory fortnight-long wait for unemployment assistance.[69] This method of unemployment relief was particularly unsuited to rural Ireland and had 'demoralised and enslaved the worker', the labourer claimed.[70]

Yet Lemass's liberal language disguised his penchant for coercion, which again reared its head in the conditions he proposed to attach to the labour camps of 'reserve pool' workers. A man of the reserve pool would be placed on a register and 'sign an undertaking to hold himself available for employment on the production of food and fuel in any place in Éire to which at any time he may be directed to go'.[71] For this, he would receive a small weekly retainer but would be automatically disqualified from emigrating. 'Failure or refusal' to work at a particular camp due to the conditions would be 'punishable by fine or imprisonment or both', and – irrespective of mitigating circumstances – the individual would be deprived of his unemployment assistance and retainer.[72] By this point, Lemass's already extensive economic portfolio had extended even further. On 2 January 1941, the cabinet committee on emergency problems agreed that the Minister for Supplies would undertake the campaign to grow more food, and in August of that year Lemass regained control of the Department of Industry and Commerce as well.[73] He pushed strongly for the implementation of the proposals, and the cabinet eventually granted them. However, the authoritarian nature of Lemass's scheme ensured that it was ultimately unsuccessful: not enough men proved willing to sign up to the conditions of the reserve pool.

Despite the creation of employment by the government through its turf schemes, the availability of men to save the turf and the harvest was threatened by the presence of agents of British construction firms. These men operated in western Irish towns, placed there to lure dissatisfied men to the high wages of the British war economy.[74] Consequently, the government granted turf workers eligibility for unemployment insurance, but farm workers remained ineligible; between 1943 and 1946, turf workers also received better wages than agricultural labourers.[75] In common with their urban counterparts, the rights of rural labourers were undermined under the key piece of Emergency labour legislation: the Wages Standstill Order of May 1941, which prevented strikes and wage increases.

While the devolution of turf production to county councils between 1941 and 1947[76] provided a ready source of rural employment, other Emergency measures interfered with labour patterns in the hope of improving productivity. In western counties where there was a stronger tradition of seasonal migration, the sporadic embargoes on the migration of agricultural labourers caused greater disruption to life and work.[77] The need for turf as fuel had become so important that in 1944 emigration from towns with a population of 5,000 and less was banned,[78] another example of the extraordinary ordering and restriction of bodies during the Emergency.

Like Lemass, Todd Andrews, the head of the Turf Development Board, saw camp labour as the best method of ensuring productivity and reducing unemployment. He argued that, in their innovative character, camp labour schemes were preferable to the 'trite old objection of administrative impracticability trotted out by elderly boy clerks'.[79] Here, again, was an example of the common distaste for bureaucracy, or 'stuffed shirts' as Seán O'Faoláin put it, during the Emergency.[80] Nonetheless, the 'shovel ready', streamlined schemes favoured by the likes of Andrews and Lemass contained drawbacks borne of impatience. The 'Kildare Scheme', for instance, which involved the cultivation of a 250-square mile area of turf in that county, provided employment for some 4,000 men from western counties between 1943 and 1947, as Andrews boasts in his memoir.[81] It also involved the housing of these labourers in camps in which conditions, as Andrews himself conceded, were 'more typical of refugee camps'.[82]

A government interdepartmental conference of 1942 agreed that conditions in state camp labour schemes like that in Kildare would have to improve.[83] It was also noted that of 180 workers from Donegal recruited to the camp, one third had left citing 'dissatisfaction with the food and other reasons'.[84] Young unemployed men – predominately from the congested districts of Galway, Donegal and Mayo – were billeted in farms and tents on the bogs because the hostels to house the workers had not been built. The Turf Development Board eventually constructed wooden huts near the bog, but due to the abysmal conditions and poor wages on offer in Kildare, these could not be filled.[85]

Along with other labour camps in counties Offaly, Kerry and Laois, the camp was supervised by the Turf Executive, which was controlled by the parliamentary secretary to the Minister for Local Government and Public Health, Hugo Flinn. Flinn, who had been given the title Turf Controller by Lemass, also set production targets for each county. He was able to sidestep questions by Labour TDs over the conditions in turf camps by stating that bog shelters were controlled by county surveyors and that national turf camps were separate. Flinn argued that the local administration of turf schemes meant 'conditions were so varied that it was impossible to make a general rule'.[86] Flinn's response belied the strong influence that central government had on the recruitment, wages and conditions of the turf drive. This central control was strengthened the following year when Flinn died, and the Department of Supplies, under Lemass, took charge of turf quotas.[87]

Relative to Lemass's preferred designs for camp labour, the 'refugee camp' living conditions of the Kildare Scheme turf camp seem almost comfortable. The government adopted Lemass's reserve pool of labour proposals as well as operating the embargoes favoured by MacEntee. However, demonstrating how far from the liberal centre Lemass had strayed, the coerciveness of his scheme was significantly diluted by cabinet. It would apply to men over the age of twenty-two, not men of eighteen as Lemass had envisaged; refusal to work at a camp would not be met with fines or imprisonment or the removal of the retainer but with the means-tested cessation of unemployment assistance for a short period; and participants would be allowed to apply for removal from the register at any time.[88]

Lemass's was a mindset at loggerheads with most people's sensitivities at the time. Even Stormont, which under the Emergency Defence Act (1940) had the power to coerce labour in the interests of the war economy, held back from introducing compulsion in labour of the kind he advocated.[89] Camp labour proved extremely unpopular. Of 400 unemployment assistance recipients in Mayo offered employment in the reserve pool, only four took up the offer.[90] At the end of the Emergency, the unsuccessfulness of Lemass's camp labour schemes was seized on by MacEntee, who smugly highlighted 'the difficulties inherent in the problem of labour mobility on an extensive scale as proved in connection with the turf development scheme'.[91] These remarks were telling of the divisions in cabinet between Lemass, who clearly relished the role of 'economic overlord', and his more cautious colleagues. While admiration for authoritarian regimes such as Salazar's Portugal was widespread among the Irish political and religious elite of the era, most looked to the ostensibly harmonious pre-war social order achieved by the Portuguese New State. Lemass, by contrast, was pursuing policies more in line with the less attractive tenets of Salazarism, which emerged during the war. These included the militarisation of labour – where Portuguese workers were subjected to military discipline in the workplace and strike activity was elevated to the status of military desertion[92] – and state requisitioning of grazing land.[93]

Cabinet divisions surface

Lemass's advocacy of camp labour was just one plank in his broader approach towards Irish agriculture during the Emergency. The issue of fair pricing provides another good example. The prices the government set for wheat were consistently lower than those recommended by the Department of Agriculture. Although farmers and the general public were unaware of the fact, this was due to the conflicting priorities of Minister for Agriculture Ryan and Minister for Supplies Lemass. While Ryan was keen to secure as high a guaranteed price for wheat as possible to stimulate production, Lemass was concerned at the impact of higher wheat prices on the price of bread and flour for consumers.[94] In 1944, the Department of Finance weighed in on Lemass's side of the argument, arguing that financial inducements to farmers were unfair because farmers' incomes had increased with periodic increases in the fixed price of wheat, whereas wage rises to those in industrial employment were forbidden under the Wages Standstill Order (1941).[95]

These disagreements over pricing policy formed just part of a broader difference of opinion between Ryan and Lemass over the nature of state intervention in the rural context. Lemass's advocacy of camp labour was also part of this battle of wits within the cabinet over the best way to increase food and fuel productivity in the countryside. De Valera's decision to place the campaign to grow more food in Lemass's hands in early 1941 represented an expansion of the already extraordinarily broad powers Lemass enjoyed. On hearing of the decision, Ryan complained angrily to de Valera of the overlapping of ministerial responsibilities that this entailed.[96] Ryan often maintained a central position in cabinet between the extremes of Lemass and MacEntee. On this occasion, however, he swapped sitting on the fence for leaping off it. His angry response was symptomatic of the resentment among other ministers at the extent of the controls that Lemass was accumulating.

Lemass was to accrue yet more power, however. In the cabinet reshuffle of August 1941 necessitated by the resignation of the Minister for Local Government and Public Health, P.J. Ruttledge, Lemass regained control of his old department, Industry and Commerce, while retaining the Supplies portfolio. This development was to the further chagrin of MacEntee, who was moved from Industry and Commerce to fill Ruttledge's vacancy. Lemass gained even greater leverage when the cabinet committee on economic planning was formed in November 1942. It was composed of de Valera, the Tánaiste and Minister for Finance Seán T. O'Kelly and Lemass.

This private battle rumbled on throughout the Emergency. In 1941, there was a major disagreement between Lemass and Ryan over the purchase of wheat. Supplies was keen to monopolise grain supply and distribution under a semi-state body. Agriculture favoured keeping the existing and popularly disliked system of grain purchase through merchants and middlemen because it provided farmers with credit. When the issue was raised at cabinet level in mid-1941, the status quo prevailed.[97] Ryan was forced, however, to make some concessions to Lemass, who favoured a stronger role for the state in the sector.[98]

The significant disagreement between Lemass and Ryan over wheat price and supply contributed towards a bad-tempered exchange of views on the broader question of agricultural productivity between the two ministers in 1944. In a memorandum on full employment, drawn up after the 1944 British White Paper on Employment Policy, Lemass made a number of observations about Ireland's agricultural economy, declaring himself for 'the improvement, reorganisation and mechanisation' of agriculture. He made it clear that he favoured continued government intervention in the market to guarantee stability of price.[99] However, he unequivocally placed price secondary to the reorganisation of the entire sector, declaring himself for the nationalisation of many industries where agricultural goods were processed: 'to ensure that the stimulation of a larger demand for its products will not be frustrated by the incapacity of the industry to organise itself'.[100] Citing the high number of uneconomic holdings in the country, he argued that 'land policy must be geared towards ownership based on ability to work the land'.[101] Most significantly, Lemass wanted the dispossession of farmland by the state to continue after the Emergency. The state must complete the 'elimination of incompetent or lazy farmers', he argued.[102] Lemass's enthusiasm for widespread dispossessions was probably only matched by that of James Larkin, the trade union leader and socialist deputy, who urged that any farmer who 'will not farm scientifically' be dispossessed by the state.[103]

The enthusiasm for dispossession was challenged, however, by the man responsible for the enforcement of the tillage orders: Ryan. Ryan had mounted a robust public defence of the necessity for such expropriations when informed of tales of hardship in the Dáil, but he privately quelled the enthusiasm within the Fianna Fáil parliamentary party for more stringent enforcement of compulsory tillage.[104] On receiving Lemass's memo, he questioned his enthusiasm for land dispossession as a means of improving efficiency. Ryan realised that a deep-seated resentment existed against the more coercive measures used by the department to increase the wheat yield and warned against the idea.[105] During the Emergency, such displacements had proved 'a delicate and difficult matter', he claimed.[106] He went on to warn that if displacement was pursued on the same scale post-war, there would be 'a danger of serious agitation and public disturbance'.[107] Ryan recognised that the threat of dispossession was viewed by the farming community as hostile encroachment rather than work ensuring the fair operation of the market.

Lemass's desire for greater state intervention in the sector to guarantee productivity was unsuited to Ireland, Ryan claimed. Farmers, unlike coal miners, did not 'slack' after having attained a certain income.[108] This was clearly an attack on Lemass's downplaying of the distinctions between agricultural and industrial economies in discussions on full employment in 1944.[109] Likewise, steps to ensure the limitation of production and the elimination of waste were dangerous because in farming this was 'hard to gauge'. He argued that if compulsory tillage was extended to include the mandatory requisition of all unproductive farm units, it would see the state take over holdings where a good farmer was merely going through a lull in productivity, due to the time involved in raising a young family, for instance.[110] 'In cases where the farms are practically derelict for reasons such as complete lack of capital, or the incapacity of the owner because of senility or mental trouble, there would be a good case for the state taking over and arranging new ownership', Ryan asserted. Moreover, 'there are a number of holdings in every parish falling below a reasonable productive capacity due to some fault on the part of the present farmer.' But in these cases, a young family member 'would in time pull the place together and become a first class farmer'. It would, therefore, be 'unthinkable to disturb the family in such cases no matter how much below the desired standard the farm might be'.[111]

The discussion between Lemass and Ryan over this issue brought the former's developmentalist priorities into conflict with the latter's concern for family and farmstead. Such a clash is typically juxtaposed by Garvin as pitting Lemass's progressive, developmentalist agenda against the backward and conservative ideals of his peers.[112] John Horgan, too, sees Ryan's 'fatalism' as 'deeply disturbing'.[113] However, both neglect to mention the crucial backdrop of disruption that Fianna Fáil's pursuit of compulsory tillage had wrought. Ryan was right to point out the social disruption that the continuation of the scheme would cause and to highlight the misconceptions underlying Lemass's view of farmers as 'lazy'. Lemass's use of the word rested on his conviction that too few farmers had met tillage quotas and those that did halted work when they had ploughed the required percentage. The inaccuracy of this view is encapsulated in a 1943 *Dublin Opinion* cartoon which imagined a horse sitting down and stopping the minute after the statutory 37.5 acres tillage quota had been ploughed.[114] Ryan pointed out that Lemass's conclusion had been reached by comparing statistics for agricultural output from 1935 with those for 1942. The difference was that in 1942 there was a dearth of fertilisers and feeding stuffs.[115] In an early memo on compulsory tillage, Ryan had stressed the critical importance of the availability of chemicals and machinery if the order was to be executed successfully.[116] Although he stopped short of saying so, compulsory tillage had been seriously compromised by Lemass's failure to stockpile these essentials of agricultural productivity at an earlier stage.

The issue of agricultural productivity raised broader questions about the measures to increase output that wartime exigencies produced. A range of commentators at the time compared Ireland unfavourably to other agricultural economies, most frequently Denmark.[117] This argument was often articulated by those sympathetic to vocationalism, who exaggerated Ireland's anti-materialistic Christian society and the inability of her smallholders to adapt to change and innovation.[118] The conservatism of farming methods in the Irish countryside was a problem, but, as head of the Irish Agricultural Organisation Society (IAOS) Henry Kennedy – himself a critic of the conservative and unproductive farm unit – stated, the urban population during the Emergency had 'good reason to be grateful for the farmers' adjustment to the production of unfamiliar crops'.[119] In fact, in Denmark, hailed as the modern efficient agrarian small nation to which Ireland's farmers should aspire, there was overt and successful resistance to the Nazi-imposed policy of slaughtering livestock to increase grain output.[120] Despite lacking vital equipment and despite resistance, Ireland's farmers proved remarkably productive, as discussed in the previous chapter.

Within the cabinet, Lemass was the harshest critic of the decentralised impulse of the broad vocationalist movement.[121] In general terms, he argued that the Irish needed a strong central government to counteract what he called their 'fissiparous tendencies'.[122] His attitudes towards farmers were in keeping with this conviction and expressed in cold economic terms. Lemass was not naïve when it came to the agricultural economy. His 1944 memorandum on full employment noted that the imposition of state trading and regulation upon the cattle trade was unsuitable due to the 'variable nature of the product', the long period of time involved in the production of the 'finished article' and because cattle transactions between farmers tended to be 'very complicated'.[123] His economic reductionism, however, ensured that he placed productivity first, without due concern for social or, indeed, *political* implications – which are now discussed.

'Get-rich-quick gentlemen living on the farmers' sweat': the political economy of rural productivity

The national effort to overcome the threat of starvation during the Emergency represented a unique national unity of purpose typical of wartime conditions. All parties and interest groups were in agreement: more wheat needed to be grown. Yet the memory of relative prosperity during the First World War intensified the sense of grievance felt by the nation's farmers during the Second. The economic conflict between the state and its farmers was heightened by the recurrent perception of the farming community that they were viewed as small and insignificant by a stridently interventionist, arrogant and unthinking Dublin bureaucracy. These conditions ensured that the farmer – the archetypal hard-working, frugal man – enjoyed continued primacy in political discourse. Most significantly, the uncomfortable measures taken to increase agricultural productivity enhanced the considerable political premium of siding with him.

Due to the prevailing nationalist interpretation of the Famine as an historical crime perpetrated by Britain, both the Fianna Fáil hierarchy and the common man or woman held the essentially moral economic belief that famines were greatly aggravated by, and in some instances caused by, selfish market behaviour. When it came to supply shortages in general, human agency was accorded primacy. Ostensibly, this provided a fillip to the government's attempts to unify the country behind its version of moral economy. It is evident, however, that state involvement in the agricultural marketplace prompted disagreements over the fairness of the government's methods.

Typically, the farmer was extolled by politicians of all colours. A 1940 Dáil speech by Patrick Belton – farmer, Fine Gael TD and president of the anti-communist Irish Christian Front – typified the opposition's slant on the issue. Recruitment for the Defence Forces was, he felt, secondary to 'the first and most important local and national security force: the ploughmen of this nation', 'the fellow who is muck up to his neck producing the food that will keep this nation independent of the submarine or any other warfare'.[124] In this description, Belton may have been muck up to *his* neck in rhetoric, but the importance he placed on the farmer was reflected in the government's prioritisation of supply over security in the next few years. After the Battle of Britain ended in British victory in October 1940, the threat of German invasion was diminished. In December 1941, the United States entered the war on the Allied side; by February 1943, the Soviet Union had triumphed at Stalingrad; and by July 1943, the Allied invasion of Axis-controlled Europe had begun in Sicily. Consequently, as the threat of foreign invasion steadily receded, the intensity of recruitment efforts to Ireland's Defence Forces abated also, and from 1942, the strength of Éire's permanent force fell into slow but steady decline.[125] As Belton had urged, the 'Step Together!' drive was overshadowed by the 'Grow More Food' campaign.

As the Emergency progressed, then, the rhetorical war to claim the ruralist mantle through the invocation of famine intensified. But as Fianna Fáil's productivity drive intensified, the government's use of emergency powers also came under greater scrutiny. Many Dáil Debates centred on the issue of the 'fairness' of government measures such as price controls. When it came to greed, the middleman was commonly represented as the greatest detriment to the honest farming community by deputies on both sides of the house. A Dáil debate of 1941 encapsulates neatly how far such notions of 'fair' norms and obligations permeated political discourse. That year, a motion was brought by two Fine Gael TDs, who claimed that the price fixed by the government for wheat was too high. It was neither 'fair' nor 'just' to ask Ireland's farmers to grow wheat at £2 a barrel, argued Fine Gael's James Hughes.[126] In reply, Fianna Fáil's interventionism was justified by both James Ryan, Minister for Agriculture, and Martin Corry, Fianna Fáil TD for Cork South–East. Both invoked the folk devil of the middleman, the scourge of the honest small farmer: in Corry's words, those 'get-rich-quick gentlemen living on the farmers' sweat'.[127] Ryan, for his part, resisted calls from both his own ranks and those of the opposition to revert to laissez-faire, arguing that this would enable the middleman to 'corner supplies'.[128]

Underlying much of the debate over pricing was a familiar tension between urban centre and rural periphery. Many country folk perceived themselves as victims of an insidious Dublin centralism, and this sentiment was often repeated in political debate. In one of the frequent debates on agricultural prices, Labour TD James Hickey quite reasonably claimed that 'the people in the cities are concerned in this matter also'.[129] Martin Corry, a fellow Corkman, bellowed back: 'the only concern the city people have, or ever had, is how to drag as much as they can out of the farmer'.[130] Although often expressed with a rhetorical flourish, anti-centralism was grounded in the nature of central intervention in the Irish countryside during the Emergency. The *Report of the Commission on Vocational Organisation* asserted that Irish agriculture was still regulated on bureaucratic lines.[131] In *The Standard*, a newspaper which vigorously advocated corporatism, the consultative council established to discuss Emergency conditions by Ryan in September 1939 was described as meeting infrequently and being 'useless' in providing dialogue with farmers.[132]

Typically, collective action among farmers during the Emergency exhibited a unifying, if somewhat narrow-minded, 'agin the government' mentality which served as an anti-centralisation umbrella when more specific concerns arose.[133] In late March 1940, *The Connacht Tribune*'s headline was 'Great Athenry Rally: 20,000 Farmers Unite to Protect Their Profession'.[134] Addressing the meeting, the headline speaker announced 'Thank God that hatred and bitterness between us have died away and that we now know our security lies in co-operation among ourselves and not with the politicians'.[135] A Garda report described a protest of 1,200 farmers in Tralee in 1940 at which a speaker complained that the youth of the country had 'flown like swallows' but 'unlike the birds', they did not return. They could not be blamed, he said, as those who remained were 'unable to earn a livelihood on the land'. Conspicuously undermining the anti-materialism of moral neutrality, he went on to question the good of neutrality when people were forced 'to pay twice the amount for a sack of flour as in England'.[136]

At the local organisational level, grievances were expressed by protest but, more commonly, through resolution. Farmers' representative bodies complained of the negative effect on productivity caused by petrol rationing. In 1941, for example, Kerry County Committee of Agriculture joined the chorus of county committees of agriculture complaining about the 'inadequate' petrol allowance county agricultural instructors had received from Supplies.[137] For agricultural instructors, the accessibility of many farms was compromised by petrol rationing. Despite a pervasive dislike of central intervention, there was a general appreciation of the improvement to farming methods provided by 'college graduates from the department with degrees and bachelors in agriculture degrees, with a good knowledge of how things should be done', as one farmer put it.[138]

A more concrete criticism that was levelled at the government was its failure to extend credit to farmers more fairly and more accessibly. Alfred O'Rahilly's popular book *Money*, which sold out within six months, argued that 'many farmers have primitive ideas about banking; they imagine their deposits are tucked safely away behind the barred windows of the local bank'.[139] He proposed instead an agricultural savings bank in which farmers could deposit money. The state could use this 'dead money' for national development: 'borrowing, production and housing'.[140] He also advocated the provision of credit to farmers at a fairer rate. Calls for the more ready availability of credit to farmers intensified after the government initiated compulsory tillage, accompanied by tough quotas which necessitated greater outlay on labour and machinery. Opposition politicians and vocational lobby groups urged the government to provide credit for tillage free of interest or at more favourable rates. This would, *The Standard* claimed, meet the 'social obligation' of the scheme.[141] Seán Ó Faoláin repeated these concerns in *The Bell*, claiming that Irish farmers had to be educated against viewing credit as a form of usury: an anxiety attributable to a landlord-cum-famine mentality.[142] Fine Gael's James Dillon, the most impressive political antagonist of the government during the Emergency, argued for a preferential system of credit for farmers to eliminate the interference of middlemen and speculators,[143] a system which, rather than governmental pressure to produce the maximum yield, would result in greater productivity.[144] Martin Corry lamented the poor availability of credit in Irish agriculture by stating 'Any hair-brained individual with an industrial scheme in mind can walk into a bank or into the Industrial Credit Corporation and draw out all he requires, and yet, when a poor farmer goes in for a loan, they almost lock the door and send for the Guards.'[145] According to another deputy, 'it would be almost as easy for a camel to get through the eye of a needle as it is for the ordinary farmer to approach any of the existing lending organisations and borrow twopence'.[146]

In reply, James Ryan argued that the finance needed for tillage was less than that needed for dairy.[147] This line of argument ignored the costs incurred in the transition to tillage for dairy farmers and the mounting expenses as the state's tillage quotas increased year-on-year. During the Emergency, loans were available to farmers through the Agricultural Credit Corporation, but were hard to obtain. The expansion in production in the agricultural sector due to the need for self-sufficiency begs the question why Ryan did not initiate a broader credit system for struggling farmers to avail of. In not doing so, it would appear that Fianna Fáil's chief concern was with Ireland's ailing agricultural exports, with the government worried that the mass extension of credit to farmers would have an adverse effect on export prices.

The criticisms levelled at Fianna Fáil's record in agriculture during the Emergency were often veiled by censorship. This had the effect of masking the political impact of such agrarian dissent. Such concerns were, however, closely linked to the emergence of the farmers' party Clann na Talmhan on the national political stage during the period. That the land issue and agrarianism were at the heart of the independence struggle has led some commentators to speculate that the death of agrarian radicalism occurred with Irish state formation following the end of the Civil War in 1923.[148] That this date marked the end of the political prominence of Irish farmers was repeated by Farmers' Party senator Patrick Baxter in a 1939 debate.[149] Farmers, he warned, had 'never got a chance to pull themselves together since 1923'.

This would only continue to be the case 'if Ministers approach this problem of getting increased production from the land without applying the big stick from buildings in Merrion Street'.[150] In years to come, though, many farmers perceived the
emergence of the big stick through compulsory tillage.

The growth of Clann na Talmhan during the Emergency, a party founded in the
west of Ireland in 1938 which aimed to give a parliamentary voice to farmers, provides evidence of the re-emergence of bottom-up rural political agitation. In their
account of the rise of Clann na Talmhan, Tony Varley and Chris Curtin attribute its
growth to a delayed reaction to the Economic War of the 1930s. They base their
assessment on a 1943 Dáil speech by the movement's leader, Michael Donnellan, in
which he criticised the policies pursued by James Ryan as responsible for the party's
very existence.[151] However, it is crucial to consider that in that speech Donnellan
referred to the policies adopted by the Minister for Agriculture 'during the last ten
years', half of which included Emergency regulations.[152] Therefore, while Varley and
Curtin's account of reasons for the Clann's popularity derived from both the
Economic War (such as rising costs) and broader post-independence conditions (a
collective occupational identity based on a dislike of establishment figures), they
neglect the major and immediate factors in Clann na Talmhan's popularity: compulsory tillage; price controls; shortages in feed, fertiliser and fuel; censorship; labour
controls; and the intensification of state pressure in the sector from 1939 to 1945 –
collectively, coercion in the countryside during the Emergency. It is important to
note that these factors were repeatedly highlighted by Clann na Talmhan before and
after their relatively strong showing in the 1943 election.[153]

These are significant and overlooked reasons for the party's growth in this period.
Clann na Talmhan owed much of its support and, to a considerable extent, its very
raison d'être to resentment among western farmers to the government's coercive
approach to agricultural productivity during the Emergency. By 1938, Fianna Fáil's
vote had started to decline among smallholders in the rural west and south-west.[154]
The result of the 1943 general election confirmed this trend. Although Fianna Fáil
did better in 1944, the period witnessed the emergence of parties that concentrated
on a specific issue or narrow range of issues.[155] Clann na Talmhan, and compulsory
tillage, certainly fit this bill. Compulsory tillage played a significant but overlooked
part in the 1948 election too, which saw Fianna Fáil removed from office. The powers
exerted through compulsory tillage prompted the government to pass a 1946 act
which gave the Land Commission greater power to repossess land.[156] These developments were grist to the Clann's anti-centralist mill. Notes prepared for the 1945
Fianna Fáil Ard-Fheis recorded that one of Clann na Talmhan's main arguments
against the government was that 'officials of the government have every man at their
mercy and could put a farmer out of business with a stroke of the pen'.[157] One of its
deputies, Joseph Blowick, warned the Dáil: 'too many sacrifices have been made in
the past for the land of this country'. His party were no longer willing 'to allow anybody to come in to a farmer and tell him that he is working his farm well or badly'.[158]

Conclusion

The *Report of the Commission on Vocational Organisation* favoured the replacement of 'the state's despotic control of production and labour' with 'voluntary collaboration for the good of the nation at a critical time'.[159] In response, the government cited the exigencies of the Emergency in its exercise of measures resembling 'despotic control'. Fianna Fáil's message of 'moral neutrality', which appealed to people to pull together against famine while reminding them that the geopolitical inferno causing the hardship was not of its doing, inspired many people in the Irish countryside to redouble their labour in the national interest. Its accompaniment, the moral economic imperative, was trumpeted by Dáil deputies of all colours in discussions on issues affecting the Irish countryside. The supply crisis and the discursive power of state propaganda had delivered a totalising hegemony that ensured that dissenting voices to the state's coercive productive measures were drowned out. That the uncomfortable methods the Irish state took in agriculture were exceptional was repeatedly stressed by the Irish government. In Britain, by contrast, there was an implicit assumption that wartime agricultural policies would be continued post-war.[160] In Ireland, the Catholic Church's acceptance of the state's insistence on the exceptionality of the Emergency helped to explain why the clash between Catholic social thinkers and the government never occurred. This discomfort was a temporary aberration; normalcy would soon return.

Many refused to excuse coercion in the countryside during the Emergency as a regrettable but exceptional necessity, however. If the government's intention to ensure fair food distribution and increase agricultural production during this period sat comfortably with 'the good of the nation', the same cannot be said of its methods. While commenting on Ireland's 'essential planning problem' in 1944, a contributor to the Jesuit periodical *Studies* noted, 'Except in a purely Totalitarian state no government could apply the regimentation necessary to ensure that the farming community on a whole would reorganise itself', 'except', he added, 'as a last resort in a national emergency'.[161] Whereas the majority of Ireland's farming community and agricultural labour force would have similarly regarded the implementation of this 'regimentation' during the Emergency as a 'last resort' – a painful but exceptional experience – to Lemass, it seems, it was the expression of an exciting opportunity. Regrettably, the price of such progress was often the suffering of the small man.

Notes

1 Lemass to McQuaid, 8 January 1941. DDA, McQuaid papers, AB8/B/XVIII/51.
2 Cited in Daly, *Agriculture*, 230.
3 McQuaid to Lemass, 3 March 1943. DDA, McQuaid papers, AB8/B/XVIII/51.
4 McQuaid to Twomey, 23 January 1942. DDA, McQuaid papers, AB8/B/Agriculture.
5 De Valera to McQuaid, 21 September 1947. DDA, McQuaid papers, AB/B/XVIII/4/6/297.
6 Daly, *Slow Failure*, 148.

7 Susana Pinar, 'The Emergence of Modern Genetics in Spain and the Effects of the Spanish Civil War (1936–1939) on Its Development', *Journal of the History of Biology* 35, 1 (Spring 2002), 111–148.

8 Bowen, *Spain*, 104.

9 de Meneses, 'Investigating Portugal', 406.

10 *The Standard*, 17 January 1941.

11 *Irish Press*, 24 February 1941.

12 *Irish Press*, 22 January 1941.

13 *Connacht Tribune*, 21 February 1942.

14 *Irish Press*, 24 February 1941.

15 *Irish Press*, 16 February 1941.

16 *Irish Press*, 24 February 1941.

17 *Irish Independent*, 18 January 1944.

18 *Muintir na Tíre* was founded in 1931 by Father John Hayes of Tipperary and re-emerged in 1937.

19 *The Standard*, 21 November 1941.

20 *The Standard*, 1 August 1941.

21 *The Standard*, 8 August 1941.

22 E.J. Coyne, 'A Workers' Republic', *Irish Monthly*, 67 (1939), 7–15.

23 Alfred O'Rahilly, *The Standard*, 31 January 1941.

24 *Commission on Vocational Organisation*, 349–350.

25 O'Leary, *Vocationalism*,127.

26 *Commission on Vocational Organisation*, 130.

27 *Commission on Vocational Organisation*, 339–350.

28 'Observations of the Department of Agriculture on the *Report of the Commission on Vocational Organisation*', NAI, DT/S13552.

29 Seán Lemass, *Dáil Debates*, vol. 77, col. 921, 8 November 1939.

30 Wills, *Neutral Island*, 237.

31 James Ryan, Seanad Éireann, vol. 24, col. 2063, 3 July 1940.

32 Daly, *Agriculture*, 58.

33 Patrick Cogan, *Dáil Debates*, vol. 78, col. 23, 22 November 1939.

34 MA, OCC/8/7.

35 Patrick Cogan, *Dáil Debates*, vol. 78, col. 164, 23 November 1939.

36 MA, OCC/8/24.

37 MA, OCC/8/21.

38 *Dáil Debates*, vol. 85, col. 1752, 4 February 1942.

39 *Dáil Debates*, vol. 85, col. 1753, 4 February 1942.

40 Ryan, *Dáil Debates*, vol. 85, col. 228, 30 October 1941.

41 Patrick McGovern, *Dáil Debates*, vol. 84, col. 715, 2 July 1941.

42 MIOA, Mairéad Dwyer, b. 1929, Gooldscross, co. Tipperary. Interviewed 7 April 2000, p. 4.

43 *Dáil Debates*, vol. 84, col. 715, 2 July 1941.

44 James Hughes, *Dáil Debates*, vol. 82, col. 31, 5 March 1941.

45 *Dáil Debates*, vol. 83, col. 2013, 17 June 1941.

46 Hughes, *Dáil Debates*, vol. 84, col. 551, 1 July 1941.

47 *Dáil Debates*, vol. 84, col. 1253, 9 July 1941.

48 *Dáil Debates*, vol. 84, col. 2508, 17 September 1941.

49 *Irish Times*, 28 September 1941.

50 Wills, *Neutral Island*, 237.

51 Ryan, *Dáil Debates*, vol. 84, col. 551, 1 July 1941.

52 *Dáil Debates*, vol. 84, col. 2507, 17 September 1941.

53 Lemass to de Valera, 17 November 1938. NAI, DT/S10927.

54 156 (23 March 1940) Dublin Garda Index to Special Files, 1929–1945.

55 De Valera to Irish Trade Unions Congress representatives, 14 May 1941. NAI, Irish Trade Union Congress collection, 6100.

56 Wages for turf cutters were kept at artificially low levels because, in the words of Turf Controller Hugo Flinn, 'If the turf wage is set at a higher level than the agricultural wage, then there is going to be competition between the two, to the detriment of agriculture.' *Dáil Debates*, vol. 86, col. 634, 16 April 1942.

57 Lemass to de Valera, 17 November 1938. NAI, DT/S10927.

58 Memorandum by the Minister of Labour and National Service, Ernest Bevin, 6 November 1940. NAUK, CAB/67/8/84.

59 Evans, 'The Construction Corps', 19–31.

60 *Irish Independent*, 4 March 1943.

61 Cabinet minutes, 3 October 1941; 19 May 1942. NAI, DT/S13029 A.

62 Dublin Garda Index to Special Files, 1929–1945.

63 Cabinet minutes, 3 October 1941; 19 May 1942. NAI, DT/S13029 A.

64 Cabinet minutes, 3 October 1941; 19 May 1942. NAI, DT/S13029 A.

65 Seán MacEntee, untitled memo, of 30 September 1942. NAI, DT/S13029 A.

66 Lemass, untitled memo, 13 May. NAI, DT/S13029 A.

67 Lemass, memorandum for the government, October 1942. NAI, DT/S13029 A.

68 Seán Cawley, 'The Case for the Rural Unemployed Worker Stated with Some Suggestions for Remedying His Condition', included in memorandum from Lemass to de Valera, 3 February 1940. DT, S10927.

69 Michael Keyes, *Dáil Debates*, vol. 85, col. 2046, 4 March 1942.

70 Cawley, 'The Case'. NAI, DT/S10927.

71 Lemass, memo, October 1942. NAI, DT/S/13029 A.

72 Lemass, memo, October 1942. NAI, DT/S/13029 A.

73 Farrell, *Lemass*, 64.

74 Daly, *Slow Failure*, 145.

75 Daly, *Agriculture*, 242.

76 Andrews, *Man of No Property*, 176.

77 NAI, Social Welfare Files/CP/1943/4400.

78 NAI, Social Welfare Files/CP/1944/4607.

79 Andrews, *Man of No Property*, 177.

80 Seán Ó Faoláin 'The Stuffed-Shirts', *The Bell*, 6, 3 (June, 1943), 182–192.

81 Andrews, *Man of No Property*, 179–183.

82 Andrews, *Man of No Property*, 180.

83 Conclusions of Interdepartmental Conference on Conditions in Turf-Cutting Labour Camp Schemes, 27 July 1942. NAI, DT/S13029 A.

84 E.J. MacLaughlin to Hugo Flynn, 8 May 1942. NAI, DT/S13029 A.
85 NAI, DT/S13029 A.
86 *Irish Press*, 17 April 1942.
87 Daly, *Buffer State*, 265.
88 Emergency Powers (no. 243) Order 1942. NAI, DT/S13029 A.
89 Blake, *Northern Ireland*, 421. As in independent Ireland, checks were introduced in Northern Ireland to halt the drift of labour from agriculture to industry in 1941.
90 E.J. MacLaughlin to Hugo Flynn, 8 May 1942. NAI, DT/S13029 A.
91 Seán MacEntee, 'Observations of the Department of Finance on British White Paper on Employment Policy', 31 October 1944. NAI, DT/S13101 A
92 de Meneses, 'Investigating Portugal', 400.
93 Richard Black, 'Regional Political Ecology in Theory and Practice: A Case Study from Northern Portugal', *Transactions of the Institute of British Geographers*, 15, 1 (1990), 38.
94 Daly, *Agriculture*, 226.
95 Daly, *Agriculture*, 232.
96 Ryan to de Valera, 13 January 1941. NAI, DT/S11402B.
97 Daly, *Agriculture*, 229.
98 Ryan, *Dáil Debates*, vol. 91, col. 685, 20 October 1943.
99 Lemass, Memorandum on Full Employment. UCDA, MacEntee papers, P67/264 (4).
100 Lemass, Memorandum on Full Employment Policy, 17 January 1945. NAI, DT/S13101 A.
101 Lemass, Memorandum on Full Employment. UCDA, MacEntee papers, P67/264 (4).
102 Lemass, Memorandum on Full Employment Policy, 17 January 1945. NAI, DT/S13101 A.
103 James Larkin, *Dáil Debates*, vol. 93, col. 396, 28 March 1944.
104 UCDA, Fianna Fáil Parliamentary Party papers, P176/440, May 1940–May 1942. Cited in Daly, *Agriculture*, 229.
105 Ryan, Observations of the Minister of Agriculture on the Memorandum by the Minister for Industry and Commerce. UCDA, MacEntee papers, P67/264 (5). See below.
106 Ryan, Observations. UCDA, MacEntee papers, P67/264 (5).
107 Ryan, Memorandum on Full Employment, 14 March 1945. NAI, DT/S13101 A.
108 Ryan, Observations. UCDA, MacEntee papers, P67/264 (5).
109 Lemass, Observations on Memorandum Circulated to Cabinet Committee by the Department of Finance on the British White Paper on Employment Policy, 21 November 1944. NAI, DT/S13101 A.
110 Ryan, Observations. UCDA, MacEntee papers, P67/264 (5).
111 Ryan, Memorandum on Full Employment, 14 March 1945. NAI, DT/S13101 A.
112 Garvin, *Judging Lemass*, 51.
113 Horgan, *Enigmatic Patriot*, 115.
114 *Dublin Opinion*, November 1943.
115 Ryan, Memorandum on Full Employment, 14 March 1945. NAI, DT/S13101 A.
116 Ryan, Memorandum on Increased Food Production, 21 September 1939. NAI, FIN/S90/35/39.
117 See, for instance, Seán Ó Faoláin, 'One World', *The Bell*, 7, 4 (January, 1944), 288.

118 See Cornelius Lucey, 'The Beveridge Report and Éire', *Studies* 32 (1943), 43; George O'Brien, 'Some Lessons for Irish Agriculture from Western Europe', *Studies*, 29 (1940), 376.

119 Henry Kennedy, 'Agricultural Prosperity', 72.

120 Milward, *War, Economy and Society*, 267.

121 O'Leary, *Vocationalism*, 130.

122 Ferriter, 'A Peculiar People', 88.

123 Lemass, Memorandum on Full Employment. UCDA, MacEntee papers, P67/264 (4).

124 *Dáil Debates*, vol. 81, col. 1258, 12 December 1940.

125 Duggan, *A History of the Irish Army*, 215.

126 *Dáil Debates*, vol. 84, col. 2367, 23 July 1941.

127 *Dáil Debates*, vol. 84, col. 2334, 23 July 1941.

128 *Dáil Debates*, vol. 84, col. 2355, 23 July 1941.

129 *Dáil Debates*, vol. 84, col. 2335, 23 July 1941.

130 *Dáil Debates*, vol. 84, col. 2335, 23 July 1941.

131 *Report of the Commission on Vocational Organisation*, 142.

132 *The Standard*, 8 August 1941.

133 This anti-bureaucratic attitude is captured in satire of the time. For example, *Dublin Opinion* (May 1940) depicted a farmer 'ploughin' in' a mountain of Department of Agriculture forms.

134 *Connacht Tribune*, 26 March 1940.

135 Duggan, *The Ploughman*, 88–89.

136 Garda report, Tralee, 19 February 1940. NAI, JUS/8/770.

137 Kerry County Committee of Agriculture, Minutes, 6 December 1941 and 24 March 1941. Kerry County Archives (KCA).

138 MIOA, Weeshie Corless, b. 1920, Kinvarra, co. Limerick. Interviewed 7 April 2000, p. 13.

139 O'Rahilly, *Money*, 303.

140 O'Rahilly, *Money*, 304.

141 See, for instance, *Irish Press*, 4 October 1939. The quote is from *The Standard*, 14 April 1941.

142 Ó Faoláin, 'One World', 289.

143 *Dáil Debates*, vol. 77, col. 614, 18 October 1939.

144 *Dáil Debates*, vol. 81, col. 1269, 12 December 1940.

145 *Dáil Debates*, vol. 81, col. 1283, 12 December 1940.

146 George Bennett, *Dáil Debates*, vol. 81, col. 1287, 12 December 1940.

147 *Dáil Debates*, vol. 81, col. 1293, 12 December 1940.

148 Sophia Carey, *Social Security in Ireland, 1939–1952, the Limits to Solidarity* (Dublin, 2007), 113–133. In *The Land for the People* Dooley also cites 1923 as marking the end of agrarian agitation.

149 The Farmers' Party was founded in 1922, but was no longer a political force during the Emergency.

150 Patrick Baxter, Seanad Éireann, vol. 23, col. 1121, 25 October 1939.

151 See Tony Varley and Chris Curtin, 'Defending Rural Interests against Nationalists in 20th Century Ireland', in John Davis ed., *Rural Change in Ireland* (Belfast, 1999), 66.

152 *Dáil Debates*, vol. 91, col. 64, 1 July 1943.

153 See, for instance, Clann na Talmhan press statements in the *Irish Independent*, 20 October 1939, 2 February 1940; *Connacht Tribune*, 30 March 1940.

154 Bew and Patterson, *Lemass*, 7.

155 Brian Girvin, 'The Republicanisation of Irish Society, 1932–48', in J.R. Hill ed., *A New History of Ireland*, vol. 7 (Oxford, 2003), 154.

156 Dooley, *The Land for the People*, 126.

157 Notes on opposition parties prepared for the 1945 Fianna Fáil Ard-Fheis UCDA, de Valera papers, P150/2062.

158 *Dáil Debates*, vol. 99, col. 300, 31 January 1946.

159 *Commission on Vocational Organisation*, 45.

160 Milward, *War, Economy and Society*, 268.

161 Joseph O'Neill, 'Our Essential Planning Problem', *Studies*, 33 (1944), 228–236.

9

Conclusions

I am very depressed at going ... Living in Ireland has been a wonderful experience, because it is a wholly Christian country ... Oh dear, I am sad.

John Betjeman, 16 June 1943

The nature of the interventionist state

The outbreak of war in September 1939 signalled a period of emergency in Ireland that was lifted almost exactly seven years later in September 1946. Focusing on Ireland's neutrality, the history of the Second World War in Ireland has been chiefly relayed from a security and diplomatic perspective. The under-researched social and economic history of the period concerns a period of isolation in which crime and the cost of living rose steeply, unemployment and emigration remained wearyingly high, wages were frozen and supplies of food and fuel contracted perilously. It was against this grim backdrop that the Irish state undertook its 'high-water mark'[1] interventionist project.

These measures took place in the midst of pervasive censorship and a strict application of the neutral spirit which portrayed Ireland as standing aloof from the materialism of the combatant nations. Remarkably, with a dose of hindsight, it is clear that this moral aloofness was *most* justified in the economic sphere. If the broad idea of 'moral economy' is extended to the geopolitical, Ireland emerged from the war with greater credit than the other European neutrals. Sweden allowed Nazi Germany military and economic transit, profiting from iron ore and wood exports long after the 'Final Solution' became evident.[2] Both Spain and Portugal also benefited from the combatants' demand for tungsten ore, a vital resource in steel alloys for weapons manufacturing. The Swiss, and to a lesser extent the Portuguese, profited from the mass laundering of Nazi gold, much of which originated from Holocaust victims' teeth, watches and jewellery.[3] In May 1945, Salazar wrongly recorded in his diary that de Valera had declared a day of mourning to mark the death of Adolf Hitler.[4] In fact, Ireland had fewer economic reasons than the other neutrals to lament the Führer's passing.

With the end of the war, the material relationship between Britain and Ireland was transformed. Critically, whereas Churchill had sought to punish Ireland for neutrality by restricting supplies vital to food production, new Prime Minister Clement Attlee's cabinet agreed 'it would be advantageous if the level of food production in Eire could be increased' and that the British government would do all in its power to do so.[5] The multifaceted interventionism practised by the Irish government in the early 1940s was necessitated by Churchillian economic bullying, coupled with Ireland's unique lack of natural resources. Emergency conditions excited fears of national cataclysm. Famine was present in the minds of those responsible for Ireland's material wellbeing during the Emergency like a dimly remembered but disquieting nightmare. Liam O'Flaherty's novel *Famine*, published in 1937, was a very popular read during the Emergency, and it was in 1943, after Bengal was ravaged by mass starvation, that de Valera first proposed that a history of the Great Famine be written to mark its centenary.[6]

Significantly, the Irish state's interventionist project also represented governmental and social pressure to combat shortages by establishing 'fairer' market customs. Ireland's political leaders recognised that in the interest of the greater good, there was a necessity to increase domestic production and to regulate the consumption and distribution of goods. The efforts of the Irish government to standardise consumption and increase output were influenced by noble moral considerations and endorsed – with few exceptions – by the Catholic establishment. In 1944, the editors of *The Bell* asked 'why not millions a day on peace?', writing to a series of economic experts asking if wartime expenditure could be continued, with the state channelling funds into constructive social projects. The financial editor of *The Economist* agreed, replying 'it is safe to assume that never again will finance become the master of economic policy'.[7] Lemass's civil servants shared this confidence in a brave new world of dynamic state action, concluding that 'the maintenance of supplies in any future Emergency shall depend almost wholly on government action'.[8]

Placing Ireland's neutrality to one side, the Irish state was not exceptional in instituting domestic controls that took on the dimensions of a moral economy. In the majority of heavily regulated wartime economies of the early 1940s, governments pitched the prices of rationed goods low to guarantee minimum supply. In doing so, states came to decide what level of expenditure and consumption was desirable, with government decisions based on what was socially preferable as well as technically feasible.[9] The rhetoric of moral economy, which infused Irish political discourse at this time, was by no means unique to Ireland. However, the material operation of this notion in a heavily regulated state, distinguished by a morally watchful society, a steadfast 'moral neutrality' consensus and a horse-and-cart economy, is singular in modern Irish history.

The real starting point for the renaissance in Irish government thinking and economic planning was not the 1950s, but the 1940s, with the formation of the cabinet committee on economic planning in 1942.[10] By virtue of the sweeping powers he enjoyed as Minister for Supplies and as a member of the government's Emergency Planning Committee, the principal agent in the management of

Ireland's Emergency was Seán Lemass. Along with a group of senior civil servants headed by Departmental Secretary John Leydon, Lemass attempted to protect the Irish public in a time of scarcity through spearheading an unprecedented degree of centralised economic control. The Department of Supplies dictated national purchase and distribution, instituted controls on exports and profits, introduced rationing and price controls and oversaw the policing of the black market – the omnipresent corollary of market regulation.

While the Department of Supplies was responsible for the implementation of the majority of economic initiatives during the Emergency, other departments of state were simultaneously active in the process of centralisation. Wage rises and collective bargaining were outlawed. To ensure Ireland maintained key workers and resources, migration was subject to close central control and the issuing of permits; customs controls were also tightened. As part of a drive for self-sufficiency, the government started a national turf drive, complete with labour camps and restrictions on the movement of labour, in order to provide fuel. Through a scheme of compulsory tillage, Ireland's agricultural economy was directed towards the production of wheat.

A trinity of themes emerged in this overarching interventionist process. For reasons summarised here under three broad aspects of the process, state action during the Emergency was generally unpopular and failed to secure the level of support anticipated by the government.

Firstly, economic structures overtook ministerial, and even collective governmental, agency. In the earliest stages of the Emergency, Lemass's price controls and early rationing schemes were immediately outstripped by wartime inflation. The price and availability of goods were dictated for the remainder of the Emergency by large commercial importers and the British authorities, not Lemass. And, as Ireland's monetary reformists argued, the agency of the country's policymakers was hampered by the tie to sterling. In June 1940, France fell to Nazi Germany. This pivotal geopolitical event prompted Britain to resume Economic War with renewed vigour through the trade squeeze of 1941. This move spelt economic disaster for an island nation heavily reliant on its bigger neighbour for trade. Ireland's lack of natural resources and trade dependence on Britain enabled the latter to unceremoniously prompt some of the most strident examples of Irish interventionism such as export controls and full rationing. The British squeeze meant that the tillage drive assumed heightened importance. Productivity was effectively hampered, however, by structure. The transition in Irish landowning patterns through the distribution of land to smallholders and Fianna Fáil's emphasis on tillage in the previous decade proved uneconomic. Fianna Fáil's structural policies of the Economic War era militated against its policies of the early 1940s in another key respect as well. In restricting profits, appointing civil servants to company boards and, most crucially, attempting to convince firms to lay in stocks in the national interest, Lemass and Leydon found themselves pitted against the indifference of foreign firms. While conflict with well-established pre-independence business concerns such as Guinness was predictable,

Lemass's actions also brought him into conflict with a confident and resilient native bourgeoisie that he had built up through the protectionism of the 1930s. Moreover, when it came to restricting illegal activity and fighting the black marketer, the state's action was compromised by the structural fact of the land border, the separate legislatures and subsequent pricing disparities between the two territories.

Secondly, there was a clear complacency in the government's approach to the management of the Emergency. As early as 1935, the government established a body to carry out economic planning for war, and by 1938, the Emergency Supplies Branch of the Department of Industry and Commerce was up and running. Yet Ireland underwent an acute supply crisis in the following years, which exposed Lemass's critical failure to establish a merchant marine in the 1930s. The need to appease British trade interests and the unwillingness of private businesses to lay in stocks notwithstanding, Lemass recklessly granted export licences for certain key resources in the early stages of the Emergency. His department also failed to secure sufficient quantities of productive aids vital to Ireland's agricultural economy. Supplies only established a system of centralised purchase and distribution belatedly and at the bequest of the British Board of Trade. As the Emergency wore on, this complacency was to have negative consequences for productive yields, mobility, and public health. Unlike their counterparts in the United Kingdom, Ireland's farmers were forced to fulfil tillage quotas with ploughs and horses instead of tractors. British thirst for beer helped Ireland through the Emergency as Lemass resorted to desperate barter arrangements which saw Guinness swapped for much-needed machinery. But, as his accusers during a January 1941 Dáil debate insisted, Lemass was guilty of overstating Ireland's preparedness for emergency conditions.[11] The public ethic of moral economy was also developed haphazardly. Between 1939 and 1941, Lemass implemented a system of price control which was subject to constant change and partial rationing. He declared himself for the voluntary curtailment of consumption, but this stance changed quickly after the British trade squeeze of 1941. British bullying precipitated a thorough rationing scheme, started in 1942, that went against his previous stance. By this point, it was too late for a consummate rationing spirit to take hold and displace reliance on alternative practices. Events were, to an extent, out of Lemass's control, but the overall effect was public confusion and mass reversion to the black market. The theological debate over the disparity between the state's controlled price and what constituted a 'just price' demonstrates just how far the controlled price differed from what many people considered the popular moral economic price. Prior to the trade squeeze of 1941 and to a certain extent afterwards, there was an official disregard for cross-border black market activity. Moreover, the official anti-partitionist mindset did little to deter smuggling. This attitude was publicly articulated by some members of the hierarchy, who condemned both cross-border smuggling and the border as immoral in the same breath.

Thirdly and lastly, state intervention during the Emergency was, at intervals, authoritarian in character. Lemass and Leydon oversaw the growth of bureaucracy under their department, which took on 'monstrous' proportions. Their relatively trenchant refusal to engage in patronage, particularly Leydon's, was admirable. However, Lemass encouraged voluntary adherence to his diktats while dismissing the moral economic volunteerism of the Irish Housewives Association and failing to incorporate consultative committees composed of trade or social groups in any meaningful way in the economic management of the Emergency. These moves prefigured his blunt dismissal of the *Report of the Commission on Vocational Organisation* in 1943. His department liberally applied red tape, arousing the anti-apparatchik ire of the broad vocationalist lobby. The department also took a resolutely firm stance with business. Again, this tough approach was necessary in some respects, but Supplies' hard-headed refusal to offer guarantees against loss meant firms were unwilling to lay in much-needed stocks. Frequently, it was small shopkeepers rather than major capitalists who fell foul of the department's fastidious approach to enforcing its version of a moral economy. Through controls on labour mobility, the institution of squalid turf camps and the derogation of private property through land dispossessions, the state bulldozed liberal constraints. For a broad cross section of people, these actions were seen as those of an uncaring bureaucratic machine. The enforcement of compulsory tillage took on a similarly authoritarian aspect, containing the threat of dispossession, apparently taking little account of land variations, and by 1944 applied to those with holdings of just five acres. Ireland's independence was fledgling, and the historical memory of evictions during the Famine and the Land War evoked uncomfortable historical parallels. Like Supplies, the Department of Agriculture applied significant pressure on the judiciary to punish those who failed to till their allotted quotas harshly. Its officials, like those of Supplies, were frustrated by the independence of the judiciary. Fundamentally, though, this punitive drive represented a thrust in the opposite direction to that seen in Fianna Fáil's policy of land allocation to small farmers and landless labourers. Compared to this approach, the church's vision of the moral economy was more paternalistically spiritual. Catholic intellectuals displayed an equivocal attitude to the state's moral economy. While such writers denounced the black market, they were also uncomfortable about state interventionism. A long-running theological debate provoked questions about the legitimacy of the state's version of moral economy by publishing arguments that argued that black market activity was justified in certain circumstances, that controlled prices were not always 'just' and that state power could be legitimately defied. These opinions demonstrated that an individual's contravention of the moral economy pursued by the state during the Emergency went against Catholic social, but not necessarily moral, teaching.

A very pleasant prison camp? Putting the 'economy' in 'moral community'

As the Emergency was nearing its conclusion, public intellectual Seán Ó Faoláin summarised the tensions over state interventionism during the Emergency and the direction of post-war planning as 'the one question tormenting every thinking mind of today – the problem of balancing state control and individual liberty'. Ó Faoláin welcomed state control 'when it transfers the responsibility for all public troubles – say Hunger, Poverty or Disease – to the shoulders of government'.[12] At the very least, the control wielded by the Fianna Fáil administration during the war period deserves praise for ensuring no one starved to death in Ireland. In doing so, it fulfilled one of the most fundamental goals of a humane state.

Its counterpoint, the infringement of personal liberty by the state, was also a feature of Emergency Ireland. The most ardent cabinet advocate of a policy of full employment, Lemass, was also the greatest champion of coercive labour schemes. With the threat of starvation a tangible possibility, the church publicly supported the state's means of protecting the common good, even when state interventionism in the economy encroached on property rights and free will. This involved the coercion of labour, both industrial and agricultural, and the erosion of liberties at work, whether in the factory or the farm. The immense effort to sustain the ailing Irish economy from the depredations caused by wartime trade disruption also involved the de facto deployment of juvenile labour. These measures were carried out within the framework of a principled refusal to ease trade difficulties by compromising political neutrality and thus exposing the civilian population to aerial bombardment. The presence of such unpleasant wartime conditions makes Tony Gray's reflection that Emergency Ireland was 'a prison camp, albeit a very pleasant one', appear jejune.[13]

Government in Ireland, in this era, was marked by a lack of departmental coordination or long-term, programmatic planning.[14] In this regard, Lemass represented a dynamically interventionist exception to an old mould. However, Lemass has been scrutinised most extensively for his modernising influence in the post-war period. Works that contribute towards what has become a semi-hagiography of Lemass by placing him on the 'good' side of a dichotomy between progressives and 'gerontocrats' not only overstate his agency but rather overlook the less successful features of his career in the early 1940s.[15] Lemass was not always on the 'right' side, or even the same side, of the historical divide between 'folksy Ireland' and 'Ireland Inc.', and cabinet divisions ran deeper than a narrative of Lemass, the progressive, foiled by a conservative consensus.

As both Mary Daly and Diarmaid Ferriter have asserted, what ultimately shaped government policy in this period was a more nuanced compromise between the stark reality of the economic situation and the internal and external pressures on the state from a variety of politicians, lobbyists and theorists who sought legislative manifestation of their cultural and economic ideologies.[16] Ultimately, Irish workers suffered under Lemass's willingness to engage in coercive economic planning and his complacent approach to national food supply.[17] Lemass's consistently top-down approach to the economic management of the Emergency, detailed in this work, indicates that J.J. Lee is guilty of overstating his sympathy for vocationalism or quasi-corporatism.[18] Tom Garvin juxtaposes the political decisions of Lemass against the

'Boys of the Old Brigade' – Eamon de Valera and John Charles McQuaid – whose 'collective dream of a moral community ... authentic, pious, static and intellectually homogeneous was briefly realised in the 1932–48 period'.[19] In this view, Garvin displays ahistorical condescension towards that very idea of a moral community in the Emergency period by omitting the fact that Lemass was part of it as well, for the moral community most certainly had its economic extensions. Brian Girvin makes a similar argument to Garvin, claiming that the 1937 Constitution 'broke decisively' with liberal constitutionalism by recognising the special place of the Catholic Church. Under Fianna Fáil 'the content of the moral community became more limited, more authoritarian and less tolerant of those who did not share the values expressed by Fianna Fáil in its constitution'.[20] Girvin's concept of moral community is rightly based on the homogeneity of ethnicity, religion and race and the hegemony of Fianna Fáil's nationalism. But to situate Lemass as a dissident in the ranks is more problematic because it underplays Lemass's application of moral values to market practices: an integral part of the moral/political schema in this period.

The Emergency cannot be taken as a slice of history viewed at a complete remove, but the social and economic conditions pertaining to the era created a conviction among all sectors that an economy guided by moral precepts had to be created. Although secured by constitutional parameters, the different visions of moral economy practised by church and state overlapped considerably. Often, the spiritual overtones of moral neutrality propaganda sat comfortably with the state's aim to secure the material wellbeing of the Irish population. Occasionally, however, there were significant differences between spiritual definitions of moral economy, on the one hand, and material definitions, on the other.

Although there was no major clash between church and state in this period, significant tensions existed. Notably, these did not centre on Lemass, who regularly corresponded with McQuaid to ensure the hierarchy supported the state's measures and waived rationing regulations for the Archbishop. The social ideas behind the government's economic decision-making in the era were marked by a distinctly conservative ruralist tinge, which Lemass challenged but was also complicit in. For instance, in most other European nations during the war, the regular male workforce declined, but mechanisation increased as a result, along with female employment. Ireland's farmers, by contrast, suffered disproportionately during the Emergency due to the failure to secure adequate supplies of agricultural machinery and the reliance on archaic means of production. Yet Ireland, in common with Nazi Germany, did not mobilise women into the agricultural workforce.

This situation contrasted with developments in Northern Ireland. Stormont was certainly guilty of a cold disregard for its Catholic minority during the war years, most forcefully underlined by the flight of Catholics to the hills surrounding Belfast after the German blitz of April 1941.[21] There were also, as in independent Ireland, noticeable tensions between the different bodies charged with overseeing the economy, increasing productivity and enforcing the state's security. The impact upon the

Northern Ireland administration of mass death through bombing, however, should not be understated. Although the government and civil service in the six counties contained many reactionary elements whose bigoted unionism was bolstered by adherence to the British war effort, wartime damage also fused the will to victory with aspirations for a better post-war reality. As Prime Minister of Northern Ireland from 1943, Basil Brooke was keen to align closely with Britain and portray to London the image of a progressive government focused on post-war recovery.[22] In Westminster, the war confirmed the post-war direction as welfarist. The war moved Britain towards policies of full employment, state control of production and economic planning. Despite resistance to this post-war leftward shift, Northern Ireland under Brooke followed Britain in adopting the welfare state and in the direction of public policy.[23] In independent Ireland, by contrast, the Emergency was viewed in official circles as just that: a *temporary* aberration that would engender hardships but one from which building a new order of things afterwards was not as pressing a priority. This was closely linked to the fact that Ireland did not suffer the sustained bombing and fighting that broke established social orders in other European countries in this period.

Farewell to Plato's Cave: perfunctory adherence

The governance of Plato's republic – with its elitist assumptions, control of information and authoritarian rule – provides analogy for independent Ireland at this time. Yet the interaction of the Irish people with the Emergency economy was rarely characterised by obedient observance. State intervention through rationing and price controls effectively abolished the price mechanism, but the black market represented its reassertion through illegal channels. Lyons's 'Plato's Cave' analogy can be taken as casting the Irish people during this period as, at best, insular and, at worst, ignorant and subservient. On the contrary, there was widespread flouting of Emergency regulation through engagement with the black market. The perfunctory adherence of certain clergymen to market regulation was replicated in the behaviour of the wider public, most of whom engaged the black trade to some extent. While there was popular support for the sanctions underpinning rationing and market restrictions, associated closely with a common desire to punish the unscrupulous 'middleman', this consensus was ultimately more hollow than it appeared. As the war continued, people experienced a great reduction in supplies. Despite the efforts of the state to enforce its economic vision by controlling prices and distribution and issuing propaganda, many people turned to the black market to satisfy their demand for unavailable goods. The border with Northern Ireland proved particularly porous during the Emergency as price disparities prompted a transition from cattle smuggling to the smuggling of smaller domestic goods.

Recalling the black market south of the border, one urban dweller stated 'you could get any amount of anything from butter to bacon to tea', but added 'if you had the money'.[24] This crucial caveat illustrates the hugely inflated prices which operated on the black market, which were driven by consumer demand. Paradoxically, there was widespread popular disdain for profiteering, but a significant number of people engaged with the black trade if they had enough money or enough desire for certain goods. In a rather perverse inversion of the 'Step Together!' mentality of the Emergency, it is evident that people of all classes procured items from the black market, including the concerned middle class. The moral economy of the Emergency was widely acclaimed, becoming as much a part of the popular consensus as Ireland's national right to moral neutrality. However, involvement in the black market was popularly legitimated by a mentality which despised the dishonest middleman but saw little wrong in dabbling in his trade now and again.[25]

The Historical Survey of the Department of Supplies claims that during the Emergency, there was 'very little criticism' of the system of the centralism it exercised.[26] This may have been the prevailing opinion in and around its Ballsbridge offices, but in the rural context, this assertion was inaccurate. The moral economic ethic fostered by church and state sought to protect the urban poor from the worst deprivations of supply shortages, but the attitude of people in rural Ireland towards city dwellers of all types was commonly derisive. The rural environment afforded greater natural opportunities to exploit the black market, but rural dwellers often saw themselves as victims of feckless Dublin bureaucrats. Tillage stipulations and the decline in dairying during the Emergency aroused great resentment in rural communities. Rural dislocation through supply shortages was worst in the west, where rural poverty and the low density of shops resulted in material deprivation and provoked anger. Otherwise, disparate parishes, cooperative creameries and townlands were united by a sense of grievance and a spirit of resistance to central intervention.

Patrick Kavanagh personified an atmosphere of decline, boredom and stasis in Emergency Ireland through Maguire, the protagonist of his 1942 poem The Great Hunger. Maguire should not be taken as evidence of Plato's Cave providing an apt analogy for Emergency Ireland. Rather, Maguire was the product of a literary turn from romanticism towards a socio-realist aesthetic, a transition inextricably linked to social and economic conditions in Ireland during the Emergency. Kavanagh's Maguire may be the embodiment of a tedious lifestyle that has been wrongly generalised as the norm, but through him, the poet remoulded the ethic of moral economy and moral neutrality into an 'apocalypse of clay': in doing so, he trumpeted a representative and symbolic victory of materialism over spirituality. This work has signalled a departure in the dominant historiography of Emergency Ireland by highlighting the inconsistencies and failures of short-term, top-down socio-economic thought and action at the time. In doing so, it has saved the Maguires, and the mass of people at the time, from the condescension of posterity and, in documenting the possibility of escape from Plato's Cave, has finally bid it farewell.

Notes

1 Horgan, *Enigmatic Patriot*, 110.

2 Levine, 'Swedish Neutrality', 324.

3 See Lochery, *Lisbon*, 210–246.

4 Salazar's diary, 3 May 1945. This assertion is reproduced in Lochery, *Lisbon*, 217.

5 Cabinet meeting minutes, 29 October 1946. NAUK, CAB/128/6.

6 Cormac Ó Gráda, *Ireland's Great Famine: Interdisciplinary Perspectives* (Dublin, 2006), 234. The book was eventually published by Robert Dudley Edwards and T. Desmond Williams as *The Great Famine: Studies in Irish History 1845–52* (Dublin, 1956). For O'Flaherty's novel and the Indian context, see Margaret Kelleher, 'Literary Connections: Cultural Revival, Political Independence and the Present', in Michael and Denis Holmes eds, *Ireland and India: Connections, Comparisons, Contrasts* (Dublin, 1997), 100–119.

7 Seán O'Faoláin et al., 'Why Not Millions a Day on Peace?', *The Bell*, 8, 6 (September 1944), 486.

8 'Historical Survey'. NAI, IND/EHR/3/C1, part I, p. 24.

9 Milward, *War, Economy and Society*, 284.

10 Farrell, *Lemass*, 66.

11 *Dáil Debates*, vol. 81, col. 1312, 16 January 1941.

12 Seán Ó Faoláin, 'On State Control', *The Bell*, 6, 1 (April, 1943), 1.

13 Gray, *The Lost Years*, 6.

14 See Lee, *Ireland 1912–1985*, 277; Fanning, *Independent Ireland*, 152.

15 See Garvin's *Preventing*.

16 See Daly, *Industrial Development*; Ferriter, "A Peculiar People".

17 Significantly, the British Minister for Labour during the war was a Labour Party man – Ernest Bevin, Secretary of the Transport and General Workers' Union. In Ireland, Lemass and MacEntee, neither of whom had trade union backgrounds, directed the wartime economy.

18 Lee, 'Corporatism', 331.

19 Garvin, *Preventing*, 34.

20 Brian Girvin, 'Church, State and the Moral Community', in Brian Girvin and Gary Murphy eds, *The Lemass Era: Politics and Society in the Ireland of Seán Lemass* (Dublin, 2005), 122–145.

21 Alvin Jackson, *Ireland 1798–1998: Politics and War* (Oxford, 1999), 353.

22 Jackson, *Ireland*, 355–360.

23 See discussions on post-war planning in PRONI, CAB/4A/22.

24 MIOA, Christy Hennessy, b. 1932, Waterford City. Interviewed 8 April 2000, page 5.

25 For the broader application of this mentality, see John Coakley, 'Society and Political Culture', in John Coakley and Michael Gallagher eds, *Politics in the Republic of Ireland* (London, 2009).

26 'Historical Survey'. NAI, IND/EHR/3/C1, part II, p. 46–47.

Select bibliography

Primary sources

Official publications

Dáil Debates
Report of the Commission on Vocational Organisation (Dublin, 1943)
Report of the Committee of Inquiry into Taxation on Industry (Dublin, 1955)
Report of the Inquiry into the Housing of the Working Classes of the City of Dublin (Dublin, 1943)
Statistical Abstracts 1936–1946

Newspapers

Anglo-Celt
Connacht Sentinel
Dublin Opinion
Evening Herald
Irish Independent
Irish Press
Irish Times
Leitrim Observer
Munster Express
Nenagh Guardian
Southern Star
The Times
Waterford News

Reference

Dictionary of Irish Biography

Records held at the National Archives of Ireland (NAI)
Department of the Taoiseach
Department of Finance

Department of Justice
Department of Industry and Commerce
Department of Foreign Affairs
Attorney General's Office
District Court Records
Supply Series
Social Welfare Files
Co-Operative Society records
Trade Union Records
Hilda Tweedy Papers

Public Record Office Northern Ireland (PRONI)

Cabinet papers
Agriculture files
Customs files
Personal Collections

Northern Ireland Digital Film Archive (NIDFA)

1940s collection

National Archives of the United Kingdom (NAUK)

Cabinet files
Anthony Eden Papers
Records of the Security Service (MI5)
Ministry of War Transport

University College Dublin Archives (UCDA)

Frank Aiken papers
Éamon de Valera papers
Seán MacEntee papers

Dublin Diocesan Archives (DDA)

McQuaid papers

Irish Military Archives (MA)

Central Registry Files
Office of the Controller of Censorship
Secret Files

Kerry County Archives (KCA)

Board of Health and Public Assistance
County Council Minutes, 1935–1945
County Committee of Agriculture Minutes, 1939–1945

Louth County Archives (LCA)
Paddy Mallon collection

Mary Immaculate College Limerick Oral History Archive (MIOA)
Baily, Patrick (b. 1932, co. Kerry)
Carey, Edmund (b. 1920, co. Limerick)
Corless, Weeshie (b. 1920, co. Limerick)
Dwyer, Mairéad (b. 1921, co. Tipperary)
Hannery, Vincent (b. 1926, co. Clare)
Hassett, Mick (b. 1921, co. Tipperary)
Heneghan, Patrick (b. 1926, co. Mayo)
Hennessy, Christy (b. 1932, Waterford)
Magill, Jack (b. 1927, co. Down)
O'Donovan, Donal (b. c. 1920, co. Cork)
Roche, Noirín (b. 1930, co. Clare)
Turby, Fr. Matt (b. 1933, co. Tipperary)

Courtesy of Tom Clonan
Dublin Garda Index to Special Files, 1929–1945

Interviewees
Gilbane, Mary (b. 1926, co. Leitrim)
Gunning, John James (b. 1927, co. Leitrim)
Hill, Lettie (b. 1920, co. Leitrim)
Kelly, James (b. 1924, co. Leitrim)
MacLellan, Margaret (b. 1926, co. Limerick)
Masterson, Pat (b. 1922, co. Leitrim)
McGrew, Joe (b. 1929, co. Tyrone)
O'Neill, Brian (b. 1937, co. Tyrone)
O'Neill, Sheila (b. 1928, co. Tyrone)
O'Keefe, Philomena (b. 1928, Dublin)
O'Keefe, Tom (b. 1927, Dublin)
Ó Muircheartaigh, Mícheál (b. 1930, co. Kerry)
Simms, Harold (b. 1923, co. Down)

Printed primary sources

Barton, Robert. 'The Agriculture of Leinster', *Capuchin Annual* (1940), 241–245.
Busteed, John. 'Our Sterling Assets', *The Bell*, 11, 4 (January 1946), 857–860.
Coyne, E.J. 'A Workers' Republic', *Irish Monthly*, 67 (1939), 7–15.
Coyne, E.J. 'The Papal Encyclicals and the Banking Commission', *Irish Monthly*, 67 (1939), 75–90.
Coyne, E.J. 'What Is Credit?', *Irish Monthly*, 71 (1943), 281–292.

Coyne, E.J. 'Agricultural Co-Operation', Irish Monthly, 73 (1945), 227–238.

Dillon, T.W.T. 'Slum Clearance: Past and Future', Studies, 34 (1945), 13–20.

'Extracts of Social Wisdom: Catholic Theory of the State', Irish Monthly, 69 (1941), 87–90.

Fallon, Gabriel. 'Those Dwellers in Marrowbone Lane', Irish Monthly, 67 (1939), 841–845.

Hegarty, E.J. 'The Black Market', Irish Ecclesiastical Record, 64 (July–December 1944), 38–43.

Heron, Barney. 'Winning the Turf', The Bell, 2, 6 (September 1941), 33–41.

Kennedy, Henry. 'Agricultural Prosperity and Urban Employment', Studies, 32 (1943), 63–72.

Leventhal, A.J. 'What It Means to Be a Jew', The Bell, 10, 3 (June 1945), 207–216.

Lucey, Cornelius. 'The Spending of the Living Wage', Irish Ecclesiastical Record, 55 (January–June 1940), 143–155.

Lucey, Cornelius. 'The Ethics of Advertising', Irish Ecclesiastical Record, 57 (January–June 1941), 1–18.

Lucey, Cornelius. 'The Just Profit Rate', Irish Ecclesiastical Record, 58 (July–December 1941), 385–400.

Lucey, Cornelius. 'The Beveridge Report and Éire', Studies, 32 (1943), 36–44.

Lucey, Cornelius. 'The Ethics of Nationalisation', Christus Rex, 1 (1947), 19–26.

MacEamuinn, Seán. 'Poachers', The Bell, 1, 4 (January 1941), 18–22.

Mansfield, M. 'Theologians and the Legal Price', Irish Ecclesiastical Record, 63 (January–June 1944), 301–311.

May, Sheila. 'Two Dublin Slums', The Bell, 7, 4 (January 1944), 351–356.

McCarthy, J. 'Smuggling and Profiteering', Irish Ecclesiastical Record, 58 (July–December 1941), 554–557.

McCarthy, J. 'The Just Price of Stored Tea', Irish Ecclesiastical Record, 60 (July–December 1941), 298–300.

McCarthy, J. 'The Legal Price', Irish Ecclesiastical Record, 60 (July–December 1942), 438–444.

McCarthy, J. 'Is the Legal Price a Purely Penal Regulation?' Irish Ecclesiastical Record, 62 (July–December 1943), 269–270.

McElligott, T.J. 'How the Farmers Can Organise', Irish Monthly, 67 (1939), 51–58.

McKevitt, Peter. 'The Beveridge Plan Reviewed', Irish Ecclesiastical Record, 61 (January–June 1943), 145–150.

McLaughlin, Thomas A. Christus Rex, 1 (1947), 10–18.

Muench, Aloisius J. 'Farmer Is Collaborator with the Creator', Irish Monthly, 70 (1942), 23–31.

O'Brien, George. 'Some Lessons for Irish Agriculture from Western Europe', Studies, 29 (1940), 367–381.

O'Brien, George. 'The Impact of the War on the Irish Economy', Studies, 35 (1946), 25–39.

O'Doherty, John. 'The Catholic Church in 1939', Irish Ecclesiastical Record, 55 (January–June 1940), 1–14.

O'Donnell, Peadar. The Bothy Fire and All That (Dublin, 1937).

O'Donnell, Peadar, 'Migration Is a Way of Keeping a Grip', The Bell, 3, 2 (November 1941), 115–119.

Ó Faoláin, Seán. 'On State Control', The Bell, 6, 1 (April 1943), 1–5.

Ó Faoláin, Seán. 'The Stuffed-Shirts', *The Bell*, 6, 3 (June 1943), 182–192.

Ó Faoláin, Seán. 'One World', *The Bell*, 7, 4 (January 1944), 281–291.

Ó Faoláin, Seán. 'One World', *The Bell*, 7, 5 (February 1944), 373–381.

O'Faoláin, Seán *et al.*, 'Why Not Millions a Day on Peace?', *The Bell*, 8, 6 (September 1944), 480–486.

O'Keefe, Denis. 'Catholic Political Theory', *Studies*, 30 (1941), 481–487.

O'Neill, Joseph. 'Our Essential Planning Problem', *Studies*, 33 (1944), 228–236.

Parsons, Wilfred. 'The Function of Government in Industry', *Irish Monthly*, 72 (1944), 148–161.

Paschal, Father. 'The Responsibility of Economists', *Irish Ecclesiastical Record*, 59 (January–June 1942), 422–432.

Rooney, Philip. 'dhrink!', *The Bell*, 8, 4 (July 1944), 290–297.

Ryan, John J.M. 'Is Portugal Totalitarian?', *Irish Monthly*, 68 (1940), 1–9.

Sharkey, John. 'What I Saw in Dublin', *The Bell*, 9, 2 (November 1944), 149–154.

Ulster Union Club eds. *The North: A Collection of Short Stories, Articles and Poems* (Belfast, 1945).

Ultach. 'Orange Terror: The Partition of Ireland' (Dublin, 1943).

'Vigilans', 'As I See It', *Christus Rex*, 1 (1947), 32–41.

Secondary sources

Allen, Kieran. *Fianna Fáil and Irish Labour, 1926 to Present* (London, 1997).

Andrews, C.S. *Man of No Property* (Dublin, 2001).

Arensberg, Conrad M. and Kimball, Solon T. *Family and Community in Ireland* (2nd edition, Cambridge, 1968).

Atkinson, Anthony B. and Nolan, Brian. 'The Changing Distribution of Earnings in Ireland, 1937 to 1968', *The Economic History Review*, 63, 2 (2010), 479–499.

Bartlett, Thomas. 'An End to Moral Economy: The Irish Militia Disturbances of 1793', *Past & Present*, 99, 42 (1983), 41–64.

Barton, Brian. *Northern Ireland in the Second World War* (Belfast, 1995).

Bew, Paul and Patterson, Henry. *Seán Lemass and the Making of Modern Ireland, 1945–66* (Dublin, 1982).

Black, Richard. 'Regional Political Ecology in Theory and Practice: A Case Study from Northern Portugal', *Transactions of the Institute of British Geographers*, 15, 1 (1990), 35–47.

Blake, John W. *Northern Ireland in the Second World War* (Belfast, 1956).

Bolger, Patrick. *The Irish Co-Operative Movement, Its History and Development* (Dublin, 1977).

Bowen, Wayne H. *Spain during World War II* (Missouri, 2006).

Breen, Richard. 'Farm Servanthood in Ireland, 1900–1940', *The Economic History Review*, 36, 1 (1983), 87–102.

Brennan, Robert. *Ireland Standing Firm and de Valera: A Memoir* (Dublin, 1958).

Briscoe, Robert. *For the Life of Me* (London, 1958).

Browne, Noël. *Against the Tide* (Dublin, 1986).

Calvocoressi, Peter, Wint, Guy, and Pritchard, John eds. *The Penguin History of the Second World War* (London, 1999).

Canavan, Tony. *Frontier Town: An Illustrated History of Newry* (Belfast, 1989).

Carey, Sophia. *Social Security in Ireland, 1939–1952, the Limits to Solidarity* (Dublin, 2007).

Carlgren, W.M. *Swedish Foreign Policy during World War Two* (London, 1977).

Carroll, Joseph T. *Ireland in the War Years* (New York, 1975).

Carson, Niall. 'Beginnings and Blind Alleys: *The Bell*, 1940–1954' (unpublished PhD thesis, Liverpool, 2011).

Caruana, Leonard and Rockoff, Hugh. 'A Wolfram in Sheep's Clothing: Economic Warfare in Spain, 1940–1944', *The Journal of Economic History*, 63, 1 (2003), 101–126.

Churchill, Winston. *The Second World War*, six volumes (London, 2000).

Clay Arnold, Thomas. 'Rethinking Moral Economy', *The American Political Science Review*, 95, 1 (2001), 85–95.

Clear, Catriona. *Women of the House: Women's Household Work in Ireland, 1922–1961* (Dublin, 2000).

Coillte, Teoranta. *A Social History of Forestry in Ireland: Essays and Recollections on Social Aspects of Forestry in the 20th Century* (Castlemorris, Kilkenny, 2000).

Collingham, Lizzie. *The Taste of War; World War Two and the Battle for Food* (London, 2011).

Coogan, Tim Pat. *De Valera: Long Fellow, Long Shadow* (London, 1993).

Cooney, John. *John Charles McQuaid: Ruler of Catholic Ireland* (Dublin, 1999).

Couturié, Sylvia. *No Tears in Ireland* (Ballivor, co. Meath, 1999).

Cronin, Maura. 'Class and Status in Twentieth-Century Ireland: The Evidence of Oral History', *Saothar*, 32 (2007), 33–43.

D.83222 (Walter Mahon-Smith). *I Did Penal Servitude* (Dublin, 1945).

Daly, Mary E. *Social and Economic History of Ireland since 1800* (Dublin, 1981).

Daly, Mary E. 'An Irish-Ireland for Business?: The Control of Manufactures Acts, 1932 and 1934', *Irish Historical Studies*, 24, 94 (November 1984), 259–272.

Daly, Mary E. *Industrial Development and Irish National Identity, 1922–1939* (New York, 1992).

Daly, Mary E. *The Buffer State: The Historical Roots of the Department of the Environment* (Dublin, 1997).

Daly, Mary E. *The First Department: A History of the Department of Agriculture* (Dublin, 2002).

Daly, Mary E. *The Slow Failure: Population Decline and Independent Ireland, 1920–1973* (London, 2006).

Davis, John ed. *Rural Change in Ireland* (Belfast, 1999).

Deeney, James. *To Cure and to Care: Memoirs of a Chief Medical Officer* (Dun Laoghaire, 1989).

Douglas, R.M. *Ailtirí na hAiséirghe and the Fascist 'New Order' in Ireland* (Manchester, 2009).

Duggan, John P. *Neutral Ireland and the Third Reich* (Dublin, 1989).

Duggan, John P. *A History of the Irish Army* (Dublin, 1991).

Duggan, Eugene. *The Ploughman on the Pound Note: Farmer Politics in County Galway during the Twentieth Century* (Athenry, 2004).

Dunphy, Richard. *The Making of Fianna Fáil Power in Ireland, 1923–1948* (Oxford, 1995).

Dwyer, T. Ryle. *De Valera's Finest Hour* (Dublin, 1982).

Eade, Charles ed. *Winston Churchill. The Wartime Speeches*, two volumes (London, 1952).

Earner-Byrne, Lindsey. *Mother and Child: Maternity and Child Welfare in Ireland, 1920s–1960s* (Manchester, 2007).

Evans, Bryce. 'The Construction Corps, 1940–48', *Saothar*, 32 (2007), 19–31.

Evans, Bryce. *Seán Lemass, Democratic Dictator* (Cork, 2011).

Fanning, Ronan. *Independent Ireland* (Dublin, 1983).

Farmer, Richard. *The Food Companions: Cinema and Consumption in Wartime Britain, 1939–45* (Manchester, 2011).

Farrell, Brian. *Seán Lemass* (Dublin, 1991).

Fee, Gerard. 'The Effects of World War II on Dublin's Low-Income Families, 1939–1945' (unpublished PhD thesis, UCD, 1996).

Feeney, Tom. *Seán MacEntee: A Political Life* (Dublin, 2009).

Ferriter, Diarmaid. '"A Peculiar People in Their Own Land": Catholic Social Theory and the Plight of Rural Ireland 1930–55' (unpublished PhD thesis, UCD, 1996).

Ferriter, Diarmaid. *'Lovers of Liberty?': Local Government in 20th Century Ireland* (Dublin, 2001).

Ferriter, Diarmaid. *The Transformation of Ireland, 1900–2000* (London, 2004).

Ferriter, Diarmaid. *Judging Dev: A Reassessment of the Life and Legacy of Eamon De Valera* (Dublin, 2007).

Ferriter, Diarmaid. *Occasions of Sin: Sex and Society in Modern Ireland* (Dublin, 2009).

Findlater, Alex. *Findlaters: The Story of a Dublin Merchant Family, 1774–2001* (Dublin, 2001).

Finnane, Mark. 'The Carrigan Committee of 1930–31 and the "Moral" Condition of the Saorstát', *Irish Historical Studies*, 32, 128 (2001), 519–536.

Fisk, Robert. *In Time of War: Ireland, Ulster and the Price of Neutrality 1939–45* (London, 1983).

Forde, Frank. *The Long Watch: The History of The Irish Mercantile Marine in World War Two* (Dublin, 2000).

Foster, R.F. *Modern Ireland, 1600–1972* (London, 1988).

Garvin, Tom. *Preventing the Future: Why Was Ireland So Poor for So Long?* (Dublin, 2004).

Garvin, Tom. *Judging Lemass: The Measure of the Man* (Dublin, 2009).

Gaughan, J. Anthony. *Alfred O'Rahilly*, two volumes (Naas, 1989).

Girvin, Brian. *The Emergency: Neutral Ireland 1939–45* (London, 2006).

Girvin, Brian and Murphy, Gary eds. *The Lemass Era: Politics and Society in the Ireland of Seán Lemass* (Dublin, 2005).

Gray, Tony. *The Lost Years: The Emergency in Ireland 1939–45* (London, 1988).

Greer, Alan. *Rural Politics in Northern Ireland: Policy Networks and Agricultural Development since Partition* (Aldershot, 1996).

Hargreaves, Eric Lyde and Gowing, Margaret. *History of the Second World War: Civil Industry and Trade* (London, 1952).

Harrison, Joseph. *The Spanish Economy from the Civil War to the European Community* (London, 1993).

Hayes, Alan ed. *Hilda Tweedy and the Irish Housewives' Association: Links in the Chain* (Dublin, 2012).

Heverin, Aileen. *ICA: The Irish Countrywomen's Association, a History 1910–2000* (Dublin, 2000).

Hodgson, Vere. *Few Eggs and No Oranges: The Diaries of Vere Hodgson 1940–45* (London, 1999).

Horgan, John. *Seán Lemass: The Enigmatic Patriot* (Dublin, 1997).

Hull, Mark. *Irish Secrets: German Espionage in Wartime Ireland, 1939–1945* (Dublin, 2002).

Jackson, Alvin. *Ireland, 1798–1998: Politics and War* (Oxford, 1999).

Johnson, David S. 'Cattle Smuggling on the Irish Border, 1932–38', *Irish Economic and Social History*, 6 (1979), 41–63.

Johnson, David S. 'Northern Ireland as a Problem in the Economic War 1932–1938', *Irish Historical Studies*, 22, 86 (September 1980), 144–161.

Johnston, Márín. *Around the Banks of Pimlico* (Dublin, 1985).

Jones, Greta. *'Captain of All These Men of Death': The History of Tuberculosis in Nineteenth and Twentieth Century Ireland* (Amsterdam, 2001).

Kay, Hugh. *Salazar and Modern Portugal* (New York, 1970).

Kearney, Richard. *Postnationalist Ireland: Politics, Culture, Philosophy* (London, 1997).

Kedward, H.R. *Occupied France, Collaboration and Resistance, 1940–1944* (Oxford, 1985).

Kelly, Stephen. *Fianna Fáil, Partition and Northern Ireland, 1926–1971* (Dublin, 2013).

Kennedy, Liam. *The Modern Industrialisation of Ireland 1940–1988* (Dublin, 1989).

Kennedy, Liam. *Colonialism, Religion and Nationalism in Ireland* (Belfast, 1996).

Kennedy, Walter. *Shipping in Dublin Port, 1939–1945* (Edinburgh, 1998).

Kennedy, Michael. *Division and Consensus: The Politics of Cross-Border Relations in Ireland, 1925–1969* (Dublin, 2000).

Kennedy, Michael. *Guarding Neutral Ireland: The Coast Watching Service and Military Intelligence, 1939–1945* (Dublin, 2008).

Keogh, Dermot. *The Vatican, the Bishops and Irish Politics* (Cambridge, 1986).

Keogh, Dermot. *Jews in Twentieth Century Ireland: Refugees, Anti-Semitism and the Holocaust* (Cork, 1998).

Keogh, Dermot and O'Driscoll, Mervyn eds. *Ireland in World War Two: Neutrality and Survival* (Cork, 2004).

Kreis, Georg. *Switzerland in the Second World War: Responding to the Challenges of Time* (Zürich, 1999).

Lee, J.J. 'Aspects of Corporatist Thought in Ireland' in Cosgrove, Art and McCartney, Donal eds, *Studies in Irish History* (Dublin, 1979), 324–346.

Lee, J.J. *Ireland 1912–1985: Politics and Society* (Cambridge, 1989).

Leitz, Christian. *Economic Relations between Nazi Germany and Franco's Spain, 1936–1945* (Oxford, 1996).

Leitz, Christian. *Nazi Germany and Neutral Europe during the Second World War* (Manchester, 2000).

Lochery, Neill. *Lisbon: War in the Shadows of the City of Light, 1939–1945* (New York, 2011).

Logue, Paddy ed. *The Border: Personal Reflections from Ireland North and South* (Dublin, 1999).

Longford, Lord and O'Neill, Thomas P. *Éamon de Valera* (Dublin, 1970).

Lycett Green, Candida. *John Betjeman Letters*, two volumes (London, 1994).

Lyons, F.S.L. *Ireland since the Famine* (Bungay, 1973).

Magnusson, Lars. *An Economic History of Sweden* (London, 2000).

McCarron, Donal. *Step Together! The Story of Ireland's Emergency Army 1939–46. As Told by Its Veterans* (Dublin, 1999).

McCormick, Leanne. "One Yank and They're Off": Interaction between U.S. Troops and Northern Irish Women, 1942–1945', *Journal of the History of Sexuality*,15, 2 (2006), 228–257.

McCourt, Frank. *Angela's Ashes: Memoir of a Childhood* (London, 1996).

McCullough, Arthur E. 'The Language and Legitimation of Irish Moral Outrage', *The British Journal of Sociology*, 40, 2 (1989), 227–243.

McGahern, John. *Memoir* (London, 2005).

Meenan, James. 'The Irish Economy during the War', in Nowlan, Kevin B. and Williams, Desmond T. eds, *Ireland in the War Years and After* (Dublin, 1969), 28–38.

Meneses, Filipe Ribeiro de. 'Investigating Portugal, Salazar and the New State: The Work of the Irish Legation in Lisbon, 1942–1945', *Contemporary European History*, 11, 3 (2002), 399–408.

Meneses, Filipe Ribeiro de. *Salazar: A Political Biography* (New York, 2009).

Milotte, Mike. *Communism in Modern Ireland: The Pursuit of the Workers' Republic since 1916* (Dublin, 1984).

Milward, Alan S. *War, Economy and Society, 1939–45* (London, 1977).

Muldowney, Mary. *The Second World War and Irish Women: An Oral History* (Dublin, 2007).

Neary, Peter J. and Ó Gráda, Cormac. 'Protection, Economic War and Structural Change: The 1930s in Ireland', *Irish Historical Studies*, 27, 107 (1991), 250–266.

Nesbitt, Ronald. *At Arnott's of Dublin* (Dublin, 1993).

Ní Shúilleabháin, Eibhlís. *Letters from the Great Blasket* (Cork, 1988).

Ní Shúilleabháin, Brenda ed. *Bibeanna. Memories from a Corner of Ireland* (Cork, 1997).

Nowlan, Kevin B. and Williams, T. Desmond eds. *Ireland in the War Years and After* (Dublin, 1969).

O'Brien, Flann. *The Third Policeman* (London, 1967).

Ó Broin, León. *Just Like Yesterday, an Autobiography* (Dublin, 1986).

O'Connor, Emmet. *A Labour History of Ireland, 1824–1960* (Dublin, 1992).

Ó Corráin, Daithí. *Rendering to God and Caesar: The Irish Churches and the Two States in Ireland, 1949–73* (Manchester, 2008).

O'Donnell, Liam. *The Days of the Servant Boy* (Cork, 1997).

Ó Drisceoil, Donal. *Censorship in Ireland, 1939–1945: Neutrality, Politics, and Society* (Cork, 1996).

Ó Drisceoil, Donal. ''Moral Neutrality': Censorship in Emergency Ireland', *History Ireland*, 4, 2 (1996), 46–50.

Ó Drisceoil, Donal. "Whose Emergency Is It?' Wartime Politics and the Irish Working Class, 1939–45" in Lane, Fintan and Ó Drisceoil, Donal eds, *Politics and the Irish Working Class, 1830–1945* (Basingstoke, 2005), 262–280.

Ó Gráda, Cormac. 'Primogeniture and Ultimogeniture in Rural Ireland', *Journal of Interdisciplinary History*, 10, 3 (Winter 1980), 491–497.

Ó Gráda, Cormac. *Ireland: A New Economic History, 1780–1939* (Oxford, 1995).

Ó Gráda, Cormac. *A Rocky Road: The Irish Economy since the 1920s* (Manchester, 1997).

Ó Gráda, Cormac. *Ireland's Great Famine: Interdisciplinary Perspectives* (Dublin, 2006).

O'Halpin, Eunan. *Defending Ireland: The Irish State and Its Enemies since 1922* (Oxford, 2000).

O'Halpin, Eunan. *MI5 and Ireland, 1939–1945: The Official History* (Dublin, 2003).

O'Keefe, Phil. *Standing at the Crossroads* (Dingle, 1997).

O'Leary, Don. *Vocationalism and Social Catholicism in Twentieth Century Ireland: The Search for a Christian Social Order* (Dublin, 2000).

Ollerenshaw, Phil. 'War, Industrial Mobilisation and Society in Northern Ireland, 1939–45', *Contemporary European History*, 16, 2 (2007), 169–197.

Peterson, Basil. *Turn of the Tide, an Outline of Irish Maritime History* (Dublin 1962).

Pinar, Susana. 'The Emergence of Modern Genetics in Spain and the Effects of the Spanish Civil War (1936–1939) on Its Development', *Journal of the History of Biology*, 35, 1 (Spring 2002), 111–148.

Price, Liam. *Dr. Dorothy Price: An Account of Twenty Years' Fight Against Tuberculosis in Ireland* (Oxford, 1957).

Price, Stanley. *Somewhere to Hang My Hat: An Irish-Jewish Journey* (Dublin, 2002).

Puirséil, Niamh. *The Irish Labour Party 1922–73* (Dublin, 2007).

Richards, Michael. *A Time of Silence: Civil War and the Culture of Repression in Franco's Spain, 1936–1945* (Cambridge, 1998).

Rigney, Peter. *Trains, Coal and Turf: Transport in Emergency Ireland* (Dublin, 2010).

Riordan, Susannah. '"The Unpopular Front": The Catholic Revival and Irish Catholic Identity, 1932–48' (unpublished MA thesis, UCD, 1990).

Riordan, Susannah. '"A Political Blackthorn": Seán MacEntee, the Dignan Plan and the Principle of Ministerial Responsibility', *Irish Economic and Social History*, 27 (2000), 44–62.

Ritchie, H. *The Navicert System during the World War* (New York, 2000).

Schwarz, Urs. *The Eye of the Hurricane: Switzerland in World War Two* (Boulder, 1980).

Scott, James C. *Weapons of the Weak: Everyday Forms of Peasant Resistance* (Yale, 1985).

Share, Bernard. *The Emergency: Neutral Ireland, 1939–45* (Dublin, 1978).

Sheehy-Skeffington, Andrée. *Skeff: The Life of Owen Sheehy-Skeffington 1909–1970* (Dublin, 1991).

Skinner, Liam. *Seán Lemass: Nation Builder* (unpublished manuscript, UCDA P161, 9).

Smith, Harold L. *War and Social Change: British Society in the Second World War* (Manchester, 1986).

Smyth, Hazel P. *The B&I Line* (Dublin, 1984).

Stephan, Enno. *Spies in Ireland* (London, 1965).

Summerfield, Penny. *Women Workers during the Second World War* (London, 1982).

Thompson, E.P. 'The Moral Economy of the English Crowd in the Eighteenth Century', *Past & Present*, 50 (1971), 76–136.

Thompson, E.P. *Customs in Common* (London, 1993).

Townshend, Charles. *Ireland: The Twentieth Century* (London, 1999).

Tweedy, Hilda. *A Link in the Chain* (Dublin, 1992).

Wheeler, Douglas L. 'The Price of Neutrality: Portugal, the Wolfram Question, and World War II', *Luso-Brazilian Review*, 23, 1 (1986), 107–122.

Whyte, J.H. *Church and State in Modern Ireland* (Dublin, 1971 and 1980).

Wigg, Richard. *Churchill and Spain: The Survival of the Franco Regime, 1940–1945* (Brighton, 2008).

Wills, Clair. *That Neutral Island: A Cultural History of Ireland during the Second World War* (Dublin, 2007).

Wylie, Neville ed. *European Neutrals and Non-Belligerents during the Second World War* (Cambridge, 2002).

Zweiniger-Bargielowska, Ina. *Austerity in Britain: Rationing, Controls, and Consumption, 1939–1955* (Oxford, 2000).

Index

agricultural productivity and state 159–163,
    179–181, 185
  cabinet divisions 156, 163–166
  censorship 156–159, 171
  Church perspectives 119, 153–156
  political economy 166–170
  see also compulsory tillage
Aiken, Frank 18, 135, 157
America 92, 101–102, 134–135, 167
Andrews, Todd 29, 32, 59, 161
Anglo-Irish relations
  British sea power 20–27
  failures (Dept. of Supplies) 34–38
  Lemass and enterprise 27–34
  trade squeeze 22–27, 37–38, 45, 63, 96,
    134–135, 179–180
  transformation, post-war 177–178
anti-materialism 71, 116–117, 123, 127,
    138, 166, 168, 177
anti-semitism 123–125

Betjeman, John 1, 4, 18, 44, 69, 91, 98, 114,
    134, 153, 177
bicycles 56–57, 74, 100
black market 11, 13, 69, 71–77, 80–86,
    137, 184–185
  Church and state 115–119, 122,
    124–125, 128, 181
  policing 45, 47–49, 51–64, 179, 184
  see also smuggling
'Blueshirt' movement 57, 114, 159
Boland, Gerald 69, 115, 128
bread 36, 45, 46, 57, 71, 78, 97, 107, 163
  black loaf 13, 33, 57, 71, 79, 97

  see also compulsory tillage
Britain *see* Anglo-Irish relations
Brooke, Basil 91, 95, 145, 146, 184

camp labour 156, 159–163
capitalism 13, 29, 34, 37, 81, 85
  Church and state 118, 123, 126–129
Catholic Social Service Conference 119
censorship 9, 13, 23, 45, 51–52, 59–62,
    104, 106, 177
  agricultural production 137–138,
    155–159, 169–170
  Church and state 118–119, 124–125
children
  labour 80, 139, 182
  smuggling 98–99
Church and state
  marketplace/money 115–117, 122–126
  priests and dissent 120–122
  visions 114–115, 117–119, 126–129
  see also vocationalism
Churchill, Winston 22, 37, 57, 95, 135,
    142, 177–178
Clann na Talmhan 156, 169, 170
clothing 33–34, 72–74
coal *see* fuel shortages
Commission on Vocational Organisation
    114, 126, 155–156, 171, 181
compulsory tillage 135–136, 147–148
  enforcement 138–140
  food supply, geopolitics 134–135
  genesis and implementation 135–136
  Northern Ireland, comparison 144–147
  propaganda and famine 136–138

resistance 140–144, 148
state interventionism 153–155, 160,
        164–165, 169–170, 179–181, 185
Construction Corps 158, 159, 160
consultation 32, 33, 37, 82, 147, 168, 181
cooperative creameries 80–85
Corry, Martin 167, 168, 169
Coyne, Thomas J. 23, 51, 60
credit, agricultural 168–169
crime 31, 69, 76
        see also black market
Cumann na nGaedheal 5–6, 114, 135

de Valera, Eamon 1–3, 8–10, 178, 183
        agricultural production 137–139, 141,
                147, 153, 163–164
        Anglo-Irish relations 19, 21, 22, 29–30
        Church and state 114, 121, 126, 153
        cross-border relations 91, 92, 106
Dillon, James 63, 124, 169
dispossession, of farmland 2, 136,
        139–140, 144–145, 156, 164, 181
Dublin
        conditions 57–58, 70–79, 83, 119
        rural view of 166, 168, 185
Dublin Opinion 36, 55, 72, 165

economic blockade 20–21, 24, 37
emergency powers, state 1–2, 5, 10–11, 19–20
        see also state interventionism
emigration 70, 78, 96, 126
        Britain 7, 10, 80, 126, 142
        controls (rural) 154, 160–162, 179
        cross-border movement 95–99, 111
exports 6, 20–27, 35–37, 146, 156, 158,
        179–180

fertiliser 20, 26, 27, 134–135, 140, 146,
        156, 165, 170
Findlater, Dermot 32, 34
Fine Gael 33–34, 36, 124, 157, 167, 169
firewood 72
        see also fuel shortages
Flanagan, Oliver J. 123, 142
Flinn, Hugo 155, 162
flour 46–47, 54, 56, 59, 61–62, 78–79

smuggling 92, 94, 97, 100, 103, 108
        see also bread; compulsory tillage
food access 69–71, 75–78
        see also black market; starvation
foot and mouth outbreak (1941) 6, 158
fuel shortages 72–73, 75, 77, 80, 83, 86
        controls 29, 44, 45, 51, 54, 120–122
        supplies 6, 20–22, 25–27, 135, 177
        turf drive 159–163, 179, 181
                Church on 119, 153–154
        see also petrol

Germany 1, 6, 92, 105, 108, 167, 183
        Anglo-Irish relations 21–24, 27, 32
Guinness 25–26, 179

Historical Survey 93, 98, 185
        Anglo-Irish relations 20, 24–25, 27–28,
                30, 33, 35, 37
        moral policing 46–48, 52–54, 59
historiography 2–13, 135, 148, 184–185

imports 6, 56, 73, 134–135, 146, 179–180
        see also Anglo-Irish relations
industry 5–6, 13, 27–39
        see also exports; imports; labour controls
IRA (Irish Republican Army) 1–2, 91, 101
Irish Housewives Association 58–59, 181

Kavanagh, Patrick 4, 185
Kennedy, Henry 82–85, 109, 66
Knightly, Michael 23, 51–52

labour, cross-border movement 95–99, 111
labour controls 96, 130, 156, 159–163,
        171, 179, 181–182
Lemass, Seán 2, 5, 19–20, 178–183
        agricultural productivity and state 153,
                155–156, 159, 160–163
        Anglo-Irish relations 18–21, 24–38
        Church and state 115–116, 118,
                120–121, 123, 126–128
        compulsory tillage 138, 144, 146–148
        conditions rural/urban 72–74, 79, 82–84
        moral policing 44–52, 54–64
        smuggling 93–97, 102–103, 107

Leydon, John 49–50, 59–62, 119,
        120–122, 179–181
    Anglo-Irish relations 19–21, 23–24,
        26–27, 29–30, 32, 33, 37–38
    smuggling 91, 92, 94, 95, 107
Lucey, Cornelius 118–119, 126

McCarthy, John 115–118
MacEntee, Seán 160, 162–163, 173–175
machinery
    agricultural production 135, 142,
        145–146, 154, 165, 169
    Anglo-Irish relations 25–26, 35–36, 38
McNamara, Michael 83, 85
McNamee, James (Bishop) 116, 127
McQuaid, John Charles (Archbishop)
        153–154, 119–121, 183
MacRory, Joseph (Cardinal) 106, 137
Ministry of Food (British) 24, 26, 36, 46,
        63, 94–95, 99
mobility see petrol, mobility
moral economy 9–12, 105–109, 117–119,
        177–178, 180–185
    agricultural productivity 157–158,
        167–168, 171
    Anglo-Irish relations 28, 34, 37
    conditions, living 69, 75, 79–80, 83, 90
    see also moral policing
moral policing
    critical perspectives 53–64
    Inspection Branch 48–53
    voluntary measures and rationing 44–48
Mulcahy, Richard 46, 157

nationalism 135–136, 138
neutrality
    censorship 60, 106, 157
    historiography 3–9
        reappraisals 9–13
    moral economy 9–13, 28, 129, 168,
        171, 177–178, 182–183, 185
    trade relations 21–22, 27, 37, 134–135,
        177–178
    see also Anglo-Irish relations, trade squeeze
Northern Ireland 63, 92–93, 137, 140, 142,
        144–148
    see also smuggling

O'Brien, Flann 56–57
O'Donnell, Peadar 80, 129
O'Duffy, Eoin 57–58
O'Faoláin, Seán 161, 181–182
O'Rahilly, Alfred 10, 122–123, 155, 168

Parr, G.H.E. 92, 94, 95, 110
petrol 6, 21, 28, 55, 97, 145, 168
    mobility 33, 56, 73, 75–78, 84,
        120–122
Portugal 4, 27, 48, 108, 124, 127, 135, 154,
        163, 177
post-war 107, 128, 164–165, 177–178, 184
price control 11, 12, 19, 29, 37, 178–181
    agricultural production 134, 156–158,
        163–164, 167–168
    Church and state 115–118, 129, 154
    see also moral policing
profiteering 29, 34, 39, 45, 59, 62, 83, 185
    Church perspectives 116, 118, 127–128
propaganda 28, 63, 82, 92, 95, 103,
        136–139, 171, 183–184
protectionism 28
Protestants 59, 77, 82, 105, 119, 153
public health issues 24–25, 71

railways (and smuggling) 97–98
rationing 24, 29, 33–35, 71–79
    Church and state 119, 120–122, 129
    moral economy 11, 12, 178–180, 184
    smuggling 92, 93–94, 98, 102, 106, 108
    see also moral policing
Riddell, Charlie 81, 83, 84–85
rubber 25, 56–57
RUC (Royal Ulster Constabulary) 92–100
rural conditions 69–75, 85–86
    cooperative creameries 80–85
ruralism 71, 138, 154, 155, 183
Ryan, James 136–140, 143–146, 148, 154,
        156, 158, 163–165, 167–170

Salazar, António de Oliveira 27, 48, 135,
        163, 177
shipping, Irish 20–24
smuggling
    cross-border relations 92–96, 108
    frontier as contested 91–92

modes of smuggling 102–105
moral economy 105–109
'new' smuggling 92, 96–102, 108–109
social Catholicism *see* vocationalism
Spain 4, 27, 37, 48, 124, 147, 154, 177
starvation 77–78, 135, 137–138, 160, 182
state interventionism
    economics, moral 181–184
    nature of 177–181
    popular adherence 184–185
    see also agricultural productivity and
        state; compulsory tillage;
        emergency powers, state
stocks, reserve 27–28, 31–33, 35–36, 38
Supplies, Department of, establishment 2,
    5, 10–11, 19–20
Sweden 4, 22, 27, 48, 63, 108, 124, 177
Switzerland 4, 27, 37, 48, 63, 108, 124

tea 35–36, 71, 75–76, 86
    smuggling 92, 97, 100–101, 103, 108

Thompson, E.P. 11, 85
turf *see* fuel shortages, turf drive
Tweedy, Hilda 58–59

unemployment 5–7, 11, 13, 73, 78, 80,
    85–86, 105, 160
usury 123, 124, 125

vocationalism 63, 114–116, 119, 126–128,
    181, 182
    agricultural production 142, 155–156,
        166, 168, 169

wages 7, 13, 78, 84–86, 161–163, 177
wheat *see* bread; compulsory tillage; flour
Williams, John 19, 51, 60
women 50, 54, 57, 58, 63, 71, 75, 77, 79
    smuggling 98, 99–101
    workforce 80, 147, 183
Woolton, Frederick James Marquis
    (Lord) 32, 69

Lightning Source UK Ltd.
Milton Keynes UK
UKOW06f2027061215

264200UK00001B/19/P